Learning English for Academic Purposes

JULIA WILLIAMS

DISTRIBUTED IN CANADA BY ERPI

5757, RUE CYPIHOT, SAINT-LAURENT (QUÉBEC) H4S 1R3
TELEPHONE: (514) 334-2690 ext. 232 FAX: (514) 334-0448
infoesl@erpi.com www.longmanesl.ca

DEDICATION

For my husband Wayne Parker,
for whom this dedication is a return in kind.

For my children Sam and Scott,
whose natural curiosity has led to many
teachable topics.

For my students, who helped me shape this material.

Editor
Sharnee Chait

Copy editor
Jeremy Lanaway

Production supervisor
Muriel Normand

Cover
eykel design

Book design and page layout
dessine-moi un mouton

Registration of copyright: 2nd quarter 2005
Bibliothèque nationale du Québec
National Library of Canada
Printed in Canada

ISBN 2-7613-1584-7

234567890 HLN 09876
131584 ABCD OF10

CREDITS

Chapter 1. pp. 3–6 “The High-Pressure Lives of Child Athletes” by Georgie Binks, *Canadian Family*, (March 2003) reprinted with permission of Georgie Binks. p. 4 Photograph: Marina Dodis. p. 10 “The drawbacks of Youth Sports” from *Will You Still Love Me If I Don’t Win?* by C. Andersonn, reprinted with permission of Taylor Trade Publishing. pp. 14–15 “More Sports, More Risk” copyright © 2002, *The New York Times*, reprinted with permission. pp. 21–23 “Role Models and Cautionary Tales” by Joan Ryan, *The Sporting News* (21 July, 1997) reprinted with permission of Joan Ryan.

Chapter 2. pp. 36–39 “National Sport, Calgary” by B. Bergman, “Sisler High School, Winnipeg” by B. Bergman, and “Earl Haig, Toronto” by K. Marley from *Maclean’s* (23 August, 2004). Reprinted by permission of Rogers Publishing Limited.

Chapter 3. p. 44 “Understanding Marketing Processes and Consumer Behaviour” from *Business* (5th Edition) by R.W. Griffin, R.J. Ebert and F.A. Starke (p. 530) Copyright © 2005 Pearson Education Canada, reprinted with permission by Pearson Education Canada Inc. pp. 49–55 “Consumer and Business Buyer Behaviour” from *Marketing, An Introduction* by G. Armstrong et al. (pp. 208–215) Copyright © 2004 Pearson Education Canada, reprinted with permission by Pearson Education Canada Inc. pp. 61–62, 64–65 Excerpts (pp.11, 12, 14, 15–18) from *Harness the Future: The 9 Keys to Emerging Consumer Behaviour* by S. Roberts, Copyright © 1998 John Wiley & Sons. Reprinted with permission from John Wiley & Sons Canada Ltd.

Chapter 4. pp. 69–73 Excerpt (pp. 559–563) from *Business* (5th Edition) by R.W. Griffin, R.J. Ebert and F.A. Starke Copyright © 2005 Pearson Education Canada, reprinted with permission by Pearson Education Canada Inc. pp. 78–82 Excerpt (pp. 214–219) from *Canadian Marketing in Action* (6th Edition) by K.J. Tuckwell Copyright © 2004 Pearson Education Canada, reprinted with permission by Pearson Education Canada Inc. pp. 88–89 “Buy this 24-year-old and get all his friends absolutely free” Reprinted with the permission of The Free Press, a Division of Simon & Schuster Adult Publishing Group, from DEADLY PERSUASION by Jean Kilbourne. Copyright © 1999 by Jean Kilbourne. All rights reserved. pp. 90–92 “Junk-Food Games” by Joseph Pereira, *The Wall Street Journal* (3 May 2004) reprinted with the permission of Dow Jones & Company, Inc.

Chapter 5. pp. 95, 96–105 “Alternative Medicine Joins the Mainstream,” “Homeopathy Offers Deep and True Healing,” “Acupuncture Relieves Chronic Pain,” “The Hazards Around Us,” “Chiropractors Unleash Body’s ‘Inherent Healing Ability,’” “Patient, Heal Thyself” by Elaine Kenney, *Ottawa Citizen* (30 December 2002), reprinted with permission by Elaine Kenney. pp. 117–119 “Bridging the Medical Divide” by Prithi Yalaja, *Toronto Star* (21 June, 2002). Reprinted with permission – Torstar Syndication Services.

Chapter 6. pp. 122–123 “Immunization Schedule” reprinted with permission by the Canadian Paediatric Society, www.cps.ca; www.caringforkids.cps.ca. pp. 125–130 “Vaccine Safety – Frequently Asked Questions” Source: Health Canada Website, Public Health Agency of Canada (Retrieved November 7, 2003). Reproduced with the permission of the Minister of Public Works and Government Services Canada, 2005. pp. 137–142 “Stacy’s Story,” and “Katy’s Story” reprinted with the permission of Vaccine Risk Awareness Network Inc. pp. 143–144 “Tips on Evaluating Information” from *Your Child’s Best Shot: A Parent’s Guide to Vaccination* by R. Gold (pp. 300–302) Copyright © 2002 Canadian Paediatric Society. Reprinted with the permission of the Canadian Paediatric Society. pp.147–149 Excerpt from “Hot Shots” by John Hoffman, *Today’s Parent* (March 2002). Reprinted with permission by John Hoffman.

Chapter 7. pp. 153–154, 156–158 Excerpts (pp.1, 4–5, 15–18) from RISK: A PRACTICAL GUIDE FOR DECIDING WHAT’S REALLY SAFE AND WHAT’S REALLY DANGEROUS IN THE WORLD AROUND YOU. Copyright © 2002 by David Ropeik and George Gray. Reprinted by permission of Houghton Mifflin Company. All rights reserved. pp. 165–167 “Precautionary Principle – FAQs” reprinted by permission of the Science and Environmental Health Network, www.sehn.org.

Chapter 8. pp. 173–174, 175–176 “GM Foods Are a Boon to Farmers, but Consumers Ask: So What?” by Tom Spears, *Ottawa Citizen* (3 January, 2000). Material reprinted with the express permission of “NATIONAL POST COMPANY,” a CanWest Partnership. pp. 184–189 “Fact Sheets/Frequently Asked Questions” Source: Canadian Food Inspection Agency Website (Retrieved 3 February, 2005). Reproduced with the permission of the Minister of Public Works and Government Services Canada, 2005. pp. 194–199 “Genetically Modified Foods: The Battle Comes to Canada” by Pauline Tam, *Ottawa Citizen* (3 January, 2000). Material reprinted with the express permission of “NATIONAL POST COMPANY,” a CanWest Partnership.

INTRODUCTION

This textbook was written in response to two gaps that I perceived when I moved from teaching in a non-credit, intensive, 25 hour/week ESL program, to a credit, six hour/week EAP program.

The first was a gap in teaching methodology between the intensive non-credit courses, and the comparatively reduced number of hours for EAP courses. The EAP environment was necessarily focused on evaluation in order to generate a student's final grade. As a result, there did not seem to be enough time to integrate process-type activities into the six hours of EAP study per week. I felt students had to move from one assignment to the next without allowing them time to build on and reinforce reading and writing skills. I wanted to carry process-type activities into the EAP context.

The second gap was a disconnect between what students were required to do in their content courses, and what students were exposed to in their EAP classes. In their content classes, students in areas as diverse as economics, business, history, communications, engineering, and international studies were often asked to read 80-page chapters, understand complex vocabulary, respond to abstract questions, research in the library, and write lengthy papers. Yet the materials the students were exposed to in EAP classes were short, and while unit topics were interesting, they were often simplistic. I wanted materials that could bridge the gap between EAP classes and content classes.

These chapters were designed to address these two gaps. For each chapter, you will find short *warm-up assignments* that allow students to use new vocabulary, grammatical structures, and organizational patterns before they attempt the longer *final assignments* that are necessarily graded. Furthermore, the authentic materials are longer, and the viewpoints are deliberately contradictory to simulate the complexity students will find outside the EAP classroom. These materials are supported by explicit four-skill strategies to assist students with processing the quantity of information in each chapter.

The chapters are arranged from simple to complex. In a six-hour per week context, three to four chapters could be covered in a twelve-week term. The eight chapters here should allow for two terms of learning, or teachers can select chapters based on student interest and ability.

Acknowledgements

There are a great number of people I would like to thank for help along the road to publication. My thanks go to David Wood, who went first in many arenas. Thank you to Joanne Bleasedale and Cecilia Vasilov of Humber College, and Cheryl Ende of Brock University who helped me to find the field of ESL. Thanks also to Maureen Keon at Algonquin College. My great admiration goes to many of my Carleton University colleagues for their professionalism and inspiration, amongst them Shannon Burke, Carol Garigue, Danita Medina, Wendy Fraser, Marie Brisson, Michael Leonard, Carolyn Wood, Estelle Lalonde, Suzie Dillon, Anne Pazaver, Stephanie Pinnacle, Louise Smith, Lee Kinsman, Andi Gray, Barbara Greenwood, Margaret Kersten, Linda Librande, Adrienne Soucy, Marilyn Weir, Jaffer Sheyholislami, Rocio Alvarez, Brenda Bedford, Jane Burnstein, Shirley Milling, Soo Kiak Loy and Emese Bukor. My great appreciation goes out to my University of Waterloo colleagues who have welcomed me so warmly: Judi Jewinski, John Crossley, Tanya Missere-Mihas, Stefan Rehm, John Vardon, Pat Skinner, Elizabeth Matthews, Dara Lane, Keely Cook, and Ron Champion. Thanks also to the team at Pearson Longman ESL Canada: my editor Sharnee Chait and Jean-Pierre Albert.

I must especially thank Wayne, Sam and Scott Parker, Carolyn and Ron Williams for their unwavering encouragement, and Garth and Ross Williams, Nicole Richer and Mary Gillespie for their continued support.

Highlights of *Learning English for Academic Purposes*

Stimulates students' interest by tapping into their prior knowledge.

Tasks (activities) focus on content and meaning, and often combine language skills in order to acquire language by using it.

Predominantly Canadian readings are from newspapers, academic textbooks, Internet articles and magazines.

Short warm-up writing assignments prepare students for the Final Assignment. Each chapter focuses on a different writing pattern.

Each unit includes an audio clip from CBC radio, authentic interviews or lectures (provided in the Audio CD). The listening tasks support the focus on reading and writing by improving students' listening skills and developing effective note-taking strategies.

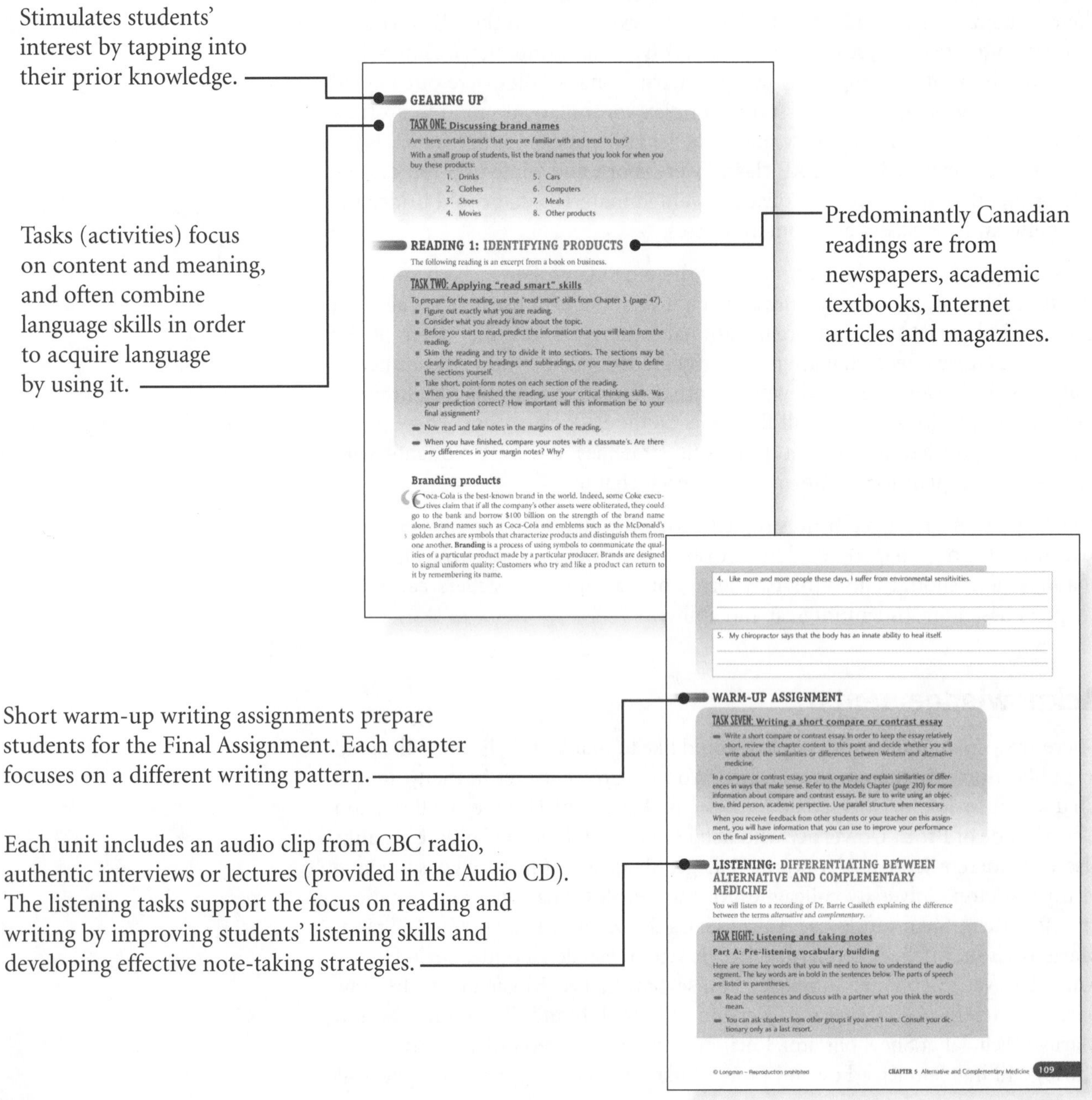

GEARING UP

TASK ONE: Discussing brand names

Are there certain brands that you are familiar with and tend to buy?

With a small group of students, list the brand names that you look for when you buy these products:

1. Drinks
2. Clothes
3. Shoes
4. Movies
5. Cars
6. Computers
7. Meals
8. Other products

READING 1: IDENTIFYING PRODUCTS

The following reading is an excerpt from a book on business.

TASK TWO: Applying "read smart" skills

To prepare for the reading, use the "read smart" skills from Chapter 3 (page 47).

- Figure out exactly what you are reading.
- Consider what you already know about the topic.
- Before you start to read, predict the information that you will learn from the reading.
- Skim the reading and try to divide it into sections. The sections may be clearly indicated by headings and subheadings, or you may have to define the sections yourself.
- Take short, point-form notes on each section of the reading.
- When you have finished the reading, use your critical thinking skills. Was your prediction correct? How important will this information be to your final assignment?

- Now read and take notes in the margins of the reading.
- When you have finished, compare your notes with a classmate's. Are there any differences in your margin notes? Why?

Branding products

"Coca-Cola is the best-known brand in the world. Indeed, some Coke executives claim that if all the company's other assets were obliterated, they could go to the bank and borrow $100 billion on the strength of the brand name alone. Brand names such as Coca-Cola and emblems such as the McDonald's golden arches are symbols that characterize products and distinguish them from one another. **Branding** is a process of using symbols to communicate the qualities of a particular product made by a particular producer. Brands are designed to signal uniform quality: Customers who try and like a product can return to it by remembering its name.

4. Like more and more people these days, I suffer from environmental sensitivities.

5. My chiropractor says that the body has an innate ability to heal itself.

WARM-UP ASSIGNMENT

TASK SEVEN: Writing a short compare or contrast essay

- Write a short compare or contrast essay. In order to keep the essay relatively short, review the chapter content to this point and decide whether you will write about the similarities or differences between Western and alternative medicine.

In a compare or contrast essay, you must organize and explain similarities or differences in ways that make sense. Refer to the Models Chapter (page 210) for more information about compare and contrast essays. Be sure to write using an objective, third person, academic perspective. Use parallel structure when necessary.

When you receive feedback from other students or your teacher on this assignment, you will have information that you can use to improve your performance on the final assignment.

LISTENING: DIFFERENTIATING BETWEEN ALTERNATIVE AND COMPLEMENTARY MEDICINE

You will listen to a recording of Dr. Barrie Cassileth explaining the difference between the terms *alternative* and *complementary*.

TASK EIGHT: Listening and taking notes

Part A: Pre-listening vocabulary building

Here are some key words that you will need to know to understand the audio segment. The key words are in bold in the sentences below. The parts of speech are listed in parentheses.

- Read the sentences and discuss with a partner what you think the words mean.
- You can ask students from other groups if you aren't sure. Consult your dictionary only as a last resort.

CHAPTER 5 Alternative and Complementary Medicine 109

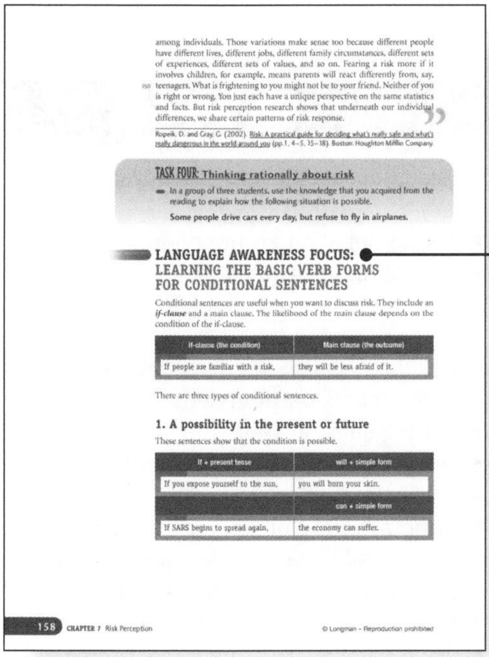

among individuals. Those variations make sense too because different people have different lives, different jobs, different family circumstances, different sets of experiences, different sets of values, and so on. Fearing a risk more if it involves children, for example, means parents will react differently from, say, teenagers. What is frightening to you might not be to your friend. Neither of you is right or wrong. You just each have a unique perspective on the same statistics and facts. But risk perception research shows that underneath our individual differences, we share certain patterns of risk response.

Ropeik, D. and Gray, G. (2002). Risk: A practical guide for deciding what's really safe and what's really dangerous in the world around you (pp. 1, 4–5, 15–18). Boston: Houghton Mifflin Company.

TASK FOUR: Thinking rationally about risk

- In a group of three students, use the knowledge that you acquired from the reading to explain how the following situation is possible.

Some people drive cars every day, but refuse to fly in airplanes.

LANGUAGE AWARENESS FOCUS: LEARNING THE BASIC VERB FORMS FOR CONDITIONAL SENTENCES

Prepares students for reading and writing assignments by focusing on strategies and grammar points.

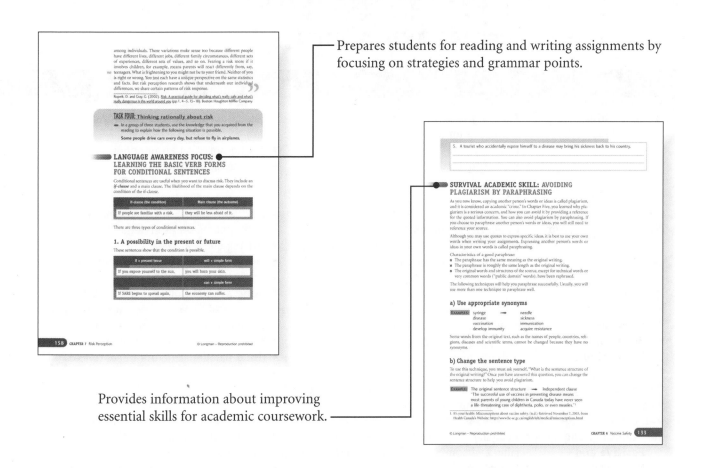

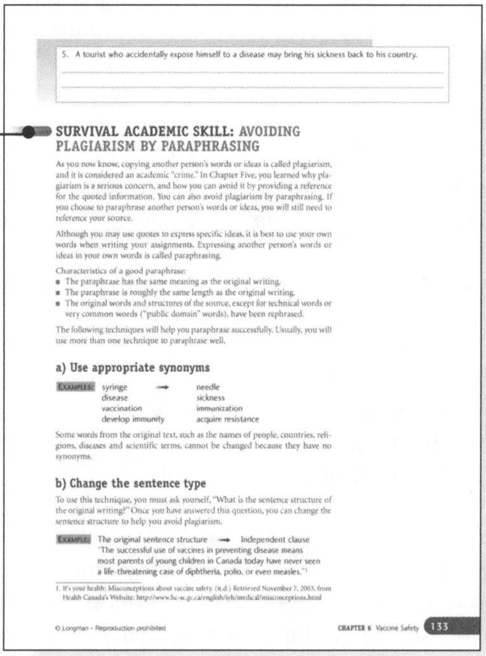

Conditional sentences are useful when you want to discuss risk. They include an ***if-clause*** and a main clause. The likelihood of the main clause depends on the condition of the if-clause.

If-clause (the condition)	Main clause (the outcome)
If people are familiar with a risk,	they will be less afraid of it.

There are three types of conditional sentences.

1. A possibility in the present or future

These sentences show that the condition is possible.

If + present tense	will + simple form
If you expose yourself to the sun,	you will burn your skin.
	can + simple form
If SARS begins to spread again,	the economy can suffer.

158 CHAPTER 7 Risk Perception © Longman – Reproduction prohibited

5. A tourist who accidentally expose himself to a disease may bring his sickness back to his country.

SURVIVAL ACADEMIC SKILL: AVOIDING PLAGIARISM BY PARAPHRASING

As you now know, copying another person's words or ideas is called plagiarism, and it is considered an academic "crime." In Chapter Five, you learned why plagiarism is a serious concern, and how you can avoid it by providing a reference for the quoted information. You can also avoid plagiarism by paraphrasing. If you choose to paraphrase another person's words or ideas, you will still need to reference your source.

Although you may use quotes to express specific ideas, it is best to use your own words when writing your assignments. Expressing another person's words or ideas in your own words is called paraphrasing.

Characteristics of a good paraphrase:

- The paraphrase has the same meaning as the original writing.
- The paraphrase is roughly the same length as the original writing.
- The original words and structures of the source, except for technical words or very common words ("public domain" words), have been rephrased.

The following techniques will help you paraphrase successfully. Usually, you will use more than one technique to paraphrase well.

a) Use appropriate synonyms

EXAMPLES: syringe → needle
disease → sickness
vaccination → immunization
develop immunity → acquire resistance

Some words from the original text, such as the names of people, countries, religions, diseases and scientific terms, cannot be changed because they have no synonyms.

b) Change the sentence type

To use this technique, you must ask yourself, "What is the sentence structure of the original writing?" Once you have answered this question, you can change the sentence structure to help you avoid plagiarism.

EXAMPLE: The original sentence structure → Independent clause
"The successful use of vaccines in preventing disease means most parents of young children in Canada today have never seen a life-threatening case of diphtheria, polio, or even measles."[1]

1. It's your health: Misconceptions about vaccine safety. (n.d.) Retrieved November 7, 2003, from Health Canada's Website: http://www.hc-sc.gc.ca/english/iyh/medical/misconceptions.html

© Longman – Reproduction prohibited CHAPTER 6 Vaccine Safety 133

Provides information about improving essential skills for academic coursework.

In-depth writing assignments synthesize the chapter readings and themes. Each chapter focuses on a different writing pattern.

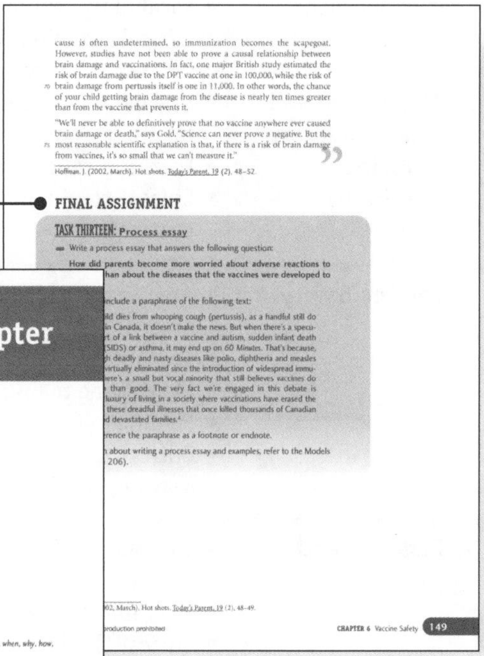

cause is often undetermined, so immunization becomes the scapegoat. However, studies have not been able to prove a causal relationship between brain damage and vaccinations. In fact, one major British study estimated the risk of brain damage due to the DPT vaccine at one in 100,000, while the risk of brain damage from pertussis itself is one in 11,000. In other words, the chance of your child getting brain damage from the disease is nearly ten times greater than from the vaccine that prevents it.

"We'll never be able to definitively prove that no vaccine anywhere ever caused brain damage or death," says Gold. "Science can never prove a negative. But the most reasonable scientific explanation is that, if there is a risk of brain damage from vaccines, it's so small that we can't measure it."

Hoffman, J. (2002, March). Hot shots. Today's Parent, 19 (2), 48–52.

FINAL ASSIGNMENT

TASK THIRTEEN: Process essay

- Write a process essay that answers the following question:

How did parents become more worried about adverse reactions to ... han about the diseases that the vaccines were developed to

nclude a paraphrase of the following text:

ld dies from whooping cough (pertussis), as a handful still do in Canada, it doesn't make the news. But when there's a specu- t of a link between a vaccine and autism, sudden infant death SIDS) or asthma, it may end up on 60 Minutes. That's because, h deadly and nasty diseases like polio, diphtheria and measles virtually eliminated since the introduction of widespread immu- ere's a small but vocal minority that still believes vaccines do than good. The very fact we're engaged in this debate is luxury of living in a society where vaccinations have erased the these dreadful illnesses that once killed thousands of Canadian d devastated families.[4]

rence the paraphrase as a footnote or endnote.

h about writing a process essay and examples, refer to the Models 206).

02, March). Hot shots. Today's Parent, 19 (2), 48–49.

roduction prohibited CHAPTER 6 Vaccine Safety 149

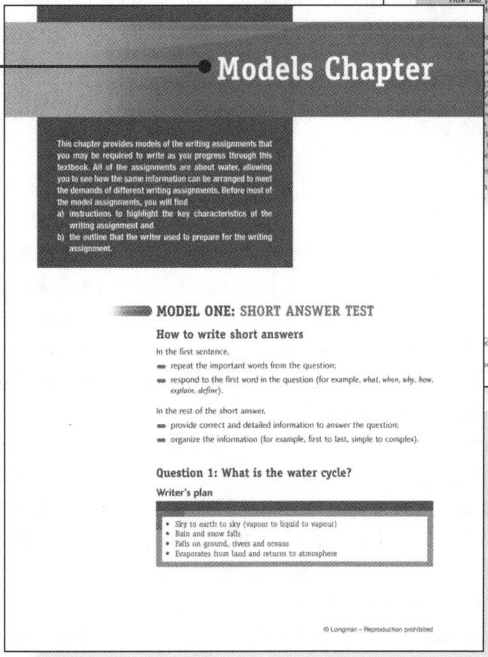

Provides students with instructions and models of all the writing patterns in the textbook.

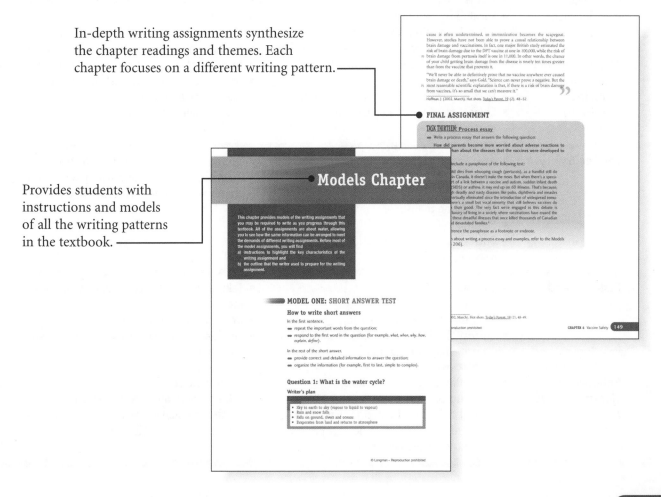

Models Chapter

This chapter provides models of the writing assignments that you may be required to write as you progress through this textbook. All of the assignments are about water, allowing you to see how the same information can be arranged to meet the demands of different writing assignments. Before most of the model assignments, you will find

a) instructions to highlight the key characteristics of the writing assignment and
b) the outline that the writer used to prepare for the writing assignment.

MODEL ONE: SHORT ANSWER TEST

How to write short answers

In the first sentence,

- repeat the important words from the question;
- respond to the first word in the question (for example, *what, when, why, how, explain, define*).

In the rest of the short answer,

- provide correct and detailed information to answer the question;
- organize the information (for example, first to last, simple to complex).

Question 1: What is the water cycle?

Writer's plan

- Sky to earth to sky (vapour to liquid to vapour)
- Rain and snow falls
- Falls on ground, rivers and oceans
- Evaporates from land and returns to atmosphere

© Longman – Reproduction prohibited

SCOPE AND SEQUENCE

Chapter	Reading Skills	Writing Skills
1. Elite Child Athletes Theme: Psychology	• Applying vocabulary strategies • Skimming for key words to read for meaning • Predicting content	• Selecting specific and descriptive vocabulary • Taking notes on an interview • Writing short answers
2. A Good Education Theme: Education and psychology	• Categorizing vocabulary • Critical thinking: Comparing and contrasting information; forming opinions	• Taking notes on interviews • Writing short answers • Designing a survey to collect information • Writing a report • Using a variety of sentence patterns
3. Consumer Behaviour and Innovation Theme: Sociology and business	• Skimming and scanning • Using subheadings to preview • Making inferences • Predicting content • Understanding content through note-taking • Critical thinking: Determining relevance	• Taking margin notes on readings • Writing short answers using margin notes • Using parallel structure in sentences • Writing process essays
4. Branding: The Positive and the Negative Theme: Sociology and business	• Applying "read smart" techniques: skimming and scanning, inferencing, predicting • Identifying collocations • Vocabulary: expressions • Critical thinking: Expressing opinions	• Taking notes on interviews • Writing short answers • Writing persuasive essays using support from texts • Using collocations and parallel structure
5. Alternative and Complementary Medicine Theme: Health science	• Understanding content through note-taking • Learning word forms and collocations • Critical thinking: Comparing and contrasting	• Taking notes on a lecture and readings • Writing compare/contrast essays using references and quotations • Using academic perspective
6. Vaccine Safety Theme: Health science	• Applying "read smart" techniques: scanning, inferences, text organization • Vocabulary: parts of speech • Identifying main ideas • Finding synonyms • Critical thinking: Evaluating information, drawing conclusions	• Taking notes on a lecture and readings • Practising paraphrasing using synonyms, changing sentence structure and voice
7. Risk Perception Theme: Psychology	• Vocabulary: Expressions • Identifying main ideas • Scanning for key information • Critical thinking: Transferring knowledge, interpreting information	• Taking notes on a commentary and readings • Organizing information in a table • Writing summaries of paragraphs, charts and short essays
8. Genetically Modified Foods Theme: Science	• Vocabulary: Word definitions • Learning collocations • Critical thinking: Detecting bias, evaluating information, forming an opinion, drawing conclusions	• Organizing information in a chart • Taking notes on a lecture and readings • Writing persuasive essays using the passive voice, collocations and references

Language Awareness Focus	Survival Academic Skill	Warm-Up Assignment	Final Assignment
• Vocabulary strategies: Context clues, root words, prefixes and suffixes, collocations • Improving writing with specific vocabulary	• Improving listening and note-taking skills	• Short answer questions	• Short answer test
• Sentence structure • Question format	• Oral and written presentation skills	• Short report based on an in-class survey	• Survey and report • Oral presentation
• Parallelism in writing	• "Read smart" techniques: Skimming, text organization, inferencing, predicting	• Short process essay	• Short process essay
• Collocations to improve fluency	• Learning independently	• Short persuasive essay	• Short persuasive essay
• Academic perspective: Using the third person to demonstrate objective viewpoint	• Referencing to avoid plagiarism	• Short compare/contrast essay	• Short compare/contrast essay with references
• Solutions to problems with writing in the third person	• Paraphrasing to avoid plagiarism	• Paraphrase	• Process essay with paraphrase and references
• Basic verb forms in conditional sentences	• Summarizing to avoid plagiarism	• Short Summary	• Extended Summary
• Using the passive voice	• Detecting bias in readings	• Short persuasive essay	• Extended persuasive essay

TABLE OF CONTENTS

Chapter 1: Elite Child Athletes 1

Chapter 2: A Good Education 24

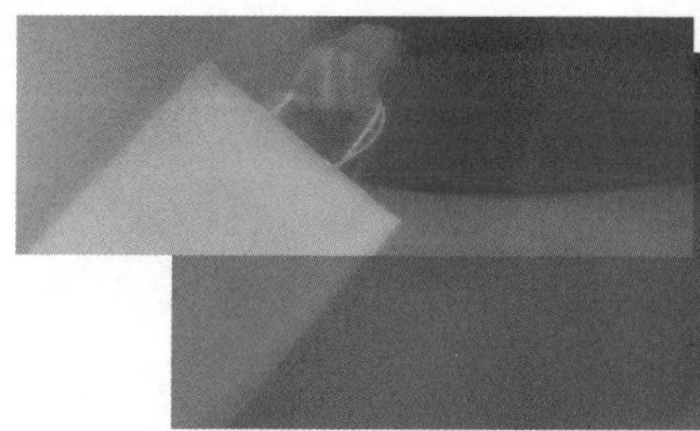

DRINK
HERE
Milkshakes
Capital
BREAD

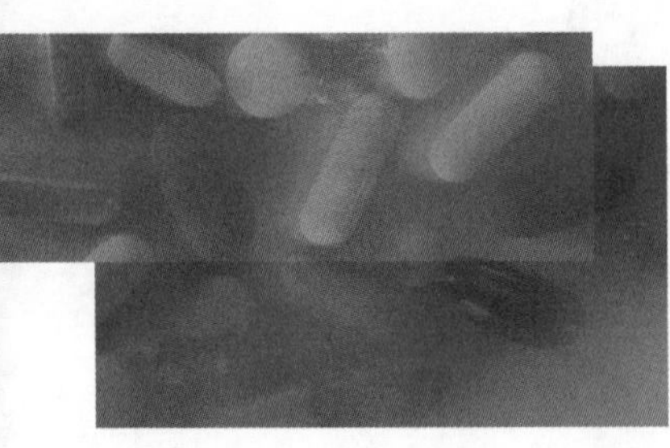

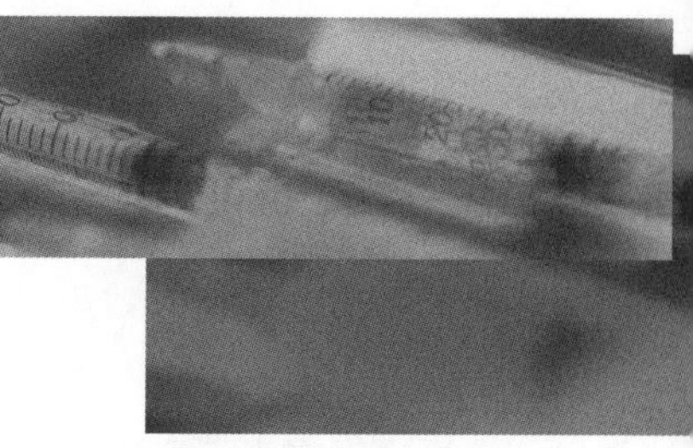

Chapter 8: Genetically Modified Foods 171

Models Chapter 200

CHAPTER 1

Elite Child Athletes

Playing sports can be a wonderful experience for children and youth; it can be especially rewarding if they are talented, hard-working, and successful. However, many young people are being asked to train long hours—even when they are injured—in order to chase international success. To win gold for their country, they often have to sacrifice their schoolwork, their friends, their family and even their long-term health. Should young athletes make these sacrifices to win big? In this chapter, you will read about elite child athletes training at the highest levels, and the pressures that they face in their quest to become the best in the world.

QUICK OVERVIEW

READING
Read excerpts from books and magazine articles in order to gather knowledge about elite child athletes while applying vocabulary strategies. Practise skimming and scanning, predicting, and reading for meaning.

WRITING
Respond to questions about the readings, take notes while listening to an interview, and write short answers in order to develop your writing fluency and learn new vocabulary.

LISTENING
Listen to a radio interview with a sports doctor and a talented young athlete. Practise listening and taking notes.

DISCUSSION
Discuss elite child athletes and exchange information about the readings and listening exercise.

LANGUAGE AWARENESS FOCUS
Learn successful vocabulary strategies (guessing meaning from context, deciding which words are important to learn and which ones are not) in order to improve your ability to read quickly for meaning. Improve your writing by selecting better vocabulary.

SURVIVAL ACADEMIC SKILL
Learn how to improve your listening and note-taking skills in order to take quick and accurate notes that capture the main points of a lecture.

WARM-UP ASSIGNMENT
Respond to questions with short answers in order to prepare you for the final assignment.

FINAL ASSIGNMENT
Complete a short answer test in order to prepare you for tests and exams.

GEARING UP

TASK ONE: Discussion about young athletes

What do you know about elite young athletes? Brainstorm with your classmates to find out more.

- In a group of three or four students, make a list of four elite young athletes.
- For each elite young athlete, fill in information in the following chart.
- When you have finished, discuss your ideas with the class.

(Suggestions: Michelle Wie in golf, Freddy Adu in basketball, Nadia Comaneci in gymnastics, Jennifer Capriati in tennis)

Name	Age	Sport	Is/Was the athlete successful?
1.			
2.			
3.			
4.			

READING 1: THE HIGH-PRESSURE LIVES OF CHILD ATHLETES: BALANCING AMBITION WITH FAMILY, SCHOOL AND FRIENDS

This article describes four child athletes who are training hard.

TASK TWO: Reading about four athletes

- In a group of three students, decide who will read about which athlete. As you read, fill in the information chart (page 3) for your athlete(s).
- When you have finished, check your information with other students who have read about the same athlete(s). Fill in any information gaps that you may have.
- Return to your group and exchange information about your athletes. As you listen to your group members, take point-form notes in the information chart.
- Try to decide which of the four athletes is best at balancing training with school, family and friends. Discuss your opinions with the class.

Student Readers

Athlete	Student Reader
A. Charlotte Makie – gymnastics	
B. Alison Hunter – skiing	
C. Patrick Chan – figure skating, Pascal Wollach – swimming	

Information Chart

Name	Sport	Number of hours spent training	How the athlete balances training with school, family and friends	Do you think this athlete can continue training like this? Why or why not?
1. Charlotte Makie				
2. Alison Hunter				
3. Patrick Chan				
4. Pascal Wollach				

Student A: Charlotte Makie

"Four days a week at noon, when her schoolmates in Langley, B.C., are heading home for bologna sandwiches and chocolate chip cookies, 9-year-old Charlotte Mackie jumps into her mother's car and digs into a container of pasta as her mom, Sue, drives off to the Omega Gymnastics Academy, 25 minutes away in Coquitlam. The Grade 4 student may have spent recess having fun on the monkey bars, but from 1 to 5 the play gets serious as the petite pony-tailed blonde dons a leotard and hits the tumbling mats, balance beams and vaults.

Since the age of 3, Charlotte has been involved in gymnastics—first tagging along as her older sister, Gael, now 14 and a Canadian junior champion, performed her routines, later as a competitive gymnast in her own right. "I like flying, doing giants around the bar—that's when you swing around. I want to go to the Olympics and win a university scholarship," she chirps in her tiny voice.

Charlotte is just one of thousands of Canadian kids trying to strike a balance between the balance beam and birthday parties, the ice rink and school work. On top of all the hours spent training each day, she has to miss her schoolmates' parties and sleepovers, but the girl is philosophical about it. "I don't really mind that much because I have closer friends at gymnastics than at school," she says.

Competitive sports are a greater presence in the lives of Canadian youngsters than ever before. From the time some kids learn to walk, their parents suit them up in hockey pads or figure skates and set them to training hours every day to be the next Wayne Gretzky or Josée Chouinard.

Sport Canada, a branch of the federal Canadian Heritage Department dedicated to promoting athletics in this country, estimates that more than two million children are involved in some type of organized athletics, with thousands taking part in regular competitive events.

The big challenge is ensuring that the athletic child—especially the one ambitious for world-class gold—achieves equilibrium amongst training, education, family time and social life.

Charlotte's mother, Sue, knows better than most how difficult that balancing act can be. Both she and her husband, Bill (now practising physicians) competed as gymnasts when they were younger. Bill qualified for the 1972 Olympic Games in Munich. "We're not normal," laughs Sue. "We spend a lot of our time in the car. Charlotte spends 90 minutes a day there. That's when she reads, does homework, sleeps. We have to be very efficient."

The competitive life for Charlotte began at age 6, when she started training nine hours a week. Those hours have since more than doubled to 20, drastically cutting into education time. So Sue has had to work out a system with Charlotte's school. "Every day, my daughter meets with her teacher at lunchtime and goes through what she will be missing and has missed, and writes it down in her agenda," she says. Not only does it take a lot of discipline on the child's part, "it takes quite a bit of parental commitment," says Sue. "I have to help out by getting missing school work." For the time being, this system is working, although her other daughter, Gael, switched to correspondence courses when she reached the eighth grade. ”

Student B: Alison Hunter

“Most children in elite sports come to realize that they must find an alternative to playing catch-up at a regular public school. For Alison Hunter, now 17, a competitive skier from Aurora, Ont., the crunch came when she hit high school and had to miss a large number of classes. The answer was to send Alison, at age 15, to live with a family in Calgary and attend the National Sport School, established for secondary-level students in 1994 by the Calgary Olympic Development Association in partnership with the Calgary Board of Education.

Since then, Alison has studied alongside more than 100 other students involved in 15 different sports, including snowboarding, figure skating, gymnastics, tennis and luge. At the beginning of each term, teachers take a look at all students' training and competition schedules for that period and plan their educational timetables accordingly.

Each teacher acts as an adviser-advocate for a small number of students, grouped by sport. All students have access to a laptop computer with dial-in access to an Internet account, allowing them to maintain contact with the school while they are away training or competing. Athletes missing big chunks of classroom time can always make up the deficits because the school offers year-round academic programs.

Alison's program makes allowance for her four hours of daily training and several months' absence each year at competitions. The great thing about the program, says her mother, Jan, is the flexibility. "At her new school, she was able to write three tests on the plane under the supervision of her coaches on her way home from a meet."

Student C: Patrick Chan and Pascal Wollach

With sports making such extraordinary demands on their time, child athletes and their parents face the challenge of making sure the interests of the children don't become too narrow. Patrick Chan is a talented figure skater at the pre-novice level who trains at Toronto's Granite Club and dreams ambitiously of "landing the first quadruple axel." Patrick has participated in just about every physical activity you could fit into 12 years— not the least of which is the several hours a day he puts in on the ice. "Because he is quite young, we wanted him to have a diversity of sporting interests, as well as time to just play," his father, Lewis, says. "So over the years he has done ballet, Ukrainian dancing, tennis, soccer, golf, skiing and basketball." Rather a full plate, yet Patrick is more than up for it. "I don't find it too much," he says gamely. "It helps me with my skating—ballet especially. I feel like I'm a much more well-rounded person."

Well and good, but what about the party and sleepover circuits? How do young athletic stars fit these in? "We try to work things in around Patrick's skating schedule," Lewis explains. "If he has to go to a birthday party, we might have him skate the morning or the night before to make up for it, rather than eliminate either the practice or the party. We think it's important for him to have friends in situations other than skating."

Sooner or later, though, something in the whirlwind life of a young elite athlete has to give. Pascal Wollach, now 15, a competitive swimmer from Melfort, Sask., who now trains in Calgary, used to immerse himself in a variety of activities. "When I was 10, I trained five to six times a week," he recalls. "That wasn't too stressful, so I joined hockey and soccer, but by the time I was 11 and training 14 hours a week, I had to drop out of those."

Two years later, he gave up piano lessons. "Last year, I even wanted to quit swimming because there was too much pressure on me," he says. "I had my school work, studying for my bar mitzvah and school sports." He then switched to a school that allows students to work at their own pace with a teacher-adviser and counts many athletes among its registrants. Currently he trains 18 hours a week but feels more in control of his life.

One of the things that contributed to the stress Pascal felt was parental expectation. "We've never been openly pushy, but without realizing it, we were exerting subtle pressures on him," admits his mother, Mychelle. "He was very close to achieving junior national standards but our talking about those standards only added stress to his life." She says parents have to know when to back off and let their child take ownership of his sport.

Pierre Beauchamp, a Montreal sports psychology consultant for Olympic and other world-class athletes, urges parents to pay attention to the signs of stress in their athlete children. "There comes a time," he says, when they will start not wanting to go to practice and be getting constant upset stomachs and headaches. They will think obsessively about their sport all the time and about the rewards rather than the pleasure." That's when the parents need to step in. ”

Binks, G. (March 2003). The high-pressure lives of child athletes. Canadian Family, 25–30.

LANGUAGE AWARENESS FOCUS: VOCABULARY STRATEGIES

TASK THREE: What to do with unknown vocabulary

When you read about the athletes in Reading 1, what did you do when you saw a word that you didn't know?

- Discuss with the class what you do when you see a word that you don't know.
- Write down both your own and your classmates' ideas in the space below.
- When you have finished, decide as a class which ideas will help you learn and remember new words most effectively.

Strategy #1: Guess the meaning from the context

One of the strategies successful students use when they come across unknown vocabulary is to try to guess the meaning of the word from the context (or the words around the unknown word).

Example: Charlotte dreams of reaching the ***podium*** at the Olympics.

You may not know the word *podium*. However, you do know some information that will help you guess the word's meaning. You know that:

- the reading is about young athletes and how they train for sports.
- the verb in the sentence is *dreams*. What do most talented athletes dream of?
- the word *Olympics* shows you Charlotte is dreaming about being successful at an international level of competition.
- *the* comes before *podium*. Therefore, you know that *podium* is a noun.

You may still not understand what *podium* means, but you have a good idea what the sentence means. Now read the sentence that follows:

EXAMPLE: Charlotte dreams of reaching the *podium* at the Olympics. She hopes she will one day climb the *podium* to receive the gold medal in gymnastics.

The second sentence gives you more information about the meaning of the word *podium*. You now know that:

- the *podium* is something that you climb onto.
- you receive medals on the *podium*.

You can probably guess that *podium* refers to the steps that winning athletes climb to receive their medals. Now you know the meaning of the word, and you didn't have to look it up in the dictionary.

Strategy #2: Guess the meaning from root words, prefixes and suffixes

You can also use what you know about root words, prefixes and suffixes to help you guess the meanings of words.

EXAMPLE: The big challenge is ensuring that the athletic child—especially the one ambitious for world-class gold—achieves ***equilibrium*** amongst training, education, family time and social life. (line 27)

You may not know what the word *equilibrium* means. However, you can figure out that the word is

- based on the root word *equal* (which you probably know means "the same").
- a noun because it is the object of the verb *achieves*.
- followed by the preposition *amongst* which indicates a middle position surrounded by a group of people or things.

You may also understand that the list of things that follows the words *equilibrium amongst* (*training*, *education*, *family time and social life*) are important parts of an athlete's life that need to be balanced. You also know that balance is a key idea in this article because *balancing* is in the subtitle of the article.

As a result, you can probably guess that the word *equilibrium* (n) means *balance* (n)—and you didn't even need to consult a dictionary!

Remember that prefixes change the meaning of a word.

EXAMPLE:

- *pre*requisite, *pre*condition, *pre*determined (*pre* means completed before)
- *re*place, *re*think, *re*store (*re* means again)
- *in*considerate, *in*consistent, *in*convenient (*in* means not)

Suffixes change the type of word (or part of speech), but the meaning remains similar to the meaning of the root word.

EXAMPLE:

- activ*ity* (noun), to act (verb), act*ive* (adjective) active*ly* (adverb)
- impress*ion* (noun), to impress (verb), impress*ive* (adjective), impressive*ly* (adverb)
- rebell*ion* (noun), to rebel (verb), rebell*ious* (adjective), rebell*iously* (adverb)

TASK FOUR: Guessing word meaning from context

- With a partner, try to guess the meaning of the boldfaced words in the sentences below.

1. The competitive life for Charlotte began at age six, when she started training nine hours a week. Those hours have since more than doubled to 20, **drastically** cutting into education time. So Sue (her mother) has had to work out a system with Charlotte's school. (line 44)

2. Alison's program makes **allowance** for her four hours of daily training and several months' absence each year at competitions. The great thing about the program, says her mother, Jan, is the **flexibility**. "At her new school, she was able to write three tests on the plane under the supervision of her coaches on her way home from a meet." (line 71)

3. "Because he (Patrick) is quite young, we wanted him to have a **diversity** of sporting interests, as well as time to just play," his father, Lewis, says. "So over the years he has done ballet, Ukrainian dancing, tennis, soccer, golf, skiing and basketball." (line 83)

4. For the time being, this system is working, although her other daughter, Gael, switched to **correspondence** courses when she reached the eighth grade. (line 51)

Strategy #3: Keep reading without knowing the meaning of every word

It may also be possible for you to continue reading without knowing the exact meaning of every word. Good students know that they may have to keep reading—even though they don't know the meaning of a certain word—in order to finish the reading quickly. Sometimes it isn't necessary to know the meaning of every word to understand the meaning of the reading.

EXAMPLE: Since then, Alison has studied alongside more than 100 other students involved in 15 different sports, including snowboarding, figure skating, gymnastics, tennis and ***luge***. At the beginning of each term, teachers take a look at all students' training and competition schedules for that period and plan their educational timetables accordingly. (line 60)

You may not know the meaning of the word *luge*. However, you can continue reading without worrying about the exact meaning because you probably know other things:

- *Luge* is a word that is included in a list of sports.
- This is the first time that you have seen the word in this article.
- The word is not repeated or referred to in the subsequent sentences.

As a result, you can probably guess that *luge* is a kind of sport. You may also realize that this word only occurs once in the article. Therefore, you probably don't need to understand its exact meaning in order to continue reading the article.

You must decide if the new word is important to understand, or if you can still understand the main points of the reading without knowing its exact meaning.

- Discuss with your class how you can decide if the meaning of a word is important to understand or not. Here are some clues.

Characteristics of a word that is not important to the meaning of the reading	Characteristics of a word that is important to the meaning of the reading
1. The word isn't repeated often.	1. The word is repeated frequently.
2. The word is included in a list of examples.	2. The word is included in the title or subheading(s) of a reading.
3. The word is an adjective that you can guess is positive or negative.	3. The word is highlighted or underlined in the reading.

READING 2: THE DRAWBACKS OF YOUTH SPORTS

This reading is an excerpt from a book about young elite athletes.

TASK FIVE: Applying vocabulary strategies

- As you read the short excerpt from this book, use your new vocabulary strategies to help you with unknown vocabulary.
- Underline the words you do not know so that you can discuss them later with your classmates. Do not use a dictionary.
  1. Guess the meaning of the word from its context.
  2. Guess the meaning of the word from its root word, or by removing its prefix or suffix.
  3. Decide if you can keep reading without knowing the exact meaning of the word.
- After reading the excerpt, discuss the underlined words with your classmates. Make a list of at least three words corresponding to each strategy.

Though there are wonderful benefits to be gained through participating in youth sports, there can also be definite drawbacks. Some are obvious, while others cannot be seen until one is already involved in the sport.

One drawback can be the time commitment and financial burden youth sports often demand. Certain sports—swimming, ice skating, gymnastics—can demand much more time than others. This time crunch can put a strain on families, especially when sisters or brothers in the same family are not involved in sports. The parents' attention can be centered around the "athlete" to the exclusion of the "nonathlete."

And even if the entire family is into athletics, another drawback that can surface in the often-hectic life of a young athlete can be the lack of time the family has to spend with each other. All the traveling, training, and competing—on top of normal school responsibilities—leave little time for family socializing or trips. Some parents, after years of being involved in sports, have regretted this loss of time together with their children.

Coaches who are too controlling, too competitive, and too much in need of success put enormous pressure upon their athletes, often humiliating and scaring them. Many young athletes are emotionally damaged by such coaches. These coaches are notorious in all sports, and sadly are allowed to continue—and are even sought out by many parents who will do anything to help their child win.

Finally, young athletes may become involved in an unbalanced program, where all the emphasis is put upon winning. In such a program, nothing is done to help an athlete learn about his or her emotional self. In fact, for the most part fear and similar feelings are usually considered weak, and it is the athlete's job to figure out how to deal with them. There is no consideration of any kind of balanced development for the athlete. It is all about winning, which gives young people the message that their worth and value is determined by how well they perform. This is the wrong message for any child to receive.

This last drawback speaks to the lack of emotional development in competitive sports programs, and specifically to the way fear is usually looked upon by many coaches (and parents) and eventually by the athletes themselves. Ultimately, this approach will severely curtail—or eliminate any real opportunity for young athletes to gain an awareness of how to deal with their emotions.

Andersonn, C. (2000). The drawbacks of youth sports. In Will you still love me if I don't win? (pp.16–17). Taylor Trade Publishing.

TASK SIX: Summarizing the drawbacks of competitive youth sports

- Summarize the drawbacks of competitive youth sports covered in the above reading.
- Make brief point-form notes.

Drawbacks of competitive youth sports

1. *Time commitment and financial burden*

2. ____

____

3. ____

____

4. ____

____

5. ____

____

LANGUAGE AWARENESS FOCUS: VOCABULARY STRATEGIES

Strategy #4: Learn more words faster with collocations

You can increase your reading, speaking and writing fluency, as well as your listening comprehension, by learning pairs or small groups of words at the same time. In English, many words often appear together in recognized mini-expressions. These groups of words are called ***collocations***.

In the last reading, there were several collocations related to *time*.

EXAMPLE: time commitment, time crunch, lack of time, leave little time for, loss of time

In the last two readings, there were a number of collocations related to *pressure*.

EXAMPLE: put (enormous) pressure on, high-pressure, under (too much) pressure, to exert pressure on (someone)

- Try to fit the appropriate collocation from the above examples into the blanks in these sentences:

1. All of the training ______________ school, family, and friends.
2. The coaches ______________ the gymnasts until the athletes are exhausted.
3. Going to the skating rink six times a week was a ______________ that his parents couldn't make.
4. Competing at the Olympics is a ______________ activity.
5. In the end, the child athlete was ______________. She became too sick to compete.

READING 3: DOCTORS' RECOMMENDATIONS

This reading is an excerpt from a newspaper article about how children suffer overuse injuries in sports. This excerpt quotes a number of doctors and sports psychologists who work with young elite athletes.

TASK SEVEN: Reading for meaning

- Read the questions. Then read the excerpt and answer the questions.

  Reading the questions first can help you complete the task faster. Identify the key words in the questions that you can skim for in the reading. The key words in the questions are in bold to help you.

- Discuss your answers with another student. Make sure that you have understood the recommendations of the medical experts.

1. Give three reasons why children are being **injured** playing sports today.

   ~~did not play so many organized sports~~
   longer training
   practice with rigor
   sports are played all year

2. How does **early specialization** in a single sport cause **overuse injuries** in children? Why are children injured most often when they are **growing** rapidly (during peak growth spurts)?

   Creates muscle imbalance
   When
   still growing

3. Children who specialize in one sport are **at risk** for what other problem? Why?

   for mental burnout

4. What are the sources of **pressure** on young athletes?

   parents
   coaches
   ch. themselves

5. Why is it difficult for a doctor to recommend "**benching**" a child (asking an injured child to sit on the bench and rest rather than play)?

   w. p. & c. consider this child the best on the team

“Doctors who specialize in the new field of sports medicine for children say more young people are getting injured playing sports, and they point to a number of causes. First, in previous generations, children did not play so many organized sports. There was much more unstructured play—a pickup basketball game here, some neighbourhood baseball there—but children didn't practice with the rigor they do today, with repetitive drills, lap running and scrimmages. In earlier days, when a child became tired of playing, he or she stopped. Today, practices for children can run three hours.

A generation ago, specific sports were played during one season. Boys may have played football in the fall and baseball in the spring. But now, many sports are played all year. Baseball leagues play and practice in the spring, summer, winter and fall; so do some soccer and lacrosse teams.

Children are also specializing in one sport at younger ages. Children as young as 10 are encouraged by parents and coaches alike to devote themselves to whichever sport they show the most promise in, be it ice hockey or tennis. In sports like gymnastics and dance, the pressure to specialize comes even earlier.

Early specialization contributes to overuse because it tends to create muscle imbalance, Dr. Small said. [Dr. Eric Small is the director of the Sports Medicine Center for Young Athletes at Blythedale Children's Hospital in Valhalla, NY] If only one sport is played constantly, one muscle—the quadricep, for instance—may be highly developed while the hamstring is not. When there is too much pull on the less developed muscle, injury can occur.

Children and teenagers are also particularly vulnerable to overuse injuries because they are still growing, Dr. Small said. Growth plates, which are made up of soft tissue, are at the tips of maturing bones, and they often aren't strong enough to handle constant pounding or the stress of a repetitive motion. Many overuse injuries occur when children are at their peak growth spurts, Dr. Small said.

Children who specialize in one sport early are not only at risk for overuse injuries but also for mental burnout, said Rick Wolff, a sports psychology expert in Armonk [NY], who discusses parenting issues on “The Sports Edge,” his Sunday morning talk show on WFAN-AM (660).

“I know of no study that says if your child specializes in one sport at an early age, that's going to guarantee them to be a star when they get to be in high school or college,” Mr. Wolff said. “Conversely I know of many studies that say that kids who specialize in one sport run a very serious risk of burning out and leaving the sport by the time they're 13 or 14.”

Mr. Wolff said that he often hears children say things like, “I play soccer seriously but I play basketball for fun,” raising the question of when sports for children became more of [a] job than an activity for fun and fitness.

Thomas Burns, a certified athletic trainer at Fox Lane High School in Bedford [NY], said that for college athletes, sports often becomes a full-time job, with football players beginning practice in July, and workouts continuing throughout the off season. But now, he said, this phenomenon seems to be spreading to younger athletes.

“This is starting to spill back from college into high school, and now sometimes into the middle school,” Mr. Burns said. “I think it's too much.”

Where is the pressure coming from? Everywhere, say those who work with young athletes. Parents want their children to succeed on the athletic field. Coaches want the best performances out of their teams. And children themselves want to perform at high levels. Those who love sports want to play for as many hours a day as they can. When an injury occurs, doctors report that families often have a difficult time accepting that the child needs a rest.

"Benching a child is a very difficult thing to do from my side," Dr. Luks said. [Dr. Howard Luks is chief of Sports Medicine at the Westchester Medical Center in Valhalla, NY] "It's not as easy as talking to a parent and saying, 'O.K., your kid can't play,' because that night I'm going to get a phone call from the father saying I'm an idiot and he's going to get a second opinion, and you're definitely going to get a call from the coach, because everyone's child is the best on the team and has the prospect to be the next Tiger Woods."

Dr. Small said he often is providing the second or third opinion to young athletes and their parents who just can't accept that the child needs to cut back on the activity or at least do some cross training.

"I was the third opinion for one 15-year-old girl who was running 50 or 60 miles a week, which is more than adult marathoners run," Dr. Small said. "In the past year, she'd had knee braces and orthopedics and ankle supports. None of them worked. It was just that she was running too much."

Lombardi, K.S. (2002, September 22). More sports, more risk. The New York Times, p. WC14.

LANGUAGE AWARENESS FOCUS: IMPROVING YOUR WRITING

You can quickly improve your written and spoken English by selecting specific and descriptive vocabulary. This will allow your readers and listeners to "see" your exact meaning, which is useful not only for them but also for you. However, selecting better vocabulary is more than just useful for academic writing—it is *essential.* Academic writing is used to express complex ideas. If you use words that are not specific, your reader may not understand your exact meaning.

You do not need to spend a lot of time looking in a dictionary or a thesaurus to find better vocabulary. Think of the words that you already recognize but have yet to use in your own writing. The words don't have to be long or fancy. Spend time searching your mind for better words; consult a dictionary or thesaurus only as a last resort.

Look at these sentences that coaches might say to their athletes. The underlined words indicate non-specific and inaccurate verbs, adjectives, and nouns.

1. If you do these recommendations, you will get success.

   With better vocabulary:
   If you ***follow*** these recommendations, you will ***achieve*** success.
   If you ***work at*** these recommendations, you will ***enjoy*** success.
   If you ***accomplish*** these recommendations, you will ***reach*** the Olympics.

2. You can do better in swimming if you work when you are very tired.

   With better vocabulary:
   You can ***improve your swimming*** if you ***train*** when you are ***completely exhausted***.

You can ***decrease your swim times*** if you ***push yourself*** when you are ***fatigued***.
You can ***increase your endurance*** if you ***swim*** when you are ***extremely tired***.

Now look at these sentences that athletes might say to their coaches.

- Work with another student to make the sentences more accurate.
- Identify the words that are non-specific, and then select better verbs, adjectives, and nouns.

1. I will work hard to get the goal.

   ____

   ____

2. The work is very difficult and the pressure is too much.

   ____

   ____

WARM-UP ASSIGNMENT

TASK EIGHT: Responding to short answer questions

In many of your classes, you will be asked to respond in writing to questions with short answers. Short answers may be as brief as one or two sentences, or as long as half a page, depending on the content. In order to write a successful short answer, you will need to follow this advice:

- Review what you know and decide on the content that you want to include in your short answer.
- Look at your content and organize it so that the information is presented in a recognizable way—from simple to complex, in chronological order, or from beginning to end. Your challenge is to organize the information so that it is not only brief but also logically presented.
- Your first sentence should clearly refer to the question.

Refer to the section on short answers in the Models Chapter (page 200) in order to learn how to write a complete short answer.

- Write a short answer to the following question:

  What should elite child athletes be careful about as they progress in their sports?

Be sure to select accurate and specific vocabulary when you write. When you receive feedback from your teacher or your classmates on this warm-up assignment, you will have some information that you can use to improve your writing on the final assignment.

SURVIVAL ACADEMIC SKILL: LISTENING AND TAKING NOTES

Listening and taking notes are essential academic skills that you will use as you attend classes throughout university. Read the following tips before you complete the listening task (page 17).

Listening

Listening is often your first source of information about a topic.

1. Think about how these points affect your ability to listen:
   - The speed and accent of the speaker
   - Your familiarity with the topic and the vocabulary
   - Your interest in the topic
2. Think about how these physical conditions affect your ability to listen:
   - Your view of the speaker and the number of speakers
   - Your ability to interact with the speaker
   - The number of speakers with similar voices
   - The background noise
3. Think about how your feelings affect your ability to listen:
   - How alert you are
   - How interested you are

Tips to help you listen better

Prepare ahead:

- Scan newspaper headings before listening to the news on television or radio.
- Scan the Internet for news items before listening to the news on television or radio.
- Read assigned readings before attending a lecture.

Predict what you will hear:

- Consider what you know about the topic.
- Listen for signals. (*The final point is, Unfortunately*)
- Listen for connectors. (*However, Therefore*)
- Listen for sequencers. (*First, Finally*)
- Listen for rising and falling intonation. (Rising intonation signals questions; falling intonation signals the end of an idea.)

Taking notes

Your notes should be accurate enough to help you review the main ideas in your courses in preparation for tests and exams. Here are some ideas that may help you improve your note-taking skills.

1. As with listening, prepare ahead so that you can anticipate new vocabulary and predict what the lecturer will say. Read the required readings for the class, and review your notes from the previous class.
2. Be organized. Date your notes. Keep them in order.
3. Write less, but write what is essential. Most classes follow a similar pattern. The lecturer will
   - introduce a general topic,
   - make a statement about the topic (the main point), and
   - present details about the statement.

   These are all important to write down.

4. Don't write in full sentences. You don't need full sentences to record the essential points.
   - Use point form.
   - Use abbreviations and symbols for long words, or repeated key words.
5. Use visual representations. Sometimes you can represent ideas with diagrams, flow charts, or bubble-diagrams, which are faster to put on the page than full sentences.
6. Write down everything that the lecturer writes on the board. Write down ideas that are repeated.
7. Compare your notes with those of a friend. Fill in any gaps that you might have. Check to make sure that you have understood the main points of the lecture.
8. Review your notes in order to help you remember content, and to predict the content of the next lecture.

LISTENING: KARA LANG – NO FREE RIDE

Kara Lang is the youngest member of the Canadian women's World Cup soccer team. Away from the field she is a high school student who is shy about her all-star reputation. You will listen to an interview from the radio program "The Inside Track."

TASK NINE: Listening and taking notes

Part A: Pre-listening vocabulary building

You will hear these sentences in the interview.

- Match the sentences from the audio segment with the correct meanings. Compare your answers with a classmate.
- Then predict what you will hear, based on the meanings of these sentences.

Sentences		Meanings
1. She is touted as one of the rising stars of soccer.		a) Each person must complete his or her work. Everyone is treated equally.
2. It is a heady experience for a 16 year old.		b) People say she will be famous in the future.
3. There's no free ride.		c) A powerful and exciting experience for a young person.

Part B: Listening for details

- As you listen, take notes in the note-taking outline below. Listen as many times as you wish.
- When you are satisfied with your notes, discuss them with a classmate. Fill in any gaps that you might have. Do you think Kara Lang can balance soccer, school and family life successfully?

When you are listening to a lecture, your notes will probably be longer, with more details about each topic and statement. You will have other opportunities to practise your note-taking skills in the following chapters.

Note-taking outline

Introduction: Kara Lang is ...
Kara's separation of school (home) life from soccer life
The opinions of young autograph seekers
The demands on Kara's time: Kara's principal, Joe Lucciani
A normal 16-year old life: Kara's basketball coach, Mike Johnston
Kara's feelings about being a role model for young children
Living away from her family

Completing homework

teaches herself

between ... ass-over the Internet

READING 4: ROLE MODELS AND CAUTIONARY TALES

TASK TEN: Predicting and reading for meaning

- Before you read the article, read the questions that you will be asked to answer. Remember to look for key words in the questions in order to help you while you read the article.
- Then read the article and apply the vocabulary strategies discussed in this chapter.
- Answer the questions.
- Discuss your answers with the class.

1. Read the title of the article. Predict the topic of the article.

cases – that should be kept in mind – serve as a warning sign

models – typical standard

2. There are three examples of child athletes in the first paragraph. What opinion do you think the author has of these three cases?

The sit. is wrong

The sit. when the y. ath. are under high pressure coming from their p. should not

does not support

3. Who are the two role models the author uses as examples of young successful athletes? (paragraphs 2 and 3)

world – fam. athletes

Tiger Woods

Martina Hingis

tales are role models

4. Why does the author think they are good role models? (paragraphs 4 and 5)

talents

& sport skills

they managed to succeed

5. What proof is there that training at a very young age will produce successful elite athletes? (paragraphs 6,7, and 8)

The statistics shows that many would few people, [illegible]

studies

6. What are the conflicting hopes that most parents have for their children? (paragraph 9)

hope that their kid

will manage at the same time to have

7. How can we explain parents who push their children to succeed? (paragraphs 10 and 11)

want the best

8. Why does the author see these examples of successful athletes as cautionary tales? (paragraph 12)

9. In her conclusion, how does the author think children should view these successful athletes? (paragraph 13)

as a positive example
as an ex. of what they can

10. Was your prediction in question 1 correct?

1 "I know a mother who sent her third-grader 50 miles away to sleep in a college dorm for a week to attend tennis camp. I see a little boy almost every Saturday afternoon on the school baseball field crouching behind the plate in full catcher's gear, throwing a hundred fireballs to his father at second base. I talked to a mother who sat near the balance beam during gymnastics practice because she knew her nervous daughter was more afraid of her than of the beam.

2 I thought of these children and parents when Martina Hingis, 16, won Wimbledon and Tiger Woods, 21, won the Western Open. The future for each had been decided by their parents at birth, mapped out as though they were long-range NASA projects. Hingis' mother named her after Martina Navratilova and coached her to tennis stardom. Woods' father had him swinging a golf club before he was out of diapers. Their entire lives have been spent in the hands of driven but loving parents guiding them in a singular pursuit.

3 Fortunately for Hingis and Woods, their talents were as large as their parents' dreams. They are millionaires many times over, on the covers of magazines, sought after by fans and media as if they were royalty.

4 But as I watched each beaming in victory, each handling the pressure as if they had basked in the spotlight forever, I couldn't decide if Hingis and Woods were role models or cautionary tales.

5 Their success no doubt will send even more parents onto tennis courts and driving ranges, into gyms and pools, urging little Jason and Jennifer to push hard, be tough, stop crying, grow up, bear down. If a kid is going to be the best, the parents reason, they have to start young. Look at Hingis and Woods, and Steffi Graf and Michael Chang and Tara Lipinski and Michelle Kwan—the list of prodigies seems endless.

6 And, the truth is, studies support the starting-very-young theory.

7 Dr. Anthony Kalinowski, a researcher at the University of Chicago, found that national-level swimmers began training at age 10, on average. Olympic-caliber swimmers, though, began at age 7.

8 In a study of Chinese Olympic divers, a Florida State researcher found that some of their 11-year-old divers had spent as many hours training in their lifetime as had some 21-year-old American divers, thus accounting for the Chinese divers' greater skill at younger ages. What seems to matter most are cumulative hours over a childhood. The same theory holds true for musicians. A study found that internationally acclaimed solo violinists began practicing their instrument at an average age of 5. Violinists of only national prominence began practicing at age 8. "It can take 10 years of extensive practice to excel in anything," Dr. Herbert Simon, professor of computer science and psychology at Carnegie-Mellon University, told the *New York Times* a few years ago. He led a research team in studying expertise. "Mozart was 4 when he started composing, but his world-class music started when he was about 17." Few of us take the extreme step of immersing ourselves and our children in a single, all-consuming dream. But we're all a little wild-eyed with our kids, living as we do in a culture driven to produce the best-looking, brightest, winningest kids on the planet. The success of Hingis and Woods only reinforces the push for children to grow up faster. Their success feeds on the adult mind-set that has 6-year-old girls dressing like vixens to win beauty contests and second-graders piloting airplanes.

9 This is the push-me-pull-you of parenthood, isn't it? We don't want our kids to lose the wonderful innocence of childhood, yet we often expect them to behave and perform like little adults. We fear for all the traps that await them as teenagers and beyond, yet we beam at their precociousness in flying across the country, reading Mark Twain in first grade, sashaying down a runway in heels and mascara, winning a three-setter against an opponent twice their age.

10 We have looked in the friends' box at Wimbledon and seen the Stefano Capriatis and Roland Jaegers and Jim Pierces who have hitched their wagons to their daughters' careers, living in their reflected glory. But there's a little bit of stage mom and dad in each of us; we cover it under the guise of "wanting the best for our children."

11 We holler from the backstop for our child to choke up on the bat, watch the ball, raise your shoulder just a bit, swing—my god, swing level! We enroll them in after-school computer and art classes when they have no interest in computers and art, and we insist they are put in the gifted programs at school though the work load is crushing. Without the gifted program, they might not get into the right high school, which will get them into the right college, which will launch them into perfect lives.

12 As I watched Hingis and Woods, I began to think they were both role models *and* cautionary tales. We need to see beyond the money and fame to the sacrifices and risks of achieving so much so young. We need to remind ourselves that, despite what we see on TV, we can't package our own children into perfect little tennis players and golfers and baseball players and beauty queens as if they are rooms we can decorate and show off. We are likely to wind up instead with children who feel like failures for not measuring up to some unrealistic standard.

At the same time, we shouldn't discourage our children from celebrating these

13 two extraordinary athletes. Let them learn about grace and the joy of performing, about discipline and heart. Then maybe, if we've done our jobs well, they'll apply those qualities to their own dreams. ”

Ryan, J. (1997, July 21). Role models and cautionary tales. The Sporting News. [electronic copy].

FINAL ASSIGNMENT

TASK ELEVEN: Short answer test

Use this short answer test to help you prepare for assignments, tests, and exams that you must write in your other classes. Refer to the Models Chapter for more information on how to write short answers (page 200).

- Complete all the questions in forty minutes. Write the answers in your notebook.
- Plan your time carefully so that you don't run out of time at the end of the test period. Leave some time to proofread your answers.
- Use specific vocabulary and try to include some of the collocations that you have learned relating to time and/or pressure.

1. **What are some of the negative consequences that elite child athletes face?**
2. **Why do parents and coaches push children to succeed in sports?**
3. **What recommendations do doctors have for child athletes and their parents?**

CHAPTER 2

A Good Education

QUICK OVERVIEW

READING
Read articles about different educational experiences, and use the information to form your own opinions about education.

WRITING
Practise different forms of writing: Take notes while listening, write short answers to questions, write a short report, develop a survey, and write an extended report.

LISTENING
Listen to two people talk about their educational experiences in order to compare and contrast information.

DISCUSSION/SPEAKING
Discuss your own educational experiences with classmates in small groups, and ask other university students questions about their opinions on education in order to generate information for a report. Report your results in an oral presentation.

LANGUAGE AWARENESS FOCUS
Learn basic question format and review sentence structure in order to write in a more interesting way.

SURVIVAL ACADEMIC SKILL
Practise forming grammatically correct questions in order to reduce your anxiety about asking questions. Brainstorm how to prepare an oral presentation.

WARM-UP ASSIGNMENT
Write a short report based on in-class student responses.

FINAL ASSIGNMENT
Prepare a survey, write an extended report based on information collected from your survey, and present the report orally.

Going to school is a common experience for almost everyone in the world. However, there are so many different kinds of schools, teachers and teaching methods that you may each have very unique school experiences. It seems that everyone has different ideas about what makes a good education. This chapter will allow you to express your opinions about education, and survey others about their opinions. You may have a hard time agreeing about what is the best educational experience.

GEARING UP

TASK ONE: Building a vocabulary base

- Read the following story and underline the vocabulary related to schools/education and teaching methods.
- List the vocabulary in the chart below. Put a check mark beside the words that you already know. If you don't have enough room, use your notebook.
- In small groups, exchange information with your classmates in order to figure out the meanings of the words that you don't know, or guess the meanings from the context of the sentence or word components. Use the vocabulary strategies from Chapter 1 (page 6) to help you.

Vocabulary words

School/Education words	Teaching method words

My school experiences

"When I first started elementary school, I was sent to a public school where I was enrolled in a French immersion program. This meant that my class spoke and worked only in French for most of the day. My oral French became very good; however, although my teachers were excellent, my written French was not as strong as my oral ability.

When my primary education was over, I enrolled in a private secondary school with a reputation for strict discipline, quality academics and mandatory participation in sports. My parents paid a lot of money to send me to this independent school, and I loved the teachers, the students and the athletics. When exam time arrived, I passed the standardized exams with reasonable grades. I was able to choose between a design career at a local college and an arts program at a university.

Once I began my university courses, I recognized that the teaching methods were completely different from those my teachers had used at high school. This was most noticeable in the French courses I took. My secondary school teachers had favoured grammar drills and translation techniques to teach written French. My knowledge of grammar improved, but I still made lots of mistakes when I wrote my assignments.

However, my university professors used the communicative language teaching method which encouraged reading real French books and articles, discussing with small groups of students and writing that was graded for content rather than grammatical correctness. My oral ability remained strong, and my writing skills increased.

I changed from being a passive student, listening to my teachers using the Socratic method, to an active student, participating and controlling the progress of my own learning.

At first, this new teaching methodology was quite a shock, but once I realized that my skills were improving, I began to save money for a long-imagined trip to France. ”

TASK TWO: Asking questions to learn information

- Using some of the vocabulary from Task One, think of some questions that you would like to ask your classmates about their education. Your teacher will write the questions on the board.
- Then, in groups of three students, write the questions in the left-hand column of the chart below. Write the names of your teammates at the top of the columns to the right.
- Take turns asking and answering the questions.
- As you listen to your classmate's responses, write brief, point-form notes in the columns to the right.
- After completing the chart, think about the most interesting piece of information you discovered about education. Discuss this information with the class.

Questions	Name:	Name:	Name:
1.			
2.			
3.			
4.			
5.			
6.			

7.			
8.			
9.			
10.			

LANGUAGE AWARENESS FOCUS: ASKING QUESTIONS

Asking questions is an essential skill that will help you become educated. During your years of study, you will need to ask questions of other students, your teaching assistants, your instructors and your professors. When you ask questions, it is important to use correct question format as this will increase your confidence, your chances of being understood and your receiving the information that you need.

Although it may be hard at first, don't be afraid to ask other students or your teachers for help. Remember that it is easy for other students to help you, and it is your teachers' job to provide you with the information that you need. A good way to ask for information is to say, "Excuse me," and then ask your question. Don't forget to smile. The students or teachers will be glad to help you.

Yes/No questions

Generally, for questions with simple yes or no answers, an auxiliary (*to be, to do, to have*) or a modal auxiliary (*can, could, may, might, must, shall, should, will, would*) precedes the subject of the sentence.

When you ask a question that has a yes/no answer, raise your pitch at the end of the question.

Auxiliary • to be • to do • to have	Subject	Rest of sentence
Was	she	happy at school?
Is	the government	funding public schools?
Has	your school	changed since you were there?
Do	students	study hard in your country?

OR

Modal auxiliary • can/could • shall/should • may/might • will/would • must	Subject	Verb	Rest of sentence
Can	you	recommend	the best professor?
Should	music	be	part of the curriculum?
Would	she	send	her children to that school?

Information questions

Generally, for questions that request information, a question word (*what, where, why, when, who, how*) is followed by an auxiliary or modal auxiliary, which is followed by the subject of the sentence.

When you ask a question that requires information, do not raise your pitch at the end of the question.

Question word • what • where • why • when • who • how	Auxiliary / Modal auxiliary	Subject	Verb	Rest of sentence
What	did	you	learn	in high school?
Why	are	so many students	failing	calculus?
How	should	the government	calculate	school taxes?

- Return to Task Two and take a look at the questions that you asked your group members. Look at the position of the verbs and the subjects in these sentences.
- Try to match your questions from Task Two with the general question patterns above.

WARM-UP ASSIGNMENT

TASK THREE: Collecting information and writing a short report

In order to prepare you for your final assignment, you and your classmates will collect information and write a short report on the results. You will think about the importance of sports in education and complete a chart showing your class's opinions. Finally, you will use this information to write a short report about how the male and female students in your class feel about sports and education.

Step 1: Discuss

- Discuss with your class if you think sports (or physical education classes) should be included in the school curriculum. Do young people need to participate in sports at school, or should they practise sports after school hours?
- Take notes as your classmates express their opinions.

Step 2: Collect information

Your teacher will ask the class the following questions.

- Record the answers in the chart.
- Designate one student to calculate the percentages as you complete the chart.

Questions	Total number of male students		Total number of female students	
1. Are sports (or physical education classes) an important part of the school curriculum?	Yes	No	Yes	No
	% of total men	% of total men	% of total women	% of total women
2. Should sports education be included in elementary schools?	Yes	No	Yes	No
	% of total men	% of total men	% of total women	% of total women
3. Should sports education be included in secondary schools?	Yes	No	Yes	No
	% of total men	% of total men	% of total women	% of total women
4. What are the benefits of sports education?				

Step 3: Write your report

Now you have enough information to write a short report of approximately two pages. Your report should include the following sections: an introduction and sections on methods, results and discussion. See the Models Chapter (page 203) to find an explanation of how to write a report.

When you receive feedback from your teacher or classmates on this warm-up assignment, you will have some information that you can use to improve your performance on your final assignment.

LANGUAGE AWARENESS FOCUS: LEARNING SENTENCE STRUCTURE AND VARIETY

Understanding basic sentence structure makes it easier to move on to more complex language tasks such as paraphrasing and summarizing. Simple sentences are the building blocks of writing. After you learn how to write simple sentences, you can make your writing more interesting by combining simple sentences in various ways.

A simple sentence is an **independent clause** (IC). It includes:

- a subject,
- a verb and
- a full thought.

EXAMPLES: An IC can be very short:
Students study. (subject + verb + full thought)

An IC can have compound subjects and verbs:
Marina and Olga study and work during the day. (subject + verb + full thought)

Here are some patterns that you can use to combine independent clauses and make your writing more interesting.

1. Combine a *phrase* with an IC.

phrase + IC	*In the beginning,* she was a good student. *In 2004,* he decided to study at university. *At the end of the day,* Hirumi was exhausted. *At first,* this new teaching methodology was quite a shock.
IC + phrase	She was a good student *in her home town.* Her parents were not happy *with her decision.* Paola left her books *near the photocopy machine.*

2. Combine a *dependent clause* (DC) with an IC.

A DC includes:

- a subordinate conjunction (e.g., *when*),
- a subject,
- a verb and
- an incomplete thought.

DC, IC	*When she started,* she was a good student. *After Xi finished the exam,* she went home to sleep. *Since exercise is important,* sports should be part of school.
IC (no comma) DC	She was a good student *when she started.* Mohammed registered early for classes *although he didn't know anyone else in the school.* He left the lecture *before the instructor assigned the homework.*

Here is a list of the most common subordinate conjunctions. It is useful to be familiar with these words.

after	because	if	until	whereas
although	before	since	when	wherever
as	even though	though	whenever	whether
as if	even if	unless	where	while
as though				

TASK FOUR: Practising sentence patterns

- On a separate sheet of paper, write four sentences. Two sentences should include phrases at the beginning or end of an independent clause and two sentences should include dependent clauses joined to independent clauses.
- When you have finished, exchange your sentences with another student. See if you can recognize the sentence combinations written by your partner.
- Help correct any errors.

3. Combine an IC with an IC using a coordinate conjunction.

When combining independent clauses, a comma is inserted before the coordinate conjunction.

IC, coordinate conjunction + IC	She was a good student, *and* she worked hard. She was a good student, *but* she didn't like her teachers. She was a good student, *for* she reviewed her notes after every class.

Here is a list of coordinate conjunctions. It is also useful to be familiar with these words.

Coordinate conjunction		Meaning
and	➟	in addition
but	➟	in contrast
for	➟	because
nor	➟	not either
or	➟	either, a choice
so	➟	as a result
yet	➟	in contrast

4. Combine an IC with an IC using a *semicolon (;)*.

Use a semi-colon when the meanings of the two independent clauses are very close.

IC + semicolon + IC	He was a good student; he always had good study habits. The essay was long and complicated; there was too much information to organize.

5. Combine an IC with an IC using a *semicolon and an adverb conjunction.*

In these cases, a comma is used after an adverb conjunction.

IC + semicolon + adverb conjunction, IC	He was a good student; *however*, he became sick. He was a good student; *consequently*, he received high marks.

Here is a list of the most useful adverb conjunctions. Once again, it is useful to be familiar with these words.

consequently	however	in fact	nevertheless
furthermore	indeed	moreover	in addition

TASK FIVE: Adding interest by using a variety of sentence patterns

You now know five different ways to join independent clauses together.

- Look at this paragraph written using only independent clauses. Writing like this is grammatically correct, but boring to read.
- Working with another student, use your knowledge of how to combine independent clauses to make the paragraph more interesting. Please note that there will be many correct answers.

"Quohong and Peter were students in a university writing course. They were worried. They had heard that academic writing was different in North America than in their own countries. They had heard that copying was bad. Using ideas from another writer without identifying the writer was bad. It was called plagiarism. Plagiarism was not acceptable in their North American university. Students who plagiarized could be punished.

Their teacher carefully explained how to avoid plagiarism. They could use three methods. They could use quotes and reference the source of the quotes. They could paraphrase a source. They could summarize a source. For paraphrasing and summarizing, they either needed a reference or not. Unique research results or statistics required a reference. Information that was common knowledge did not require a reference. They felt better. They knew how to avoid plagiarism. They were ready to write their first essay."

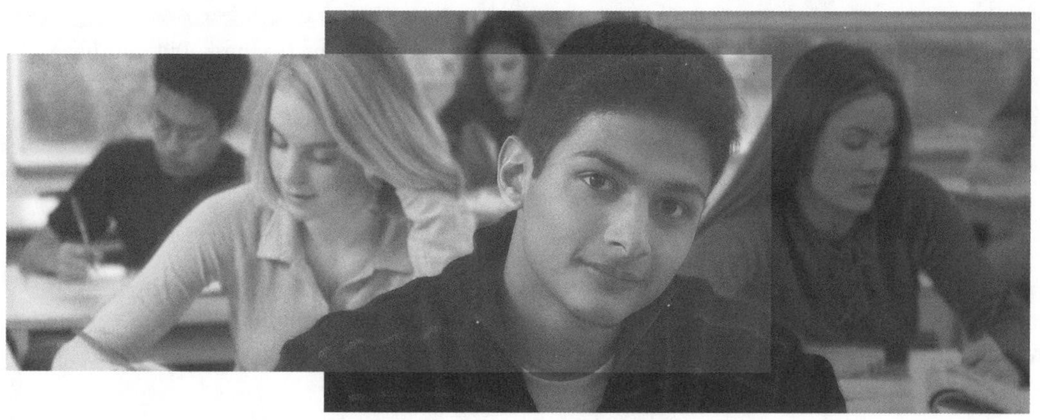

LISTENING: INTERVIEWS ABOUT SECONDARY EDUCATION

TASK SIX: Listening and taking notes

- Listen to the two interviews about secondary education. Notice how the interviewer asks questions.
- As you listen, take notes in the columns below. Use the tips about listening and note-taking from Chapter 1 (page 15) to help you.
- Once you have completed the chart, compare your notes with two other students.
- Discuss your answers. Fill in any gaps that you might have. Think about the similarities and differences in the two speakers' educational experiences.

Interview 1: Ayanna Roberts	Interview 2: Edward De Langen
1. Where did you go to school?	1. What high school did you go to?
2. Was it a big school?	2. Did you have a lot of friends?
3. Was it a positive experience?	3. Were you involved in sports or a lot of things in high school?
4. What kind of after-school activities were you involved in?	4. I hear you had a pretty famous teacher. (André Trudel, former bodyguard for Prime Minister Pierre Trudeau)

5. Tell me about some of your teachers. Did you have any favourites?	5. Tell me about some of your teachers. Did you have any favourites?
6. Tell me about your friends. Are you in touch with your friends from high school?	6. Today you're a computer programmer. Were you involved in computers back then?
7. This May you've got a big high school reunion ... Tell me about it.	7. I know two years ago you had a high school reunion. How was that?

TASK SEVEN: Comparing and contrasting information

- In your groups, discuss the similarities and differences in the interviewees' educations.
- In order to express your ideas clearly, use your knowledge of conjunctions and sentence structure from the Language Awareness Focus (page 30).
- Refer to the chart below for help.

Type of conjunction	To express similarity	To express contrast
Subordinate conjunctions		although though even though while whereas
Coordinate conjunctions	and so	but yet
Adverb conjunctions	moreover furthermore in addition	however nevertheless

- Write four sentences to demonstrate the similarities and differences in the interviewees' educational experiences.

- Show your sentences to either a classmate or your teacher. Check to make sure that your sentence structure is correct.

EXAMPLE: While Edward went to an exclusive private high school, Ayanna attended a large public school. (DC, IC)

1. ______________________________

2. ______________________________

3. ______________________________

4. ______________________________

READING: SELECTING A SECONDARY SCHOOL

Each of these articles is about a school that is based on distinct beliefs about what constitutes the "best education."

Group Work

TASK EIGHT: Reading to form an opinion

For this task, you will need to pretend that you are a parent trying to select a secondary school for your 13-year-old child. You will need to read the following information, select the best school for your child and then explain your choice.

- Form a group of three students. In your group, divide up the articles so that each student reads one article.

Article	Student reader
Student A: National Sport, Calgary	
Student B: Sisler High School, Winnipeg	
Student C: Earl Haig, Toronto	

- Look at the questions preceding your article before you start reading. Predict the topic of your article.

- Look for the characteristics of each school as you read. Use the vocabulary strategies that you learned about in Chapter 1 to help you deal with words you don't know.
- After you have read your article and answered all the questions, meet with two or three other students who have read the same article. Make sure that your answers are complete.
- Return to your first group and exchange information with your group members.
- Discuss the choices of schools. Compare and contrast the information. Decide which school offers the best education for your child. Which school would your child attend and why?

Questions for Student A: National Sport, Calgary

1. Read the title of this article and predict the special characteristic of this high school.

national sport
special in sport activ.
Provide the st. with opport. to go in for sports
sport facilities

2. What is the goal of this school?

is not only to pr. students with prof sport results
excel academ

3. What are some of the advantages for students attending this school? List as many as you can.

class sizes are small
negotiable deadlines

Student A: National Sport, Calgary

Athletes' ABC's

"What do short-track speed skater Alanna Kraus, freestyle skier Deidra Dionne and hockey player Jennifer Botterill have in common? In addition to being Olympic medal-winning athletes, all are graduates of the National Sport School. Building on the legacy of the 1988 Winter Olympics in Calgary, the National Sport School was founded in that city in 1994 as a way of giving aspiring elite athletes a chance to complete their high school education while meeting their training and competition commitments.

Operated jointly by the Calgary Board of Education and the Calgary Olympic Development Association, the public school serves 110 students, ages 14 to 19, from more than 20 sports. Class sizes are small, homework deadlines are negotiable and tutorial and online services are available for when the student athletes are otherwise occupied—which is much of the time. “There’s probably not one day in the whole year,” says Rick Pressé, the school’s outgoing principal, “where all 110 students are here at the same time.”

The school isn’t just a staging ground for superb athletes; it also produces students who excel academically. “Any high-performance athlete must become goal-oriented, manage their time effectively and be very focused,” says Pressé. “Those are all skills crucial to academic success.”

The students, who each pay an annual $4,000 program fee, also benefit from being with those who have similar interests. “We all have the same goal—to excel in athletics,” says swimmer Pascal Wollach, 16, who just finished Grade 11. “We’re friendly to each other; there are no enemies here.” Pascal, who has his sights set on the 2008 Olympics, credits his teachers with helping him keep up with his studies. “They are really supportive. Because classes are smaller, they’re always available if you have questions.”

Pressé says the school strives to instil a sense of balance in students as they juggle the demands of sports and education. “These kids do sacrifice a lot in terms of their social life,” he says. “But they also get to experience something many other students don’t. There’s a joy and passion that drives them. And it’s great to see.” ”

Bergman, B. (2004, August 23). National Sport, Calgary. Maclean’s, 117 (34), 36.

Questions for Student B: Sisler High School, Winnipeg

1. What are this school’s remarkable achievements?

2. What is the advantage of a principal who has worked at the same school for 24 years? Give an example.

Student B: Sisler High School, Winnipeg

Plain great

“It all starts at the top, according to everyone at Winnipeg’s Sisler High School. Everyone, that is, except the top himself, principal George Heshka, who’s more inclined to credit his staff and nearly 1,600 students for his school’s remarkable achievements. Sisler teachers have won six Prime Minister’s Awards for excellence. Its choirs and dancers hold numerous arts prizes, while a group of 39 students won the Canada FIRST Robotics competition in 2003. The school teaches Construction Technology for Women and university-level courses in calculus, physics and Latin. Its innovative Refugees and Exile program, which not only instructs students in one of the contemporary world's major issues but also includes a 24-hour "experiential learning component"—some students play soldiers while others are cast as desperate refugees—brought a Lieutenant Governor of Manitoba Classroom Teacher Award to Chris Bandfield, the instructor who developed it. Sisler even has a cricket team. And its students go on to post-secondary education at a level twice the national average.

But it is Heshka who has set the tone during his 24-year term as principal, a tenure well beyond the Canadian norm—Ontario parents can expect to see two or three principals during their child's K to 8 life. That longevity has allowed him to "sink roots and start working co-operatively with the teachers." That's crucial, technology co-ordinator Dennis Mogg says: "George supports people's ideas and lets them go with them, even when they're controversial." English teacher Kristin Peterson, who started the school's successful series of all-girl classes, couldn't agree more. "I brought the idea to him in May of 1992, and he said 'Sounds good, start in September.'" According to Peterson's tracking, students in the all-girl classes—which include power mechanics (auto)—achieve marks 10 per cent higher than those in mixed classes, showing what can be gained "by leaving their hormones in the hall."

Bergman, B. (2004, August 23). Sisler High School, Winnipeg. Maclean's, 117 (34), 37.

Questions for Student C: Earl Haig, Toronto

1. What does this school do to help students "fit in" with the large number of students?

offers group activities

2. What are some of the advantages for students attending this school? List as many as you can.

Student C: Earl Haig, Toronto

Club kids

"Being a member of two school councils and two charity drives would be enough for most students, but recent Earl Haig Secondary School graduate Golnoush Hassanpour wanted more. "I figured out at the beginning of this year that I hadn't really got the full high school experience," says the 17-year-old. But after adding another five projects to her plate last year, as

well as co-founding an environmental club, she really felt like part of the school.

Fitting in at the huge north Toronto school, home to more than 2,000 students, isn't easy. But because the school offers so many group activities, there's a real community atmosphere. Earl Haig, also home to the Claude Watson arts program, offers some 60 student clubs, many yearly trips and often several arts evenings in a single week. "It's really rewarding seeing so many students involved," says teacher Walter Raemisch, who also holds the position of staff clubs leader. "They take ownership of the school and its activities." A selection of Earl Haig's extracurricular offerings:

Manga and Anime Club: Thirty or so members meet weekly to discuss Japanese comics, writing their own co-operative manga by year's end. "Manga has its own style—it's real life, not just superheroes and stuff," says president Jessica Li, 18.

Mango and Animal Club: Started after Raemisch misheard the name of the previous club, this small group meets to obsess over their comedic hero, Conan O'Brien.

Leadership Council: Over a hundred students, divided into six subcommittees, organize as many as an astounding five school-spirit activities a week.

A Minor Variation: This art and literature magazine takes advantage of the art school's talent, not to mention students dedicated to creative writing.

Boku Chinese Magazine: This teen magazine, which features articles on fashion, trends and music, first appeared last year and is now projected at four issues annually. "One lunchtime, we decided to start a magazine," says co-founder Carol Hung, 17. "Then we realized how hard it would be."

VIBE: The 13-member hip-hop dance crew had 200 people audition in the past school year. "Any time on stage is our favourite time," says choreographer Kimmy Ross, 19. "Especially when we can't even hear the songs because the audience is going so crazy."

Zoom Student Film Festival: Started eight years ago for Haigers only, the festival now features 14 shorts from students across Toronto. Entries are judged by such luminaries as SCTV alumnus Joe Flaherty and TVO producer Risa Shuman. ”

Marley, K. (2004, August 23). Earl Haig, Toronto. Maclean's, 117 (34), 42.

SURVIVAL ACADEMIC SKILL: PREPARING FOR AN ORAL PRESENTATION

As part of your final assignment for this chapter, you will be asked to

- design a survey in order to discover opinions on an education-related topic,
- write a report and
- present your results to the class in an oral presentation.

Most students have given oral presentations at some point in their academic careers. Here is an opportunity to learn from each other's experiences.

- Work together in small groups to fill in the table below with your recommendations for oral presentations.
- Discuss your recommendations with the class. Which recommendations do you think are the most helpful?

What should you do …

before an oral presentation?	during an oral presentation?	after an oral presentation?

Organization of presentations

As with any academic work (written or oral), your challenge is to organize your information so that it is easy for your readers or listeners to understand. Your organization will depend on the type of information that you are presenting.

When you present survey results, even in an oral presentation, you may use report format (introduction, methods, results, discussion) to organize your material. Your organization should be clear.

It is generally good advice to begin your presentation with a point-form outline showing the organization of your presentation. This will help your listeners follow the information that you present, and predict what they will hear next.

FINAL ASSIGNMENT

TASK NINE: Designing a survey, writing an extended report and presenting your results to the class

Use what you know about question format and what makes the best education to design a survey. By asking people about their opinions on education, you will generate information that you can use to write a report.

1. Decide what education-related topic you would like to ask people about. There are many excellent possibilities. Here are some good ones:
   - Should students learn a foreign language as part of a good education?
   - Should students study art at school?
   - Should music be part of the school curriculum?

2 Begin by selecting *two distinct groups of people* to survey. These people are called participants. You can select men and women (as in your warm-up assignment), older people and younger people, or English-speaking people and foreign-language speaking people. There are also many other groups that you can select.

3 Create a series of questions (at least five) to discover the participants' opinions about education. Your first question should ask the participants to identify themselves as belonging to one of your two distinct groups. The other questions should ask them about their opinions. You can ask *closed* questions, *Likert Scale* questions and *multiple choice* questions.

- Closed questions are questions that have yes or no answers.

EXAMPLE: Are sports an important part of education?
Yes____ No____

- Likert Scale questions ask people to rate their opinions on a scale of one to five.

EXAMPLE: How important is small class size (20 students or fewer) to a good education?
a) Very important
b) Somewhat important
c) Neither important nor unimportant
d) Unimportant
c) Completely irrelevant

- Multiple choice questions provide possible answers for your participants.

EXAMPLE: What is the most important goal of a good education?
a) To provide high quality academics
b) To develop self-esteem and confidence
c) To develop a love of learning
d) To promote community involvement
e) To encourage participation in sports

4 Once you have a set of questions, ask a classmate or your teacher to preview your questions. Make sure that you are using correct question format. Write the questions on a separate sheet of paper. Leave space to record the participants' answers to your questions.

5 Conduct your survey. Ask at least twelve people—six from each distinct group.

6 List your results in a table on a separate sheet of paper.

7 Write a report based on the information that you gather. Your report should include the four sections that are common in reports: introduction, method, results and discussion. Use your knowledge of the structures of comparison and contrast to express your ideas clearly.

8 Prepare a short oral presentation to inform the class of your survey results.

CHAPTER 3

Consumer Behaviour and Innovation

QUICK OVERVIEW

READING
Read excerpts from textbooks in order to learn about cultural influences on consumer behaviour and the forces that motivate it. Learn how to skim and scan in order to read strategically.

WRITING
Write short answers to questions, take notes while listening, write a short process essay and a final essay.

LISTENING
Listen to interviews of factory owners explaining how they innovate in order to attract consumers.

DISCUSSION
Discuss the factors that influence your buying decisions, talk about possible innovations and share information from the readings and listening task.

LANGUAGE AWARENESS FOCUS
Learn how to create parallel structures to list similar items in a sentence by using similar grammatical forms.

SURVIVAL ACADEMIC SKILL
Practise "read smart" techniques in order to help you read faster and remember more.

WARM-UP ASSIGNMENT
Write a short process essay based on the readings from the chapter.

FINAL ASSIGNMENT
Write a process essay based on the readings and listening task from the chapter.

In the world of business, nothing is more important than knowing what the consumer will buy. Companies may spend a significant amount of time and money trying to figure out how consumers behave, and why they will purchase one product but not another. A business must understand the behaviour of its consumers if it is to be successful. Once a company really knows its consumers, it can create new products, or innovate, in order to motivate its consumers to buy.

12001

GEARING UP

TASK ONE: Discussion about buying

When you decide to purchase an item, what influences your decision?

- With a small group of students, discuss the factors that will influence your decision to buy a new pair of shoes.
- Note each factor that you discuss.

· style
· price
· brand
· comfortable
quality

READING 1: UNDERSTANDING MARKETING PROCESSES AND CONSUMER BEHAVIOUR

This reading lists a number of influences on consumer behaviour, and groups them into four categories.

TASK TWO: Reading and comparing information

- After reading the excerpt, fill in the table below to show the four categories and the factors influencing consumer behaviour.
- When you have finished, return to your notes from Task One. Place the influences that you discussed into the four categories defined by the reading.

Category	Influences from reading	Influences from group discussion (Task One)
1. Psychological	Ind's motivation, perception, ability to learn, attitude	
2. Personal	personality, lifestyle,	
3. Social	family, opinion leader, reference groups	
4. Cult.	culture, subculture, social class	

Understanding Consumer Behaviour

Market research in its many forms can be of great help to marketing managers in understanding how the common traits of a market segment affect consumers' purchasing decisions. Why do people buy DVDs? What desire are they fulfilling? Is there a psychological or sociological explanation for why consumers purchase one product and not another? These questions and many others are addressed in the area of marketing known as consumer behaviour. Consumer behaviour focuses on the decision process by which customers come to purchase and consume a product or service.

Influences on consumer behaviour

To understand consumer behaviour, marketers draw heavily on the fields of psychology and sociology. The result is a focus on four major influences on consumer behaviour: psychological, personal, social, and cultural. By identifying the four influences that are most active, marketers try to explain consumer choices and predict future purchasing behaviour:

- *psychological influences* include an individual's motivations, perceptions, ability to learn, and attitudes

- *personal influences* include lifestyle, personality, economic status, and life-cycle stage

- *social influences* include family, opinion leaders (people whose opinions are sought by others), and reference groups such as friends, co-workers, and professional associates
- *cultural influences* include culture (the "way of living" that distinguishes one large group from another), subculture (smaller groups, such as ethnic groups, with shared values), and social class (the cultural ranking of groups according to criteria such as background, occupation, and income)

Although these factors can have a strong impact on a consumer's choices, their effect on actual purchases is sometimes weak or negligible. Some consumers, for example, exhibit high brand loyalty—they regularly purchase products because they are satisfied with their performance. Such people (for example, users of Craftsman tools) are less subject to influence and stick with preferred brands. On the other hand, the clothes you wear and the food you eat often reflect social and psychological influences on your consuming behaviour.

Griffin, R.W., Ebert, R.J., & Starke, F.A. (2005). Understanding marketing processes and consumer behaviour. In Business (5th ed., p. 530). Toronto: Pearson Education Canada.

LANGUAGE AWARENESS FOCUS: USING PARALLELISM IN WRITING

These sentences are all taken from the reading. Look at them carefully and explain what they have in common.

EXAMPLES:

- The result is a focus on four major influences on consumer behaviour: psychological, personal, social, and cultural. (line 11)
- Psychological influences include an individual's motivations, perceptions, ability to learn, and attitudes. (line 15)

- Personal influences include lifestyle, personality, economic status, and life-cycle stage. (line 17)
- Social influences include family, opinion leaders, and reference groups such as friends, co-workers, and professional associates. (line 19)
- Cultural influences include culture, subculture, and social class. (line 22)

You probably guessed that all these sentences list items. Now take a closer look at how the items are listed.

- *The result is a focus on four major influences on consumer behaviour: psychological, personal, social, and cultural.*

  Each item is a one-word adjective used to describe the kind of factor (psychological factor, personal factor, social factor, cultural factor), and all the adjectives end in *–al.*

You may notice that the way this list is written creates a parallel structure in which the reader can easily see the similarity of the listed items. This similarity—or parallel structure—makes it easy for the reader to understand, and even creates a rhythm that is pleasing and easy to say. This is called *parallelism.*

Parallelism is the listing of similar items using similar grammatical forms. It is a good idea to write in parallel structure whenever you can, as it helps your reader to understand, and it shows that you have good language control.

Now look at another of the above examples:

- *Personal influences include lifestyle, personality, economic status, and life-cycle stage.*

  Each of these items is a noun, which creates parallelism in the sentence. However, this sentence could be made even "more parallel." If you look carefully, the first two items are one-word nouns. However, the second two items are *adjective + noun* combinations. We can try to improve the parallel structure in the sentence by making all the items adjective + noun combinations:

- *Personal influences include lifestyle* ***preference****, personality* ***type****, economic status, and life-cycle stage.*

  This sentence has improved parallel structure, making it easier to understand and giving it a smoother rhythm.

- Try to modify another of the above sentences by improving the parallel structure.

  Psychological influences include an individual's motivations, perceptions, ability to learn, and attitudes.

  After the word *individual's,* four items are listed. Three of them are one-word nouns. Can you change the third item into a one-word noun to match the other items?

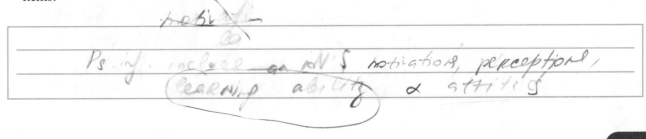

TASK THREE: Using parallelism

You should use parallel structure whenever you are listing items for your reader's consideration, especially in thesis statements and passages containing statistical information.

- Try to improve the following sentences by using similar grammatical forms to list items. Hints for the first four sentences are in parentheses.

  Note: These sentences were adapted from Reading 2, page 48.

1. Subcultures include nationalities, religions of all kinds, groups from different races, and people from different geographic regions. (Match one-word nouns.)

2. Canadian natives, consumers from unique ethnic groups, and Internet users are just three of Canada's important subcultures. (Match adjective-noun combinations.)

3. Canada is becoming more multicultural and people speak many different languages. (Find a one-word adjective to match *multicultural*.)

4. The shift toward informality has resulted in more demand for clothing that is more relaxed and furniture that is simple for our homes. (Find adjective-noun combinations for both items.)

5. Canada is a country that believes in freedom, dignity, respect for other cultures, equality of all people, fair treatment for everyone, and opportunity to participate.

6. Today's visible minorities include Chinese (23 percent), 19 percent are South Asians, Blacks are also at 19 percent, 13 percent are West Asians/Arabs, Filipinos (8 percent), Southeast Asians comprise 5 percent of the population, 6 of 100 are Latin Americans and others make up 7 percent of the total population.

SURVIVAL ACADEMIC SKILL: "READ SMART" TO READ FASTER AND REMEMBER MORE

Generally, for most of your academic reading, you will want to read fast and remember what you read. In order to accomplish this, you should "read smart." Here are some tips that can help you read quickly, understand the main points and think critically about what you read so that you will remember the content.

1. **Figure out exactly what you are reading.** This is important because different kinds of writing will be organized in different ways. If you know how the writing is organized, you can find the main points quickly. This type of reading is called *skimming*.
   - Textbooks are usually very structured. They will have headings and subheadings, and the topic sentence of each paragraph will clearly express the main point of the paragraph. The concluding sentence for each paragraph is also important, as concluding sentences often restate the main points of the paragraph. Of course, you should also look at pictures and read captions (the writing below the pictures).
   - Magazine and newspaper articles, including Internet articles, are organized to attract attention. Generally, the main points appear in the first few paragraphs, and the details are discussed at the end of the article. Again, you should look at pictures and read captions.
   - Scholarly essays may be found in academic books, magazines and newspapers; they may also be found on the Internet. Scholarly essays are organized according to essay structure, with an introduction and thesis, clear topic and concluding sentences and a conclusion, which restates the main points. See the Models Chapter for examples of scholarly essays.
2. **Consider what you already know about the topic.** If you are reading a textbook, looking at the table of contents can help you see how the information in the chapter relates to the information that comes before and after the chapter. For other types of writing, try to recall the information that you already know about the topic, and then figure out how it relates to the new information.

3. **Before you start to read, predict the information that you will learn from the reading.** What do you expect the writing to tell you? If you try to predict what you will read, you will read with greater attention in order to see if your prediction was correct or not. Either way, you will read with greater attention.
4. **Take short, point-form notes on each section of the reading.** The section might consist of one paragraph, or it might consist of several. Use your judgment. Keep your notes short so that they are quick to review. Write in the margins. Highlight key points. Remember, however, that if you highlight too much information, it will be difficult to review quickly later on.
5. **When you have finished the reading, use your critical thinking skills.** Judge whether your prediction was correct or not. Write short notes about your impressions of the content. Don't write notes about the content itself; instead, write notes about what you think of the content. For example, how important is this information for your course; does the information complement your prior knowledge of the topic; was the information surprising in any way; did you agree or disagree with the information; do you think there was a bias in the writing? All of these observations can help you not only remember the information, but also decide how important it is to your academic success.

READING 2: CONSUMER AND BUSINESS BUYER BEHAVIOUR

This reading is an excerpt from the textbook, *Marketing: An Introduction.*

TASK FOUR: Applying "read smart" skills

This is a long reading, providing you with a perfect opportunity to practise the "read smart" skills.

1 **Figure out exactly what you are reading.**
Skim the reading. Skimming means looking quickly at the parts of the reading that stand out for a reader. For example, look at titles, headings, subheadings, pictures or diagrams, and captions. You are gathering information about the reading. Now you should know exactly what you are reading. What is it?

____

____

2 **Consider what you already know about the topic.**
The first reading (page 44) provided you with information about consumer behaviour. Think about what you learned in the first reading. How will this reading build on the first reading?

____

____

____

3 Before you start to read, predict the information you will learn from the reading.

Predicting the information that you will read is an important part of becoming a skilled reader. What do you think this reading will be about?

____

____

4 a) With another student, go through the reading and divide it into sections.

The headings and subheadings will indicate where the divisions are located, but you should also try to find the divisions within each subtopic. You can do this by skimming the topic sentence of each paragraph. Remember: you are reading a textbook, and the advantage of textbook information is that it is usually clearly organized with obvious divisions.

Compare your divisions with those of another pair of students. Do you agree on the divisions?

b) Take short, point-form notes on each section of the reading.

Now that you have divided the reading into sections, read the text and take short notes on each section. You should be able to find the main points without having to read every single word. Use your note-taking skills to keep your notes brief. Write in the margins of your textbook. Use abbreviations for key words and symbols. Sample notes for the first section of this reading have been provided as an example.

5 After you read the excerpt, check to see if your prediction was correct.

Answering this question is a good way to review information in the reading, and fit it together with the information that you already had.

Characteristics affecting consumer behaviour

Consumer purchases are influenced strongly by cultural, social, personal, and psychological characteristics, shown in Figure 6-2. For the most part, marketers cannot control such factors, but they must consider them. To help you understand these concepts, we apply them to the case of a hypothetical consumer—Jennifer Wong, a 26-year-old brand manager working for a multinational packaged-goods company in Toronto. Jennifer was born in Vancouver, but her grandparents came from Hong Kong. She's been in a relationship for two years but isn't married. She has decided that she wants to buy a vehicle but isn't sure she wants to buy a car. She rode a motor scooter while attending university and is now considering buying a motorcycle—maybe even a Harley.

Consumers influenced by cultural, social, personal and psychological factors.

Figure 6-2: Factors influencing consumer behaviour

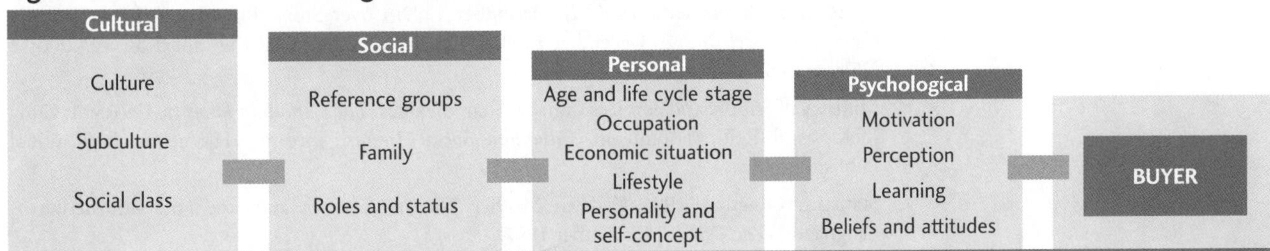

Cultural Factors Cultural factors exert a broad and deep influence on consumer behaviour. The marketer needs to understand the role played by the buyer's *culture, subculture,* and *social class.*

Culture
The set of basic values, perceptions, wants, and behaviours learned by a member of society from family and other important institutions

Culture Culture is the most basic cause of a person's wants and behaviour. Human behaviour is largely learned. Growing up in a society, a child learns basic values, perceptions, wants, and behaviours from the family and other important institutions.

Maclean's 1999 and 2000 polls of Canadian values and attitudes revealed that more than 90 percent of Canadians believe that our country has a distinct culture and distinct values. Almost 80 percent of Canadians believe that our identity is based on a strong sense of our own history, rather than simply a desire not to be Americans. The majority of Canadians noted that our flag, the achievements of prominent Canadians such as artists and scientists, our climate and geography, our social safety net, our international role, and our multicultural and multiracial makeup are symbols of our uniqueness. Canadians want the government to take a tough stand on law and order and see rebuilding our social institutions as a government priority. They strongly favoured investments in the CBC and our health care and education systems over tax cuts in the 2000 poll. Furthermore, we are becoming an increasingly confident and optimistic people who no longer see ourselves as boring or sexually repressed.[1]

Another recent study outlined some other basic values shared by Canadians: "Canada is a country that believes in freedom, dignity, respect, equality and fair treatment, and opportunity to participate. It is a country that cares for the disadvantaged at home and elsewhere, a country that prefers peaceful solutions to disputes. Canada is a country that, for all its diversity, has shared values.[2]

Canadians still see government as the leader in the fight to protect unique Canadian values from the inroads of American influence. Respect for diversity has also long been part of our heritage. Canada had three founding nations: Aboriginal people, England, and France. More than four million Canadians report that they can speak both English and French. The proportion of francophones who are bilingual is almost five times that of anglophones who are bilingual. Not surprisingly, Quebec has the largest number of bilingual Canadians (35 percent). New Brunswick is the second most bilingual province.[3]

Canada is becoming more multicultural and multilingual. Because of increased immigration, our population comprises a rich mix of people from around the globe (for example, Canada is home to 4.2 million Scots, 2.7 million Germans, 1.2 million Italians, 900 000 Chinese, 300 000 Russians, and 200 000 Jamaicans). The number of visible minorities almost doubled from 1991 to 2000 and now comprises 5.7 million people (about 17.7 percent of the population). By 2016 it is estimated that the group will grow to 7.7 million people and will comprise

1. Allan R. Gregg, "Coming of Age: After a Rough Ride, Canada's Mood Has Returned to the Confident Outlook Found in 1984's First Year-End Poll," Bruce Wallace, "What Makes a Canadian? We're Certain We're Unique, but We Don't Seem to Know Precisely What Sets Us Apart from Others," *Maclean's*, 20 December 1999: Cover Story; Robert Sheppard, "We Are Canadian," *Maclean's*, 25 December 2000: Cover; accessed online at www.macleans.ca/2000/12/25/cover/45320.shtml.

2. Ministry of Supply and Services Canada, Shared Values: *The Canadian Identity*, 1991, p. 1; Craig McKie and Keith Thompson, *Canadian Social Trends*, Toronto: Thompson Educational Publishing, Inc.

3. Statistics Canada, "1996 Census: Mother Tongue, Home Language and Knowledge of Languages," *The Daily*, 2 December 1997.

almost a quarter of Canada's population. Today's visible minorities include Chinese (23 percent), South Asians (19 percent), blacks (19 percent), West Asians/Arabs (13 percent), Filipinos (8 percent), Southeast Asians (5 percent), Latin Americans (6 percent), and others (7 percent).[4]

Marketers are always trying to spot *cultural shifts* in order to discover new products. For example, the cultural shift toward greater concern about health and fitness has created a huge industry for health and fitness services, exercise equipment and clothing, and lower-fat and more natural foods. The shift toward informality has resulted in more demand for casual clothing and simpler home furnishings.

Subculture
A group of people with shared value systems based on common life experiences and situations

Subculture Each culture contains smaller subcultures, or groups of people with shared value systems based on common life experiences and situations. Subcultures include nationalities, religions, racial groups, and geographic regions. Many subcultures make up important market segments, and marketers often design products and marketing programs tailored to their needs. Native Canadians, ethnic consumers, and Internet users are just three of Canada's important subcultures:

1. *Native Canadians.* Native Canadians are making their voices heard both in the political arena and in the marketplace. There are 416 000 status Indians living in Canada. When Métis, nonstatus natives, and Inuit are added to this group, the number swells to 712 000. Not only do Native Canadians have distinct cultures that influence their values and purchasing behaviour, but they have also profoundly influenced the rest of Canada through their art, appreciation of nature, and concern for the environment.

Banks have been particularly responsive to the unique needs of Aboriginal Canadians.[5] Scotiabank, for example, has maintained its relationship with First Nations people through its three on-reserve branches and 24 Aboriginal banking centres. It also uses grassroots marketing and public relations efforts, including its sponsorship of the Aboriginal Achievement Awards and 10 annual scholarships of $2500 for young Aboriginal entrepreneurs. CIBC found that cultural symbols can better link a firm with its native customers. On its Aboriginal Banking Web site, CIBC features a medicine wheel to symbolize CIBC's "holistic and integrated approach" to achieving "balance and harmony in relationship with Aboriginal people." The symbol was selected as an indication of CIBC's respect for the cultural integrity and diversity of Aboriginal people in Canada.

2. *Canada's ethnic consumers.* Consumers from ethnic groups represent some of the fastest-growing markets in Canada. In Toronto, for example, close to 42 percent of the population comprises visible minorities, and its four major ethnic population groups—Chinese, Italian, Portuguese, and South Asian—account for $13 billion in consumer spending. Marketing to ethnic communities isn't just an issue for marketers working in Vancouver, Toronto, and Montreal. Even smaller centres, such as Ottawa, Edmonton, and Calgary, have

4. Jo Marney, "Counting Ethnic Canadians In," *Marketing Magazine* (Online edition), 4 June 2001; Top 25 Ethnic Origins in Canada (1) 1996 Census, Statistics Canada, available online at 222.statcan.ca/English.census96/feb17/eolcan.htm, accessed 24 May 2002; Malcolm Dunlop and Christine Comi, "Multicultural Explosion," *Strategy Magazine*, 11 February 2002, p. 25; Astrid Van Den Broek, "Fighting Cultural Face," *Strategy Magazine*, 2 February 2002, p. 21.

5. Carey Toane, "Veering off from the Mainstream: Marketers Are Finding Divergent Ways beyond Traditional Advertising to Reach Ethnic Consumers," *Marketing On-Line*, 5 June 2000; Patrick Lejtenyi, "Underlying Differences: Market Researchers Must Be Diligent about Identifying Subcultures within Ethnic Groups," *Marketing On-Line*, 5 June 2000.

growing ethnic populations. The Canadian Advertising Foundation suggests that visible minorities have as much as $300 billion in purchasing power.[6]

Specialized media have been springing up across Canada to serve these communities. Besides newspapers targeting these communities, a growing number of local multiethnic broadcasters, like Toronto-based CFMT International are being established. Several national television services are aimed at specific cultural groups, such as Black Entertainment Television, Telelatino Network, and the Asian Television Network.

Some marketers have seen the wisdom of targeting religious communities as well as visible minorities. For example, 351 705 people across Canada in 2000 identified themselves as being of Jewish ethnic origin. Hallmark Canada saw an opportunity to serve this market. Although it has offered cards for Jewish holidays for many years, it now also offers such products as Star of David cookie cutters, wooden dreidel toys, themed wrapping paper, and paper party items subbranded under its Tree of Life brand to give them a unique identity.[7]

Marketers must track evolving trends in various ethnic communities. Consider Chinese-Canadians, for example. In the past, most members of this ethnic group came from Hong Kong. Today they are arriving from Taiwan and mainland China. Why should marketers be concerned where Chinese immigrants come from? Primarily for language reasons. Although the Chinese who come from Hong Kong speak Cantonese, people from Taiwan and mainland China often speak Mandarin. Marketers must also be aware of the differences between new immigrants and those who are "integrated immigrants"—people who are second-, third-, fourth-, fifth-, and even sixth-generation Chinese-Canadians. Although marketing information often must be translated into the language of new immigrants, integrated immigrants communicate mainly in English. Although Chinese-Canadians are influenced by many of the values of their adopted country, they may also share some values rooted in their ethnic history: trust family, work hard, be thrifty, save, and have liquid and tangible goods. Air Canada used its knowledge of these values in a campaign that linked Chinese-Canadians' need for security and the desire to keep connected to their homeland with Air Canada's services.[8]

Many ethnic groups believe that they have been neglected or misrepresented by marketers. A Canadian Advertising Foundation study revealed that 80 percent of people belonging to visible minorities believed that advertising has been targeted almost exclusively at "white" people. Yet 46 percent of this group stated that they would be more likely to buy a product if its advertising featured models from visible minority populations.

Let's consider our hypothetical consumer. How will Jennifer Wong's cultural background influence her decision about whether to buy a motorcycle?

---

6. Sinclair Stewart, "Special Report: Multicultural Marketing: A Long and Winding Road: While the Numbers Suggest Canada's Ethnic Communities Are Well Worth Wooing, National Advertisers Are Still Reluctant to Embark on a Multicultural Mission," *Strategy*, 17 August 1998, p. 20.

7. Carey Toane, "Veering off from the Mainstream: Marketers Are Finding Divergent Ways beyond Traditional Advertising to Reach Ethnic Consumers," *Marketing On-Line*, 5 June 2000.

8. Jennifer Lynn, "Approaching Diversity," *Marketing*, 30 July 1995, p. 15; David Menzies, "TD Bank Opens a Branch in Cyberspace," *Marketing*, 19 June 1995, p. 11; James Pollock, "Opening Doors of Opportunity," *Marketing*, 18 September 1995; Isabel Vincent, "Chasing after the Ethnic Consumer," *The Globe and Mail*, 18 September 1995; Craig McKie and Keith Thompson, *Canadian Social Trends*.

Jennifer's parents certainly won't approve of her choice. Tied strongly to the values of thrift and conservatism, they believe that she should continue taking the subway instead of purchasing a vehicle. However, Jennifer identifies with her Canadian friends and colleagues as much as she does with her family. She views herself as a modern woman in a society that accepts women in a wide range of roles, both conventional and unconventional. She has female friends who play hockey and rugby. Women riding motorcycles are becoming a more common sight in Toronto.

3. *Internet users.* People who "surf the Net" also have a culture that marketers ignore at their peril. Internet users have their own language, norms, values, and etiquette or "netiquette." One recent *Globe and Mail* headline claimed, "Internet has transformed life!" [9] Although this may be hyperbole, the Internet has certainly revolutionized the way we shop, communicate, and learn. One 16-year-old Ottawa teenager, for example, claimed, "I spend a lot of time on the computer talking to people. My life sort of revolves around it."

About 54 percent of Canadians used the Internet during March 2002, compared with 59 percent of Americans. The first Canadian Internet audience information and usage data from Nielsen/NetRatings indicate that, in one month, Canadian Web surfers spent nearly two hours less time online than U.S. Internet users and averaged fewer sessions and sites visited. Table 6-1 outlines the findings from the Nielsen study.[10]

Table 6-1 Activity for average Internet user at home in Canada versus the United States, March 2002

	Canada	United States
Number of sessions per month	19	20
Number of unique sites visited	23	45
Time spent per month	9:18:28	11:02:29
Time spent during surfing session	0:29:01	0:33:30
Duration of a page viewed	0:00:50	0:00:56
Active Internet universe (had access and actually surfed)	10.0 million	105.1 million
Current Internet universe estimate (had access but did not necessarily go online)	17.0 million	167.3 million

9. Keith McArthur, "Internet Has Transformed Life!" *The Globe and Mail*, 22 March 2000, p. B11.
10. Nielsen/NetRatings, "Canadian Internet Users Spend More Time Online than U.S. Web Surfers," *Reports on Internet Usage in Canada*, Average Web Usage, February 2002.

Canada is number two in the world in terms of the proliferation of home computers and Internet access, trailing the United States. It is not surprising that marketers are working hard to target Canadian Internet users. They must remember, however, that hard-sell marketing is definitely unacceptable on the Web, and marketers who violate this norm may be "flamed" or "mail bombed" by irate Web users.

Today's Internet users are not the stereotypical 14-year-old computer nerds, pounding away on a computer in the basement. One reason that retailers are so interested in using the Internet as a marketing channel is the compelling demographic characteristics of Internet users. First, they are above-average spenders. Internet users tend to be highly educated people in white-collar jobs who earn high incomes. In Canada, the largest group of Internet users (29 percent) fall in the 35 to 44 age group. People 25 to 35 years of age make up the next largest group (27 percent), followed by the youth market, those 18 to 24, who represent 21 percent of the Internet population. This market is highly attractive, given its technological sophistication and willingness to make Internet purchases. People aged 45 to 54 make up 15 percent of Internet users, while those over 55 constitute only 8 percent of the Internet usage group.

Historically, male Internet users have outnumbered female Internet users. Recent surveys, however, have shown that users are now equally represented between them, more closely resembling the general public.[11]

Unlike any group of consumers before them, Internet users are powerful and in control. The consumer is the one who chooses to access a Web site, and marketers must adjust to the idea that the Internet is a means of two-way communication between a customer and a vendor, not the one-way street that media advertising represents. In other words, consumers are not just listening to what the corporation wants to tell them; they're choosing the information that appeals to them. And Internet users value information.

Several articles have claimed that the Internet hasn't lived up to its promise as a marketing tool. Those who make this claim base their argument on the fact that few users actually make purchases over the Internet (even though Canadians spend $21 million annually on online purchases). However, before marketers deny the value of the Internet, they must understand how and why people use the technology. Most people who use the Internet do so for communication purposes, primarily e-mail. A third of people use it for information and reference. Ten percent use it to access online magazines.[12] The fact that many Internet users use the technology as a source of information is important for marketers, especially those selling goods and services that require extensive information searches. Auto or real estate purchases fall into this category. Purchasers of mutual funds are renowned "information hounds" who conduct extensive comparisons among competing products.

Although many consumers use the Internet in the information search stage of the purchase process, few use it in the final step in the transaction process for

---

11. Industry Canada, "Internet Usage Statistics and User Characteristics: Demographic Characteristics of Internet Users," *Canadian Internet Retailing Report*, 23 October 1998, Chapter 3.1, available online at strategis.ic.gc.ca/SSG/iro162e.html, accessed 28 October 2002.

12. Steve Ferley, "PMB '97 Reveals That Canadian Internet Usage Patterns Fall along Both Language and Demographic Lines," *Print Measurement Bureau, 1997 Study*, p. 16.

several reasons. People are worried about providing their credit card numbers when making an Internet purchase. Since consumers can't see or touch a product offered for sale over the Internet, they fear they will have little recourse if the product they order isn't the right one, isn't delivered, or arrives broken. Consumers also have privacy concerns: They are concerned that the information they provide when making a purchase or requesting information may be sold or given to another organization without their permission.

How does being part of the Internet generation affect Jennifer Wong and her purchase decision? Jennifer is highly computer literate. She uses a computer daily at work, carries a laptop when attending meetings, and has a computer in her apartment. One of the first things she did when considering a motorcycle purchase was to log on to the Internet. She learned a great deal simply by browsing the sites of such manufacturers as Honda, Yamaha, and Harley-Davidson. She especially liked the Harley site and the annual events listed for Harley owners. She was concerned that most of these events took place in the United States, however. Using their response button, she requested information on dealers in her area and information about specific models. Jennifer also found several chat groups and posted questions to members of these groups, especially female riders.

Social Class Almost every society has some form of social class structure. Social classes are society's relatively permanent and ordered divisions whose members share similar values, interests, and behaviours. Social class is determined by a combination of occupation, income, education, wealth, and other variables. In some social systems, members of different classes are reared for certain roles and cannot change their social positions. In Canada, however, the lines between social classes are not fixed and rigid: People can move to a higher social class or drop into a lower one. Marketers are interested in social class because people within a given social class tend to exhibit similar buying behaviour, showing distinct product and brand preferences in areas such as clothing, home furnishings, leisure activity, and automobiles.

Social classes
Relatively permanent and ordered divisions in a society whose members share similar values, interests, and behaviours.

In 2000, Compusearch Micromarketing and Data Systems conducted a study that allowed them to develop profiles of the top five percent of the Canadian population.[13] They grouped households based on such factors as average household income, education, and house value. The resulting 12 distinct profiles allow marketers to gain insights about groups' lifestyles, geographic locations, and media habits. For example, Compusearch labelled one group "Asian Heights" after the people of Chinese origin that compose its membership. They have large families, live in heavily mortgaged homes, attend fashion shows, enjoy eating exotic foods, and love to buy home entertainment equipment. Many are two-income families who balance the stress of commuting with the stress of their managerial and white-collar jobs.

Jennifer Wong's social class may affect her motorcycle decision. As a member of the Asian Heights group, Jennifer finds herself frequently buying brand-name products that are fashionable and popular with her friends and extended family. ”

Armstrong, G, Kotler, P. Cunningham, P. & Mitchell, P. (2004). Consumer and business buyer behaviour. In Marketing: An Introduction (pp. 208–215). Toronto: Pearson Education Canada.

13. "Lifestyles of the Rich," *National Post*, 22 April 2000, p. E11.

TASK FIVE: Using margin notes to answer comprehension questions

- Use your margin notes to answer the following questions. If you have done a good job with them, you will probably not have to return to the reading.

1. What factors are included as cultural influences on consumer behaviour?

cultural
personal
social
psychological

2. What is culture?

p. 52

3. What are some of the main characteristics of Canadian culture as identified by *Maclean's* 1999 and 2000 polls?

strong sense of Can. history
p. 50 §20

4. Why is it important to identify cultural shifts?

helps to discover new products

5. What is a subculture?

p. 51

6. What are three Canadian subcultures mentioned in this text?

Native canadians
ethnic cons.
Internet users

7. How has Scotiabank targeted Native—or Aboriginal—Canadians?

through its 3 on-reserve branches & 24 aboriginal bank centres

+

8. Why are ethnic consumers important to marketers?

9. How do ethnic groups feel about marketing and advertisements?

believe that they have been neglected or misrepresented by marketers

10. Why are Internet users an attractive market for advertisements?

11. Why are Internet users concerned about making online purchases?

12. What is social class?

WARM-UP ASSIGNMENT

TASK SIX: Writing a short process essay

- Write a short process essay to explain how cultural factors will influence the consumer behaviour of *one* of the following consumers:
    1. Fifteen-year-old Thomas Williams has been saving his paper route money for six months to buy himself a pair of the coolest basketball shoes. Thomas lives in Toronto.
    2. Twenty-three-year-old Mary Wood is an English Second Language teacher living in an apartment in Vancouver. She wants to buy a computer.
    3. Nineteen-year-old Xiaoshan Wu is an engineering student in Ottawa. She lives far away from the university campus, and wants to buy a car.

A process essay explains how to do something. Refer to the Models Chapter (page 206) to see examples of a process essay. Use parallel structure in your thesis and concluding statements, and in any other sentences that list items. When you receive feedback from other students or your teacher on this assignment, you will have information that you can use to improve your performance on the final assignment.

READING 3: INTRODUCTION TO ECONOGRAPHICS

In the first two readings of this chapter, you read about the influences on consumer behaviour that are constant—true in the past, present and future. However, there is another area that marketers study in order to predict how consumer behaviour will change in the future. This is the study of *econographics*.

TASK SEVEN: Reading strategically

Your task is to read a text about econographics and then answer a series of questions. In situations like this, it is helpful to read strategically in order to reduce the amount of time that you require to complete the task. Always read the questions first, looking for key words. Then scan the text for the key words from the questions. You can scan a reading for information when you know what pieces of information you are looking for—just as you did in Chapter 1.

Here are some tips:

- A question may ask *where*, in which case you will be able to scan for the name of a place (usually starting with a capital letter).
- A question may ask *when*, in which case you will be able to scan for a date or time.
- A question may ask *why*, in which case you will be able to scan for *because*.
- Dates and statistics are easy to find as they stand out in a text.
- Synonyms may be used to refer to key words in questions. For example, a question may ask about *consumers*, and the text might contain the synonym *purchasers*.

Read the following questions. Then scan the text to find the answers.

1. What percent of the gross domestic product (GDP) is consumer spending?

consumer spending account for 66%

2. What is econographics?

p 61

3. What can we use demographics to predict? Is it the best indicator of consumer behaviour?

shifts in cons. behavior / consumer needs

demography alone doesnot have all the answers

4. What is psychographics? Is it the best indicator of consumer behaviour?

No it is not

explains only one dimension of the emerging new consumer

5. What are the nine key drivers of consumer behaviour? Take brief notes about each driver in the table below.

Key drivers	Brief notes
1. Economy	
2.	• Consumers will learn about their buying choices through technology • Will buy through technology too
3.	
4.	
5. Environment	
6.	
7.	• Influenced by physiological, psychological, social, cultural and personal characteristics
8.	
9.	• How products are presented will motivate consumers to buy

Introduction to econographics

"Consumer spending accounts for 66 percent of the gross domestic product (GDP) in Canada and the United States, so it is no surprise that it significantly affects the economy, governments, educational institutions, the workforce, the retail sector, consumer-based manufacturers and service providers, and the financial services and investment community. Finding a way to anticipate future consumer buying behaviour would be invaluable to both the private and public sectors, given the profound effect consumers have. Econographics is a predictive model that can help business people anticipate future consumer demand. It monitors how the world is changing and is likely to change in the future, and predicts how consumer behaviour will be altered as a result.

Unlocking the mysteries about consumers

Futurists, demographers, and advertisers each claim to have the key that unlocks the mysteries about consumers. For example, demographers tell us that population age shifts are the most important factor that determines changing consumer behaviour. We cannot deny the impact the baby boom has had on North America. This is not news. Marketers have understood this power for decades, but they are now becoming increasingly aware that demography alone does not have all the answers.

Demography can explain some things. Population age shifts, the main focus of most demographic analysis, for example, are very useful in predicting some basic consumer needs. Forecasting school enrolments, the need for child care, health care and eventually, funeral services are some examples of this. However, forecasting consumer buying behaviour simply by analysing demographic shifts is very short sighted. It ignores other factors that help explain how consumers are going to change.

Advertisers believe that market segmentation based on psychographics—the study of people according to their attitudes, etc.—is much more effective than demographics in predicting consumer behaviour. Psychographics, it is claimed, uncovers the mystery about consumers—that they buy what they think they *want*, not just what they think they need. Advertisers claim that consumers' values, attitudes and lifestyles are responsible for their behaviour. However, psychographics, like demographics, explains only one dimension of the emerging new consumer. It fails to take into account the increasing diversity of consumers and to anticipate how they will change in the future in response to changes in their world.

The nine key drivers

Econographics provides a complete picture of the new consumer that is emerging because it monitors all the key factors that influence consumer behaviour. There are nine key drivers that have a significant effect on consumers:

1. Economy
2. Technology
3. Globalization
4. Government
5. Environment
6. Demographics
7. Consumer Psyche
8. Wellness
9. Retailing

Why is each of these nine drivers so critical to understanding the new consumer?

1. **Economy** affects consumers' ability and confidence to spend money, the availability of time to shop, what they buy and whether they borrow, spend or save. In addition, education is strongly linked to the economy.
2. **Technology** will affect how consumers learn about their buying options. Technological advances will affect where, what, when and how consumers buy in the future.
3. **Globalization** increases consumers' exposure to international products and increases their knowledge about different cultures and tastes.
4. **Governments** affect consumers in many ways, but especially in their pocket-books. Their ability to spend is affected by the taxes they pay and the benefits and services they receive from government.
5. **Environment** is important to consumers. Consumer awareness of environmental issues and corporate abuse of the environment will affect their buying behaviour in regard to the products they avoid and the ones they support. Threats to our environmental safety, such as skin cancer caused by exposure to the sun, also affect consumer buying behaviour.
6. **Demographics** affect consumers' needs, tastes, preferences and aspirations. Whether consumers are in a spending or saving mode is influenced by their life stage and family structure.
7. **Consumer Psyche** deals with the conscious and unconscious decisions consumers make. It is influenced by physiological, psychological, and social and cultural influences, and by an individual's personality traits. Fundamental shifts in consumers' values, attitudes, lifestyles and buying behaviour have all had a significant effect on consumer goods and services companies in the '90s.
8. **Wellness**—physical and psychological—of a consumer affects what products and services are purchased. When consumers and their families are healthy, they are in the market for entirely different products and services than when someone is sick or disabled. Attitudes towards a healthy lifestyle are also a key motivator of what products and services consumers will buy.
9. **Retailing** can be a great motivator of consumers by putting them in the mood to buy, influencing what and how much consumers buy. Retailing options, be they store or non-store environments, also affect when, where and how consumers buy. ”

Roberts, S. (1998). Harness the Future: The 9 Keys to Emerging Consumer Behaviour (pp.15–18). Toronto: John Wiley & Sons.

READING 4: THE CHALLENGE OF THE CHANGING CONSUMER

This reading demonstrates how companies can thrive or die depending on their ability to innovate. The companies that are able to use their knowledge of econographics to develop innovative new products that their consumers will want to buy can survive in a tough market.

TASK EIGHT: Scanning for information

- Read the following questions and then scan the reading to find the answers quickly. Use the tips for scanning found in the previous task (page 59).
- Discuss your answers with the class when you have finished.

1. What happens to companies that are slow to respond to changing consumer demands?

   suffer signif financial losses
   lose consume

2. Provide three examples of companies that were slow to respond to changing consumer demand.

   packaged goods manufact-res
   soft-drink companies

3. What are the rewards for companies that try new approaches to attract consumers?

   experience stunning growth
   gain strong competitive advantage

4. Provide some examples of companies that have successfully used innovation to attract new consumers?

   Dell Computers
   Microsoft Intel Harley-Davidson

5. What will the future be for companies that anticipate changing consumer needs?

   the future looks very bright

The challenge of the changing consumer

"Many examples exist of industries and individual companies that have suffered significant financial losses because they were slow to respond to changing consumer demands. The North American automobile industry in the '70s did not stay in tune with their customers. Car owners were looking for smaller, better-quality vehicles that offered fuel efficiency at an affordable price. Japanese cars filled this void and captured a significant share of the North American car market. North American car manufacturers have, arguably, caught up, but it was a costly lesson.

Packaged-goods manufacturers failed to take the threat of private-label entries seriously back in the early '90s when consumers became much more price conscious. Private labels have achieved a 20 percent share in many categories, and as high as 80 percent in a few cases. Soft-drink companies didn't anticipate that Cott Beverages, supplying private-label soft drinks to retailers, would make the inroads they did. They learned a painful lesson about profit erosion in Canada. By becoming more efficient and lowering the retail price gap compared to private-label entries, beverage companies have been able to halt the growth of private-label and return to profitability.

Trailblazers

The stunning growth of some trailblazing companies provides evidence of the rewards of new approaches. These companies prove that consumers will spend their money freely when they find what they want. Let's look at some of these successful companies. Microsoft and Intel have left their competition in the dust by fulfilling consumers' quest for faster, more powerful computing that is also more user friendly. In the case of Microsoft, providing great customer support to solve computing problems has also given them a strong competitive advantage. Dell Computers offers customized computer hardware solutions to its customers directly by telephone or on-line. Their business will likely continue to grow strongly because consumers will be looking even more for customization and simple purchase transactions.

Harley-Davidson has tapped into the consumers' increasing desire for new experiences and adventures, as well as customized products. As a result, it has had a hard time keeping up with demand. The Harley cult, reinforced by its customer magazines, *Hog Tales* and *The Enthusiast,* intensifies the Harley experience. Harley-Davidson's latest twist is to let customers build their own motorcycle from a list of options using an interactive television screen. This should increase the Harley mystique even further.[14] Yet price a Harley and you will discover that consumers will pay for what they want.

Levi's is another trailblazer that has found a way to offer consumers a personalized pair of jeans for only a small price premium. The company understands that one size does not fit all, and that consumers will expect more customized products like this in the future. Tropicana Canada is another innovative company that has broken through the barriers of mass marketing. For example, it has hit the mark with Chinese consumers. Its approach has been so successful that it has achieved higher awareness and usage among Chinese customers than among all others.[15]

Barnes & Noble is yet another success story. Their stores combine wide selection, good customer service and comfortable reading areas. Sales at Barnes & Noble have jumped to $1.3 billion in 1996 from $154 million in 1991.[16] Starbucks coffee shops are also cashing in by providing comfortable living-room environments and premium coffee. Sporting Life, a Canadian retailer, is winning the war against category-killer sporting-goods stores by offering consumers an excellent selection of higher-end sporting and casual fashion merchandise. It has clearly differentiated itself from the lower-end mass apparel found in most category killers, but at the same time, provides helpful, friendly service that consumers are looking for. Their sales volume, estimated at $30 to 40 million from two stores in 1995, is well ahead of the per-store sales volume of large sports chains.[17] On a Saturday, their outlet on Yonge Street in Toronto is one of the busiest stores I've ever been in.

What you can do

The future looks very bright for companies that anticipate the needs and aspirations of tomorrow's consumer. Of course it will not be news to you that the world and consumers are changing rapidly and that companies will need to adapt to this change. The question you may be left with is what can I *do* about it? "

Roberts, S. (1998). Harness the Future: The 9 Keys to Emerging Consumer Behaviour (pp. 11, 12, 14). Toronto: John Wiley & Sons.

LISTENING: EXAMPLES OF INNOVATION

You will hear reporter David Gutnick speaking with two factory owners. Every day, the owners struggle to attract consumers and provide quick and efficient service. They discuss how their factories have innovated in order to meet changing consumer demand and to survive in a tough market.

14. William A. Band, "Standardize to Customize for Market of One." *Strategy,* 17 March, 1997, p. 14.
15. Andrea Graham, senior product manager, Tropicana Canada, personal communication, May 1997.
16. Brian Hutchinson, "Merchants of Boom." *Canadian Business.* May 1997, p. 41.
17. John Heinzl, "Can Sporting Life Do It Again?" *The Globe and Mail,* 15 November, 1995, p. B11.

TASK NINE: Listening for key information

Part A: Pre-listening vocabulary building

Here are some expressions that you will hear as you listen to the interviews.

- With a classmate, match the definitions with the expressions.

Expression		Definition
1. Stay on top of trends		a) to make an unsuccessful business successful
2. To have a revelation		b) to reduce unwanted expenses
3. Turn a business around		c) to copy a product that is popular (or will become popular)
4. Knocked it off (to knock off)		d) to recognize what is popular and to use that knowledge to improve your business
5. On the way up		e) to discover new or surprising information
6. Cut the fat		f) to become more successful

Part B: Listening for key information

- Listen to the interviews and fill in the table below with key information. You may listen as many times as you like.
- When you have finished, compare your notes with another student and fill in any gaps that you might have.

Factory owner(s) and factory name	• Gerry and Anita Petriello • Wonderform factory	• Jack Kovinko • Jack Spratt factory
Product	• Women's underwear (bras, corsets, girdles, bustiers)	
Number of employees		
Innovation		

TASK TEN: Discussing possible innovations

Discuss the ideas that you have heard in the interviews, and add some of your own ideas about possible innovations. Try to use some of the new vocabulary and expressions that you have learned throughout the chapter.

- In groups of four or five students, discuss how the Jack Spratt blue jean company could attract more clients by innovating in these areas:
  - Design: what could the company do to make its jeans more attractive to consumers?
  - Manufacture: what could the company do to make its production process more efficient?
  - Distribution: what could the company do to make its distribution to retailers more efficient?
  - Presentation: what could the company do to present its jeans in an attractive way to retailers and consumers?
  - Marketing: what could the company do to advertise its jeans so that more consumers will buy them?

When you have finished, discuss your best ideas with the class.

FINAL ASSIGNMENT

TASK ELEVEN: Writing a process essay

- Write a process essay to explain how a business can predict changing consumer demands and produce innovative products that consumers will want to buy.

In your assignment, you should include the factors that a business must consider in order to predict consumer demands accurately. These are:

- influences on consumer behaviour, in particular, cultural influences
- econographics, and
- types of innovation—design, manufacture, distribution, presentation and marketing

Refer to the Models Chapter (page 206) to see examples of process essays. Use parallel structure in your thesis and concluding statements, and in any other sentences that list items.

handle
pick our orders
present to the customers

CHAPTER 4

Branding: The Positive and the Negative

QUICK OVERVIEW

READING
Read textbooks and articles about the methods of branding products, and the positive and negative consequences of brand marketing. Identify collocations (pairs or small groups of words) used in the readings. Use "read smart" skills to understand the texts.

WRITING
Write short answers to questions, take notes while listening to an interview and write a short persuasive essay. Write another persuasive essay to complete the final assignment.

LISTENING
Listen to a radio interview of two children discussing brand awareness and the effects of marketing on children.

DISCUSSION
Discuss your brand preferences with classmates, exchange information about the readings and listening task, suggest activities to support independent language learning and talk about new vocabulary.

LANGUAGE AWARENESS FOCUS
Understand how learning collocations can increase your fluency in all four language skill areas.

SURVIVAL ACADEMIC SKILL
Consider how learning independently (self-directed learning) can help you learn English faster. Learn several techniques to help you direct your own language learning.

WARM-UP ASSIGNMENT
Write a short persuasive essay.

FINAL ASSIGNMENT
Write a persuasive essay.

Just about every product we buy—from clothing to computers to food—has a brand. "A brand is a name, term, symbol, or design that identifies the goods and services of an organization so that they can be differentiated from those of the competition."* Companies certainly benefit from creating a brand, but what about consumers? Do they benefit from brands? Some critics argue that the answer is no. In fact, they believe that brand marketing negatively influences people, especially children.

* Tuckwell, K.J. (2004). Canadian Marketing in Action (6th ed., p. 208). Toronto: Pearson Education Canada.

GEARING UP

TASK ONE: Discussing brand names

Are there certain brands that you are familiar with and tend to buy?

With a small group of students, list the brand names that you look for when you buy these products:

1. Drinks
2. Clothes
3. Shoes
4. Movies
5. Cars
6. Computers
7. Meals
8. Other products

READING 1: IDENTIFYING PRODUCTS

The following reading is an excerpt from a book on business.

TASK TWO: Applying "read smart" skills

To prepare for the reading, use the "read smart" skills from Chapter 3 (page 47).

- Figure out exactly what you are reading.
- Consider what you already know about the topic.
- Before you start to read, predict the information that you will learn from the reading.
- Skim the reading and try to divide it into sections. The sections may be clearly indicated by headings and subheadings, or you may have to define the sections yourself.
- Take short, point-form notes on each section of the reading.
- When you have finished the reading, use your critical thinking skills. Was your prediction correct? How important will this information be to your final assignment?

- Now read and take notes in the margins of the reading.
- When you have finished, compare your notes with a classmate's. Are there any differences in your margin notes? Why?

Branding products

"Coca-Cola is the best-known brand in the world. Indeed, some Coke executives claim that if all the company's other assets were obliterated, they could go to the bank and borrow $100 billion on the strength of the brand name alone. Brand names such as Coca-Cola and emblems such as the McDonald's golden arches are symbols that characterize products and distinguish them from one another. **Branding** is a process of using symbols to communicate the qualities of a particular product made by a particular producer. Brands are designed to signal uniform quality: Customers who try and like a product can return to it by remembering its name.

branding
Process of using symbols to communicate the qualities of a product made by a particular producer.

Adding value through brand equity

brand equity
Degree of consumers' loyalty to and awareness of a brand and its resultant market share.

Many companies that once measured assets in terms of cash, buildings, equipment, and inventories now realize that a strong brand is an equally important asset. Widely known and admired brands are valuable because of their power to attract customers. Those with higher **brand equity** have greater brand awareness and loyalty on the part of consumers and larger market shares than competing brands (and are perceived to have greater quality). Because a brand adds value to a product, marketers manage brands to increase that value. In other words, they build equity in a brand by maintaining or improving brand awareness and perceived quality in much the same manner that you build up ownership equity in your house by maintaining or improving its condition and features.[1] The Irving family of New Brunswick recently embarked on a plan to increase the brand equity of Royale, a once-popular brand of tissue. The goal is to make Royale a major brand in Canada.[2]

Table 16.1 shows the rankings of the top global brands according to estimates of each brand's dollar value. It reflects the *earnings boost* that each brand delivers—that is, an index of a brand's power to increase sales and earnings, both present and the future—and shows how much those future earnings are worth today. Only *global brands*—those with sales of at least 20 percent outside the home country—are included.[3]

brand awareness
Extent to which a brand name comes to mind when the consumer considers a particular product category.

Several factors are involved in brand equity, including *brand loyalty* and **brand awareness**—the brand name that first comes to mind when you consider a particular product category. What company, for example, comes to mind when you need to send a document a long way on short notice? For many people, FedEx has the associated brand awareness.

Ebusiness branding

It takes a long time to establish national or global brand recognition.[4] After years of work, Cisco Systems Inc., the network-equipment manufacturer, reached new heights in branding for business-to-business, or B2B, e-commerce. The company's "Cisco Internet Generation" promotional campaign for 2001 stressed reliability and innovation, and in analyzing the campaign, Cisco found that its brand awareness increased by 80 percent (boosting it past rivals Lucent Technologies and Nortel Networks). The campaign also lifted Cisco's reputation as an Internet expert above that of Microsoft, IBM, and Lucent.[5]

The expensive, sometimes fierce struggle for brand recognition is perhaps nowhere more evident than in the current branding battles among dot-com firms. Collectively, the top Internet brands—America Online, Yahoo!, and Amazon.com—spend billions a year even though they have just barely cracked the ranks of top-60 global brands. Even with 210 million visitors each month,

1. Philip Kotler: *Marketing Management,* 11th ed. (Upper Saddle River, NJ: Prentice Hall, 2003) 422–424.
2. Gordon Pitts, "New Irving Generation Broadens Horizons," *The Globe and Mail,* 18 January, 2003, B1, B4.
3. Gerry Khermouch, Stanley Holmes, and Moon Ihlwan, "The Best Global Brands," *Business Week* (6 August, 2001): 50–57.
4. Eloise Coupey, *Marketing and the Internet* (Upper Saddle River, NJ: Prentice Hall, 2001), 174–179.
5. John Frook, "Cisco Scores with Its Latest Generation of Empowering Tools," *B to B* (20 August, 2001): 20.

Table 16-1 The world's 10 most valuable brands

Brand	2003 Brand Value (in billions of U.S. dollars)
1. Coca-Cola	$ 70.4
2. Microsoft	65.1
3. IBM	51.7
4. GE	42.3
5. Intel	31.1
6. Nokia	29.4
7. Disney	28.0
8. McDonald's	24.6
9. Marlboro	22.1
10. Mercedes	21.3

Yahoo! still faces formidable competitors in AOL Time Warner and Microsoft. Moreover, the costs of branding promotions are hitting all dot-coms at a time when they are trying to survive the near collapse of the industry.[6] The mounting costs of brand identity mean that many more would-be ebusinesses will probably fail.[7]

It's not just ebusinesses that are trying to catch the attention of consumers. Even traditional retailers are choosing attention-getting names such as Gadzooks, Wet Seal, Noodle Kidoodle, Koo Koo Roo, and Ugly Duckling.[8]

Firms that sell products internationally face an issue of growing importance in branding strategy. They must consider how product names will translate in various languages. In Spanish, for example, the name of Chevrolet's now-defunct Nova simply became *no va*—"it does not go." Sales were particularly poor in South America. Similarly, Rolls Royce was once going to name a new touring car "Silver Mist." Rolls changed the name to "Silver Shadow" when it discovered that mist is German for "manure."[9] Naturally, foreign companies hoping to sell in Canada must be equally careful.

6. Marc Gunther, "The Cheering Fades for Yahoo," *Fortune* (12 November, 2001) 151–158.

7. Lori Mitchell, "Branding Equals Smart E-Business," *InfoWorld*, www.InfoWorld.com/articles/tc/xml/00/12/18/001218tcbranding.xml, 15 December, 2000; Robyn Greenspan, "Brand Opening," *ECommerce-Guide*, http://ecommerce.internet.com/news/insights/ectips/article/0,,6311_557131,00.html, 10 January, 2001; Kris Wadia, "Top 10 Myths of E-Branding," *Business-Minds*, www.business-minds.com/article.asp?item=68, 17 May, 2001.

8. Eileen Kinsella "Corporate Names Go Quirky," *The Globe and Mail*, 20 May, 1997, B12.

9. Cyndee Miller, "Little Relief Seen for New Product Failure Rate," *Marketing News* (21 June, 1993): 1; Nancy J. Kim, "Back to the Drawing Board," *The Bergen [New Jersey] Record*, 4 December, 1994, B1, B4.

Types of brand names

Virtually every product has a brand name of some form. However, different types of brand names tell the alert consumer something about the product's origin.

national brands
Products distributed by and carrying a name associated with the manufacturer.

National Brands. Brand name products that are produced and distributed by the manufacturer are called **national brands.** These brands, such as Scotch tape, are often widely recognized by consumers because of large national advertising campaigns. The costs of developing a positive image for a national brand are high, so some companies use their national brand on several related products. Procter & Gamble now markets Ivory shampoo, capitalizing on the widely recognized name of its soaps.

licensed brands
Selling the right to use a brand name, a celebrity's name, or some other well-known identification mark to another company to use on a product.

Licensed Brands. More and more nationally recognized companies and personalities have sold other companies the right to place their names on products, which are **licensed brands.** Licensing has become big business. Franklin the Turtle, the subject of 26 books and an animated television series produced by Nelvana, is a Canadian product that is also popular in the United States. Nelvana and U.S.-based Sears Roebuck & Co. signed a licensing agreement allowing Sears to set up Franklin boutiques at its more than 850 stores. These boutiques market Franklin clothing and accessories that are available exclusively at Sears.[10]

private brands
Products promoted by and carrying a name associated with the retailer or wholesaler, not the manufacturer.

Private Brands. When a wholesaler or retailer develops a brand and has the manufacturer place that brand name on the product, the resulting product name is a **private brand.** One of the best-known purveyors of private brands is Sears, with its Craftsman tools and Kenmore appliances.

J. Sainsbury PLC, the largest supermarket chain in Britain, introduced its own private brand of cola in a can that looks strikingly like the one used by Coke. The two products are stocked side by side on store shelves, and Sainsbury's offering is noticeably cheaper than Coke. The product is made by Cott Corp. of Toronto. The story is much the same in North America. Under the Sam's "American Choice" label, Cott sells a billion cans of soft drinks each year at Wal-Mart.

Loblaw Cos. Ltd., owned by George Weston, has created a line of upscale products under the private brand "President's Choice." Clever advertising, fancy labels, and exotic product names differentiate the line and draw consumer attention to items such as peanut butter and cookies. Another Weston-owned company, Holt Renfrew, emphasizes its private brand. A stylish Prada suit sells for $2000 to $4000, but the Holt Renfrew equivalent is priced at only $300 to $700.[11]

Brand loyalty

brand loyalty
Customers' recognition of, preference for and insistence on buying a product with a certain brand name.

Companies that spend the large amount of money it takes to develop a brand are looking for one thing from consumers: **brand loyalty.** That is, they want to develop customers who, when they need a particular item, will go back to the same brand and buy the company's products.

Brand loyalty is measured in three stages. First, the company wants *brand recognition.* By putting the brand in front of consumers many times and associating it with a type of product, the producer hopes that consumers will become aware of

10. Brian Milner, "Canada's Franklin the Turtle Heads South," *The Globe and Mail,* 14 February, 2000, B1, B10.

11. Marina Strauss, "Holt Renfrew Brands a Strategy," *The Globe and Mail,* 20 March, 1997, B13.

its existence. Recognition is not enough, however. The owner of the brand wants consumers to start showing *brand preference* when they make a purchase. Brand preference requires not only awareness that the brand exists but also a favourable attitude toward the ability of the brand to provide benefits. Finally, because a brand may be unavailable in a store from time to time, companies seek *brand insistence.* Brand insistence is highly valued by brand owners, but it is very difficult to achieve.

A survey sponsored by Reader's Digest Canada found that Canadians have less trust in product brands than they did 20 years ago. However, some well-known brands like Becel Margarine, Robin Hood flour, Wal-Mart, and Black & Decker are still viewed positively.[12] ”

Griffin, R.W., Ebert, R. J. & Starke, F.A. (2005). Business (5th ed., pp. 559–563). Toronto: Pearson Education Canada.

TASK THREE: Using margin notes to answer comprehension questions

- Use your margin notes to find the answers to the questions below.
- Compare your answers with those of a classmate. Fill in any gaps that you might have.

1. What is branding?

p. 69

2. Besides cash, buildings, equipment and inventories, what other asset should a company consider when calculating its total value?

strong brand

3. What factors are involved in brand equity?

consumer loyalty
brand awareness

12. Marina Strauss, "Consumers Less Trusting of Brands," *The Globe and Mail,* 13 February, 2003, B3.

4. What other products and services are fighting to establish globally recognized brands?

5. Companies that sell their products internationally must be aware of what other issue?

6. What are some of the different kinds of brands? Give an example of each.

7. What are the three stages of brand loyalty?

LANGUAGE AWARENESS FOCUS: COLLOCATIONS

In Chapter 1, you found out that you can increase your fluency—in all four language skill areas—by learning words in pairs, or small groups, at the same time (see page 11). *Collocations* are words that often appear together in recognized mini-expressions. When you know how words collocate, you know how words are used together. Research indicates that collocations represent a significant amount of all language use. Therefore, when you learn a new word, you should learn not only the meaning of the word but also how the word collocates with others. Then you will know both what a word means and how to use it.

In the previous reading, there were a number of collocations with the word *brand*. The collocations follow two patterns.

1. *Brand* is used as an adjective that modifies a noun.

   EXAMPLES: brand name, brand equity

2. *Brand* is used as a noun, and is preceded by an adjective.

   EXAMPLES: best-known brand, strong brand

TASK FOUR: Reading closely to identify collocations

- Read the excerpt in Reading 1 (pages 69–73) more closely, and list all the collocations related to the word *brand*.
- List the collocations in one of the two identified patterns. You should use some of these collocations in the writing assignments for this chapter.

Brand as adjective + noun	Adjective + brand as noun
• brand name • brand equity awareness recognition preference identity	• best-known brand • strong brand national licensed private global brands

READING 2: THE BENEFITS OF BRANDS

The following reading discusses the marketing aspects of brands: benefits, loyalty and power.

TASK FIVE: Finding out more about brands through scanning and discussion

Group Work

The reading is divided into three sections.

- In a group of three students, decide which student will read and answer the questions for each section.

Section	Student Reader
A. The Benefits of Brands	
B. Brand Loyalty	
C. Brand Power: What Makes a Great Brand?	

- First, read the questions for your section. Then scan the reading for key words in order to find the answers quickly.
- When you have finished, check your answers with a classmate who has read the same section. Fill in any gaps that you might have.
- Then return to your group and exchange the answers to all the questions.
- Take notes and ask questions as other students provide information.
- When you have finished, discuss with the class why the automotive brand, Porsche, is so successful.

Questions for Student A: The benefits of brands

1. What are the benefits of brands for consumers?

2. What are the benefits of brands for marketing organizations?

3. What is the goal of developing a brand?

Questions for Student B: Brand loyalty

1. Briefly describe the three stages of brand loyalty.

2. Why is it important for a company to retain its current customers?

3. What is brand equity?

Questions for Student C: Brand power: What makes a great brand?

1. What are the principles of a great brand, as defined by Scott Bedbury, marketing director of Nike?

2. Do these principles guarantee brand success? Why or why not?

no guarantees for success

3. What is the basis of successes like Nike, Disney and Coca-Cola?

Student A: The benefits of brands

Branding offers consumers and marketing organizations several benefits. Some of the benefits for the consumer are as follows:

1. Over time, the brand name suggests a certain level of quality. Consumers know what to expect; they trust and have confidence in a brand.
2. There can be psychological rewards for possessing certain brands. For example, purchasing a BMW automobile might suggest achievement for the owner while wearing a suit with a designer label may make one feel stylish.
3. Brands distinguish competitive offerings, allowing consumers to make informed decisions. Such names as Minute Rice, Lipton Cup-A-Soup, and Post Fruit & Fibre suggest clear messages or benefits about the product.

The marketing organization also enjoys benefits:

1. Branding enables the marketer to create and develop an image for a product or service. In the automobile market, the name Lexus is associated with "excitement," while in the tea market Tetley Tea is well known for its round perforated teabag that offers a better tasting tea. The brand image is partially created through advertising. In most advertising, a close relationship exists between a brand and its slogan. In the case of Tetley the slogan is: "Tetley. Good things all round." Collectively, they help form an impression in the consumer's mind. Here are a few examples:

   Tetley—"Tetley. Good things all round."

   VISA—"All you need."

   Nike—"Just Do It."

   3M—"from need...to 3M Innovation."

   Apple—"Think Different."

2. Satisfied customers will make repeat purchases and hopefully remain loyal to a brand. This loyalty stabilizes market share and provides for certain efficiencies in production and marketing.
3. A good brand name will communicate the point of difference (USP) and highlight the distinctive value added. For example, the name Lean Cuisine addresses two strategic issues: lean communicates the low-calorie benefit, and cuisine implies that it tastes good. The name is meaningful and pleasant sounding. Household goods tend to have names that communicate what they do (e.g., Ziploc, Spray 'n Wash, Liquid Plumr, S.O.S., and Mr. Clean).

Creating and using brand names is a crucial aspect of product strategy, since the attributes of a brand—its package and logo and its image—influence other marketing activities, specifically pricing and promotion. Given the cost of marketing activities, a brand (name and trademark) must be more than just a tool for distinguishing one brand from another. It must communicate the key point of difference and highlight the distinctive value added.

Student B: Brand loyalty

brand loyalty

Brand loyalty is defined as the degree of consumer attachment to a particular brand of product or service. This degree of attachment can be weak or strong and varies from one product category to another. Brand loyalty is measured in three stages: brand recognition, brand preference, and brand insistence.[13]

brand recognition

In the early stages of a product's life, the marketing objective is to create **brand recognition**, which is customer awareness of the brand name and package. Once awareness is achieved, a brand may offer customers free samples or coupons to tempt them to make the first (trial) purchase.

brand preference

In the **brand preference** stage of a product's life, the brand is in the ballpark—that is, it is an acceptable alternative and will be purchased if it is available when needed. If it is unavailable, the consumer will switch to an equal, competitive alternative. For example, if Pepsi-Cola is requested at McDonald's and the order cannot be filled because the product is unavailable there, the consumer will usually accept the substitute, in this case, Coca-Cola.

brand insistence

At the **brand insistence** stage, a consumer will search the market extensively for the brand he or she wants. No alternatives are acceptable, and if the brand is unavailable the consumer is likely to postpone purchase until it is. Such a situation is a marketer's dream, a dream rarely achieved. Some critics insist that the original Coca-Cola product (now called Coke Classic) reached a level beyond brand insistence. So strong was the attachment that the product could not be changed. When it was, the backlash from the consumer franchise was so strong that the company had no alternative but to bring the original product back.

The task of the marketer is to keep customers loyal. Study after study has shown that it is many times more difficult and expensive to convert a new customer than it is to retain a current customer. In preserving loyalty, companies cannot take their customers for granted. Many brands are instituting customer relationship management (CRM) programs that are specifically designed to keep a customer a customer.

To illustrate how fast loyalty can fade, consider the case of Chips Ahoy, a prominent cookie product marketed by Nabisco. At one time, it was the market leader with strong brand loyalty. Its primary benefit was a chip content of 20 to 25 percent. But along came President's Choice Decadent Chocolate Chip Cookies offering 39 percent chip content. President's Choice became the best-selling cookie nationally, even though it is only sold in 20 percent of grocery stores, while Chips Ahoy's national market share dropped below 2 percent.[14] This illustration shows that premium private label brands can be a major force in consumer goods.

brand equity

The benefits of brands and the various levels of brand loyalty are what marketers refer to as brand equity. **Brand equity** is defined as the value a consumer derives from a product over and above the value derived from the physical attributes, those characteristics and associations that are linked to a brand that can add value to it. Brand equity consists of four variables: name awareness, a loyal customer base, perceived quality, and the brand's association with a certain attribute. For example, consumers' attitudes and feelings about a product, as in the above-mentioned case of Coca-Cola, help establish brand equity. Much research has been done on brand equity and its importance in marketing.

Brands also have monetary value and that value reflects the status of a brand on a global scale. There are not that many truly global brands but the top five are

13. Dale Beckman, David Kurtz and Louis Boone, Foundations of Marketing (Toronto, ON: Holt, Rinehart and Winston, 1988), pp. 316–317.

14. Jeff Pappone, "Loblaws' private label the choice of Harvard," *Financial Post,* 4 June, 1999, p. C4.

well known names: Coca-Cola (valued at $68.9 billion), Microsoft ($65.1 billion), IBM ($52.8 billion), GE ($42.4 billion), and Nokia ($35.0 billion).[15] There are no Canadian brands in the latest ranking of the top 100 global brands.

Student C: Brand power: What makes a great brand?

"Brand names, trademarks, logos, and advertising slogans all play a major role in creating an image with consumers. Whether it applies to a product or service or to a company itself, the right name can produce customer loyalty, recognition in the marketplace, and money at the bottom line. The opposite is also true. A bad brand name can bury a company in obscurity or sink a new product faster than you can say Edsel.

To illustrate, consider the case of Nike. Scott Bedbury, the man who gave the world "Just Do It," started working for Nike in 1987, when it was a $750-million company. Seven years later, Nike was a $4-billion business. In between, Bedbury directed Nike's worldwide advertising efforts and broke the "Just Do It" branding campaign. According to Bedbury, building a great brand depends on knowing the right principles. Among these principles are the following:

1. **A great brand is in it for the long haul** Thinking long term, a great brand can travel worldwide, transcend cultural barriers, speak to multiple audiences, and let you operate at the higher end of the positioning spectrum—where you can earn solid margins over the long term.
2. **A great brand can be anything** Anything is brandable. Nike, for example, leverages the deep emotional connection that people have with sports and fitness. In computers, most people do not know how processors work or why they are superior to the competition. But what they want is a computer with "Intel inside." Intel is a classic case in branding strategy.
3. **A great brand knows itself** The real starting point is to go out to customers and find out what they like or dislike about the brand and what they associate as the very core of the brand concept. The customer's view of a brand can be very different from that of company executives.
4. **A great brand invents or re-invents an entire category** Such brands as Apple, Nike, and Starbucks made it an explicit goal to be protagonists for each of

15. "The World's 10 Most Valuable Brands," *Business Week,* 6 August, 2001, www.businessweek.com/magazine/content

their product categories. Apple was a protagonist for an individual: anyone wanting to be more productive, informed, and contemporary. At Nike, Phil Knight (company founder and CEO) is the consummate protagonist for sports and athletes.

5. **A great brand taps into emotions** The common ground for great brands is not performance. They recognize that consumers live in an emotional world. Emotions drive most, if not all, of our decisions.

6. **A great brand has design consistency** They have a consistent look and feel and a high level of design integrity. Consider such brands as McDonald's, Coca-Cola and Disney. They refuse to follow any fashion trend that does not fit their vision.

7. **A great brand is relevant** Many brands try to position themselves as "cool." More often than not, brands that try to be cool fail. Being cool is not enough to sustain a brand. A brand has to be relevant—it provides what people want, and it performs the way people want it to. Consumers are looking for something that has lasting value.

These principles are fine, but there are no guarantees for success. Brands are subject to the whims of consumers, a fluctuating economy where uncertainty prevails, and the rapid pace of technological change. A brand could come out of nowhere and become a billion dollar brand or it could be humbled quickly by a changing economy.

Interbrand, a management consulting company in the United States, analyzes global brands and reports that Coca-Cola is the number one brand valued at US$68.9 billion in 2001. It is a steady performer from year to year and is not subject to the ravages of economic cycles like many other brands. Brands such as Amazon.com and Yahoo! rose to prominence with the dot.com wave but when the dot.com bubble burst, the value of these brands dropped considerably. In 2001 the value of the Ford brand name dropped 17 percent from $36.4 billion to 30.1 billion. It was literally run over by the Firestone tire controversy. In spite of the fall, the Ford brand name still ranked 8th among the world's leading brands.

Even the powerful Nike brand (which ranks 34th in global value) has had its share of problems due to bad publicity associated with production practices in the Far East. It has fallen out of favour with some, perhaps due to an oversaturation of marketing hype. For many consumers "Just Do It" has become "Just Cool It." Too much of anything may not be a good thing. Competitors, such as Adidas, are quietly taking market share from Nike. In sharp contrast, a brand like Starbucks experienced a huge increase in value, moving from $1.3 billion to $1.8 billion, an increase of 32 percent in 2001. Firmly established brands such as IBM, Microsoft, GE, Disney, and McDonald's tend to retain their top-10 status from year to year.

Do these stories imply that all brands, however big, are eventually doomed to fade? The answer is no, but it depends on the quality of marketing behind the brand. It seems that brands such as Nike, Disney, and Coca-Cola, which are often referred to as "philosophy brands," have an advantage. These brands express an attitude toward life, which can be extended into a variety of different areas. Therefore, a true brand transcends product format and has a relationship with the consumer that has more to do with the beliefs the brand expresses than the product itself. As markets change, the brand has to use the power of that relationship to expand and evolve into new formats and markets. Those that do not are destined to fail.

Adapted from "The World's 10 Most Valuable Brands," Business Week, *6 August, 2001; www.businessweek.com/magazine/content, Richard Tomkins, "Fading stars of the global stage,"* Financial Post, *8 March, 1999, p. C4; and Scott Bedbury, "What great brands do," www.fastcompany.com/10.bedbury.html.*

Tuckwell, K.J. (2004). Canadian Marketing in Action (6th ed., pp. 214-219). Toronto: Pearson Education Canada.

WARM-UP ASSIGNMENT

TASK SIX: Writing a short persuasive essay

- Write a short persuasive essay to agree or disagree with the following statement:

  Only companies benefit from brands.

A persuasive essay should try to convince others to accept your viewpoint. Refer to the Models Chapter (page 207) to see examples of a persuasive essay. Use some of the collocations from Task Four in this chapter. Try to use parallel structure in your thesis and concluding statements and in any other sentences that list items.

When you receive feedback from other students or your teacher on this assignment, you will have information that you can use to improve your performance on the final assignment.

SURVIVAL ACADEMIC SKILL: LEARNING INDEPENDENTLY

It is difficult to study at an academic level in a second language. You must constantly struggle with course content, which is always complex, as well as language uncertainty. Furthermore, you may have a limited amount of time in which to improve your English and successfully complete your degree or diploma. Not only do you need to learn English to accomplish your goals, you also need to learn English fast.

Your ESL instructors and professors are able to provide you with valuable assistance. They will do their best to develop your language learning skills during class time; they will also assign you homework that will reinforce your skill development. In the same way that a coach helps an elite athlete, your ESL instructors and professors will help you. However, like an elite athlete, you must also complete some of your training on your own. Consider yourself an elite academic athlete struggling to achieve a difficult goal.

Think about the number of hours that you dedicate to studying English in one week. It is likely that your ESL class time, together with the time that it takes you to complete your homework, does not fill up many of the 168 hours available to you every week. If you are only studying English during class time and homework periods, you may not be progressing as quickly as you would like.

If you believe that your English skills should be progressing faster, think about how you can learn independently. You may notice that studying at increasingly higher levels at a North American academic institution is forcing you to learn more independently. Like an athlete in training, you can study independently in order to accelerate your progress in learning English.

Successful language learners understand the following key points that allow them to learn quickly. They:

- practise, assessing their own strengths and weaknesses.
- make plans to help develop their weakest language skills.
- remain positive—even when faced with frustration.
- know that studying a language only during class time and homework periods may not be enough to progress as quickly as they would like.
- know what they do outside the classroom is as important to their language learning as what they do inside the classroom.
- know that they don't need to be sitting in the library or the classroom to learn a language.

TASK SEVEN: Discussing how to learn independently

- In a group of four or five students, discuss ways that you can practise and improve language skills on your own.
- Write down all the ideas that you have in your notebook. Some ideas are included here to help you.
- When you have finished, combine your best ideas with those from other student groups, and discuss them with your teacher.

What I can do to improve my listening skills

- Read newspaper headlines or skim Internet news sources before listening to the TV news. As you improve, listen to the TV news before listening to the radio news.
- Listen to the radio news as many times as possible throughout the day. There may be an all-news radio station in your area that broadcasts news a few times an hour. Many radio stations broadcast news every hour on the hour.

What I can do to improve my speaking skills

- Join a group that interests you: a sports class (tennis, soccer, yoga, aerobics), a skill development class (first aid, painting, knitting, home renovations) or a student group (international students' club).
- Pick an interesting news story and ask a native speaker about it. Promise yourself to speak to at least one native speaker each day.

What I can do to improve my reading skills

- Read in English what you like to read in your own language. Read mystery novels or sports magazines, or the entertainment, business, technology or travel section in newspapers.
- Scan the Internet and newspapers for information that interests you.

What I can do to improve my writing skills

- Use the writing tutorial services available to all students on campus.

- Read a short newspaper article several times; then hide it and rewrite the article yourself. When you are finished, compare your version with the original.

Think about your language strengths and weaknesses. Decide which areas of skill development will benefit you, and then make a plan. If you learn independently, you will soon notice an improvement.

LISTENING: MINI-CONSUMERS

In this interview, two thirteen-year old children speak about the influence that brand advertising has on children. The two children are called Tommy and Zoe.

TASK EIGHT: Listening and taking notes

Here are some of the product and brand names that you will hear:

Sponge Bob Square Pants (cartoon character)
Pizza Pizza 697-1111 (pizza brand)
Klondike Bar (ice-cream product)
Astro-Jacks (3 balls on a string for $15 dollars)
Gap (brand name - clothing)
Nike (brand name - sports)

- Listen to the interviewer's questions and take notes on the children's answers on the interview outline. You may listen to the interview as many times as you like.
- After each listening, compare your notes with those of another student. Fill in any gaps that you might have.

Interview outline
Hello again, I'm Anna Maria Tremanti, and you're listening to The Current. In this last half-hour we're looking at the marketing techniques, old and new, that are employed day in day out to capture the minds of today's children and the wallets of today's parents. We want to find out what sort of effect this marketing is having on today's media-savvy youth. A little later we're going to talk to some experts on this subject, but you can't have this discussion without talking to the core-demographic, as it were. So joining me is Tommy Paxton-Beasley and Zoe Brownstone. They're both 13 years old and they attend the Claude Watson School for the Arts here in Toronto. Good morning.
We're talking about television programming that targets a youth market. Zoe Brownstone, are these kinds of conversations, the kinds of conversations you just heard there, are they the kinds of conversations you have?

How about you Tommy? Do you talk about this stuff with your friends?

You two are pretty cynical, so you look at this stuff and they don't sway you. You don't say, "Oh, I need that to be better, smarter, prettier, more handsome"?

But it seems to me that you're watching this with maybe a lot more intelligence than we (adults) are giving you credit for too.

Tommy what about you? You say you don't watch a lot of TV. What about your friends? Are they influenced by the ads?

OK, I just want to ask you about peer pressure in all of this. Do you feel peer pressure from your friends about how you spend your money on different things?

READING 3: DEADLY PERSUASION

The title of this article (page 88) is a reference to the many advertisements you see that recommend that you "buy this product, and get another product free." Of course, you can't buy a "24-year-old" person, or "get his friends absolutely free." This information in the title should suggest to you that the author is not in favour of this kind of advertising. This excerpt is from an American anti-consumerism book.

TASK NINE: Developing vocabulary and reading for meaning

Part A: Pre-reading vocabulary building

- In a group of three, read the following sentences from the text and match the boldfaced vocabulary with the definitions in the box below.
- When you have finished, discuss your answers with the class.

1. Home pages on the World Wide Web **hawk** everything from potato chips to cereal to fast food—to drugs. (line 1)

2. Alcohol and drug companies, **chafing under** advertising restrictions in other media, have discovered they can find and **woo** young people without any problem on the Web. (line 2)

3. Marketers attract children to Websites with games and contests and then **extract** from them information that can be used in future **sales pitches** to the child and the child's family. (line 8)

4. Belgium, Denmark, Norway and the Canadian province of Quebec **ban** all advertising to children on television and radio … (line 20)

5. An effort to pass similar **legislation** in the United States in the 1970s was **squelched** by a **coalition** of food and toy companies, broadcasters and ad agencies. (line 24)

Possible meanings

- a group with similar interests
- laws
- attempts to sell products by persuasion
- legally state that something must not be done, shown or used
- sell informally
- firmly prevented
- attract people by promising them something they would like
- feeling annoyed about something
- take information to gain an advantage (shows disapproval)

Part B: Reading for meaning

- Use your knowledge about the key vocabulary and sentences in this reading (Part A) to predict what you will read (a step in the "read smart" process, page 47). Discuss this with the class.
- Read the comprehension questions. Identify key words in the questions to look for in the excerpt.
- Read the excerpt and answer the questions.
- Check your answers with two other students.
- What is your opinion about Internet advertising to children? Should it be banned, or not? Discuss this issue as a class.

1. Why is the Internet an attractive place for marketers to advertise to children?

2. How does online advertising "trick" children?

3. What do online advertisers attempt to develop in very young children?

4. With respect to advertising that targets children, what is the difference between legislation in the United States and legislation in Belgium, Denmark, Norway and the Canadian province of Quebec? What is your opinion about this issue?

5. Why are advertisers trying to form "long-term relationships" with young children? In your opinion, could this damage children?

6. What does the author mean when she writes there are products that might "end up 'owning' people"?

Buy this 24-year-old and get his friends absolutely free

"Home pages on the World Wide Web hawk everything from potato chips to cereal to fast food—to drugs. Alcohol and tobacco companies, chafing under advertising restrictions in other media, have discovered they can find and woo young people without any problem on the Web. Indeed, children are especially vulnerable on the Internet, where advertising manipulates them, invades their privacy, and transforms them into customers without their knowledge. Although there are various initiatives pending, there are as yet no regulations against targeting children online. Marketers attract children to Websites with games and contests and then extract from them information that can be used in future sales pitches to the child and the child's family.

Some sites offer prizes to lure children into giving up the e-mail addresses of their friends too. Online advertising targets children as young as four in an attempt to develop "brand loyalty" as early as possible. Companies unrelated to children's products have Websites for children, such as Chevron's site, which features games, toys, and videos touting the importance of—surprise!—the oil industry. In this way, companies can create an image early on and can also gather marketing data. As one ad says to advertisers, "Beginning this August, Kidstar will be able to reach every kid on the planet. And you can, too."

The United States is one of the few industrialized nations in the world that thinks that children are legitimate targets for advertisers. Belgium, Denmark, Norway, and the Canadian province of Quebec ban all advertising to children on television and radio, and Sweden and Greece are pushing for an end to all advertising aimed at children throughout the European Union. An effort to pass similar legislation in the United States in the 1970s was squelched by a coalition of food and toy companies, broadcasters, and ad agencies. Children in America appear to have value primarily as new consumers. As an ad for juvenile and infant bedding and home accessories says, "Having children is so rewarding. You get to buy childish stuff and pretend it's for them." Our public policy—or lack thereof—on every children's issue, from education to drugs to teen suicide to child abuse, leaves many to conclude that we are a nation that hates its children.

However, the media care about them. The Turner Cartoon Network tells advertisers, "Today's kids influence over $130 billion of their parents' spending annually. Kids also spend $8 billion of their own money. That makes these little consumers big business." Not only are children influencing a lot of spending in the present, they are developing brand loyalty and the beginnings of an addiction to consumption that will serve corporations well in the future. According to Mike Searles, president of Kids 'R' Us, "If you own this child at an early age, you can own this child for years to come. Companies are saying, 'Hey, I want to own the kid younger and younger.'" No wonder Levi Strauss & Co. finds it worthwhile to send a direct mailing to seven- to twelve-year-old girls to learn about them when they are starting to form brand opinions. According to the senior advertising manager, "This is more of a long-term relationship that we're trying to explore." There may not seem much harm in this until we consider that the tobacco and alcohol industries are also interested in long-term relationships beginning in childhood—and are selling products that can indeed end up "owning" people.

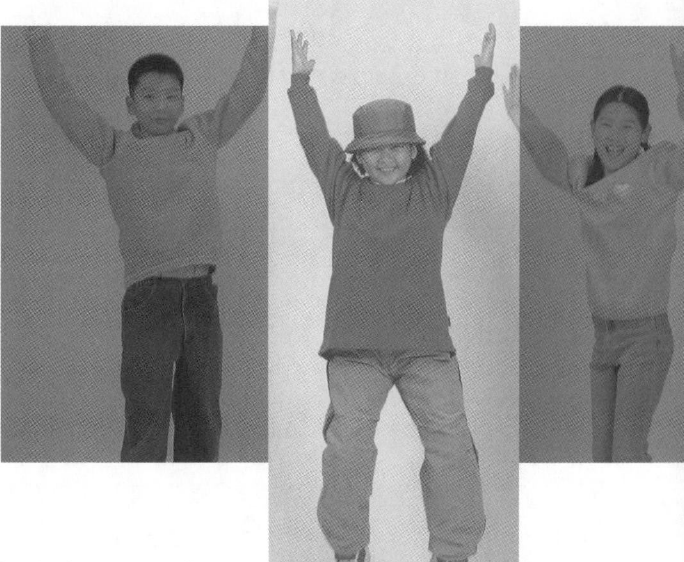

Kilbourne, J. (1999). Buy this 24-year-old and get all his friends absolutely free. In Deadly Persuasion (pp. 43–44). New York: The Free Press.

READING 4: JUNK-FOOD GAMES

This is an article about how brand-name food companies are developing online games to attract children to their products.

TASK TEN: Scanning for information

- Skim the reading's title (above) and subtitle (page 91). What expressions demonstrate that this article will be critical of brand-name companies' use of online games for children as a way of advertising?
- Read the questions and then scan the article to find the answers.

1. How does the article begin? Why did the author choose to start the article this way? This is a common way for newspaper and magazine articles to begin.

2. Why are advergames free to play?

3. Give an example of a Kraft Nabiscoworld.com game.

4. Explain how PepsiCo Inc. Frito-Lay's game works.

5. How do companies promote their advergame sites? Give an example.

6. Why are online games so attractive to marketers?

7. Why do advertising critics think advergames may have negative consequences?

Online arcades draw fire for immersing kids in ads; Ritz Bits Wrestling, anyone?

"Forest Hartmann, a Concord, N.H., 7-year-old, recently sat down at the family computer to play a game of basketball. After shooting some baskets he felt hungry. He asked his mom for some Oreos.

Sylvia Hartmann wasn't surprised. After all, her son was playing Oreo Dunk'N Slam on one of **Kraft Foods** Inc.'s Web sites, Nabiscoworld.com. Banners behind the virtual basket read "Oreo Lick 'em!!!" and "Oreo Dunk 'em!!!"

"How can you think of anything else but Oreos?" his mother asks, recalling the incident.

As the popularity of online games takes off, marketers of kids' food are turning the games into a new advertising vehicle. Brand-laden diversions, sometimes called "advergames," are emerging as a powerful and inexpensive new ad medium, cropping up on dozens of sites from marketers of cookies, candy, cereal, chips and soda.

Visitors play free of charge; but in return they soak up a heavy dose of advertising. They often are exposed to dozens of brand images and messages while playing a single game. Game creators say their users include both children and adults; the typical player spends a half-hour on a game site, often replaying a single game 15 times or more.

Kraft's Nabsicoworld.com features advergames for at least 17 brands, plus classic games such as chess, mah-jongg and backgammon. Some games integrate brands into the play. In Ritz Bits Sumo Wrestling, for example, players control either the Creamy Marshmallow or the Chocolatey Fudge cracker in a bellysmacking showdown, which results in the "S'more"-flavored cracker.

In another Kraft game, users are Planters peanut vendors at a baseball game; they have to throw bags of nuts at spectators in a ballpark festooned with Planters logos. In a Life Savers "boardwalk bowling" game, players try to roll balls over a Life Savers logo through holes shaped like the candies.

PepsiCo Inc.'s Frito-Lay unit has an auction site for kids and kids' sports teams called ePloids.com: The currency is Ploids, which kids get from bags of chips. (Most one-ounce bags are worth one ploid each.) According to the site, merchandise recently auctioned off includes a Toshiba 20-inch television set (for 5,801 ploids) and a Nintendo Game Cube system (for 5,025). Winning bidders redeem their ploids by mail.

Some sites feature survey questions and post statistical breakdowns of the responses. "What do you do after school?" the Nabsicoworld site recently asked its users. The answers: 44% went for "Starving! Got to eat!"; 12% for "out with friends"; 12% for "Sports! Time for practice" and 32% for "get online."

Companies promote their advergame sites on food packages, in TV commercials and on Yahoo and other major Internet portals. Some run sweepstakes and contests, and sponsor links between their sites and others. For instance, on the Neopets site, players can collect points for their virtual pets by clicking on links to advergames for **McDonald's** Corp., **Hershey Foods** Corp.'s Bubble Yum and **General Mills** Inc.'s advergaming site, "You Rule School!" Players can redeem points for candy, snacks and other prizes.

Marketers love Web games because they deliver brand messages cost-effectively. The cost to air a 30-second TV commercial ranges from $7.31 per thousand viewers during the day to $29.90 during prime time, according to SQAD Inc., a Tarrytown, N.Y., media-research firm. In contrast, there are no costs to "air" advergames. Spreading developments costs across the typical number of players, advergaming can cost less than $2 per thousand users, proponents say.

"As opposed to a 30-second commercial where you're being beaten over the head with the message, these games are a very benevolent approach to marketing," says David Madden, executive vice-president of sales and marketing for Wild-Tangent Inc., a Redmond, Wash., advergame developer.

But the games are drawing fire from advertising critics, including those concerned about childhood obesity. They say many advergames are designed to bombard children with snack-food ads. Dale Kunkel, a communications professor at the University of California, Santa Barbara, says children younger than eight can't tell the difference between a marketing pitch and straightforward information. "They just don't understand persuasive intent," Dr. Kunkel says. "It's a great way to put candy, chocolates and junk food in a good light. It's almost as if Dan Rather was reading the news to them."

Catherine Li, an analyst at technology market research firm Forrester Research Inc., calls advergaming a "sly" approach. It "really crosses that line between advertising and content, and that's probably why advertisers like it," she says.

Some worry that the absorbing nature of the games, the age of many of the players and the data collected in the surveys make for an uneven playing field. Advertisers are "being allowed to prey on your weakness," says Jeff Chester, head of the Center for Digital Democracy, a Washington, D.C., watchdog. Companies can create "little profiles of children and dangle ads for fast foods and snacks that they know they have a weakness for," he adds. "I consider that kind of advertising to be really unfair."

Pereira, J. (2004, May 3). Junk-food games. The Wall Street Journal, pp. B1, B4.

FINAL ASSIGNMENT

TASK ELEVEN: Writing a persuasive essay

- Write a persuasive essay to respond to this statement.

  There are no negative consequences of branding.

Start with an introduction and thesis statement presenting your view. Develop your argument with evidence from the readings in this chapter. Try to end with a conclusion that states a solution or a call for action. Refer to the Models Chapter (page 215) to see examples of persuasive essays. In your writing, use some of the collocations that you have learned in this chapter. Use parallel structure when needed, and choose accurate vocabulary to express your ideas.

CHAPTER 5

Alternative and Complementary Medicine

QUICK OVERVIEW

READING
Read newspaper articles for information about alternative and complementary medicine in order to compare and contrast information, develop vocabulary and share information.

WRITING
Write short answers to questions, take notes while reading and listening, and write compare and contrast essays using an academic perspective and references.

LISTENING
Listen to an excerpt from a radio program in order to learn the distinction between alternative and complementary medicine.

DISCUSSION
Discuss your own knowledge of alternative and complementary medicine with classmates. Exchange information and compare answers.

LANGUAGE AWARENESS FOCUS
Learn about the academic perspective and how to use the third person to demonstrate an objective viewpoint.

SURVIVAL ACADEMIC SKILL
Learn about plagiarism and how to avoid it by referencing.

WARM-UP ASSIGNMENT
Write a short compare or contrast essay.

FINAL ASSIGNMENT
Write a compare and contrast essay.

Have you ever used acupuncture to reduce your pain, tried yoga to help you relax or taken an herbal remedy to increase your energy? After discovering that their conventional doctors are unable to help them feel better, many people have begun to look for ways to help themselves. This chapter looks at why people are interested in alternative and complementary medicine; it also examines some different forms of therapy and the distinction between alternative and complementary treatments.

GEARING UP

TASK ONE: Classifying vocabulary

What kind of vocabulary is associated with Western medicine and Eastern medicine?

- In a group of four students, list the following adjectives in the appropriate column of the table:

traditional	conventional	unconventional	mainstream
Chinese	complementary	alternative	holistic

Western medicine	Eastern medicine

- Do you agree about which words belong in each column? If not, can you explain why?

READING 1: ALTERNATIVE MEDICINE JOINS THE MAINSTREAM

This short article introduces a series on alternative medicine.

TASK TWO: Reading for contrast

- Read the article using the strategies that you learned in Chapter 1 (pages 6–9) to help you with unknown vocabulary.
- List some characteristics of Western medicine during the Second World War and some characteristics of alternative medicine today.
- Once you have finished, check with a classmate to make sure that you have understood the information.
- Discuss with your partner:
  1. whether you agree or disagree with the characteristics; and
  2. why alternative medicine looks so attractive today.

Characteristics of Western medicine	Characteristics of alternative medicine

"In the book *Why Things Bite Back*, Edward Tenner describes the great strides that were made, particularly during the Second World War, when health care was mostly "crisis or emergency care." At that time, surgical techniques and the use of antibiotics dramatically cut death rates: "... medical technology has been most dramatically effective when injury has been most severe and has needed the most prompt attention." It seems that since the war, Western medicine has continued in this mode, where most maladies are dealt with by medication or surgery.

Today, much evidence suggests there is a philosophical shift towards "health maintenance and preventative health care," and away from crisis care. This shift generates an easy alliance with alternative approaches, which share some basic premises about health, including a strong conviction about the body's innate ability to heal itself.

This philosophical shift comes at a time when the medical system is stretched to the limit, so individuals, partly out of necessity, need to take more and more responsibility for their own health. Is the trend partly rooted in the baby boomers' quest for longevity and quality of life? No doubt, as this generation has always been preoccupied with living long, healthy lives.

Do you know anyone who isn't taking a vitamin, herbal or health supplement? And most people, I am sure, know the benefits of Echinacea to build the immune system and help ward off the flu.

The ancient practice of yoga is experiencing a resurgence throughout Ottawa. Yoga classes are offered at most community and recreational centres. Ottawa yoga instructor, Patricia Dymond, has initiated programs specifically for cancer and heart patients."

Kenney, E. (2002, December 29). Alternative medicine joins the mainstream. Ottawa Citizen, p. A12.

READING 2: ALTERNATIVE THERAPIES

These articles present information about five different alternative therapies.

Group Work

TASK THREE: Reading, note-taking and sharing information

- Form a group of five students. You will each read a short article about a different kind of alternative medicine and take notes in the chart following the article.

Article titles	Student reader
A. Homeopathy offers deep and true healing	
B. Acupuncture relieves chronic pain	
C. The hazards around us (environmental medicine)	
D. Chiropractors unleash body's 'inherent healing ability'	
E. Patient, heal thyself (kinesiology)	

- Once you have finished reading and taking notes, check with other students who have read your article to make sure that your information is correct and complete.
- Return to your original group and take turns presenting the information that you have learned from your article.
- As you listen to the other students, take your own notes in the charts provided.

Student A: Homeopathy offers deep and true healing

Homeopathy, a 200-year-old science, has undergone more growth in the last 20 years than any other alternative approach in terms of its application and the results it produces. Increasingly, all over Europe, India and South America, many MDs practise homeopathy along with conventional medicine.

"Homeopathy is curative—it goes to the cause of the disease or condition; conventional medicine is mostly palliative—it alleviates symptoms," says Dr. Shahram Ayoubzadeh, who practises homeopathy and naturopathy at Ottawa's Integral Health Clinic. He believes that in many cases of acute and chronic conditions, the body, if properly assisted, has the resources to overcome illness. "Homeopathy, as an alternative health practice, is my biggest love, and as a philosophy it makes perfect sense to me."

Dr. Ayoubzadeh, who has been in practice since 1988, applies its fundamental principles when treating patients.

"Treat the cause, not the symptoms. Treat the whole, not the part. The first thing I ask is: 'Why is the patient suffering?' Whether the patient is experiencing a migraine headache, high blood pressure or depression, I look at finding the root cause of the problem."'

Dr. Ayoubzadeh has helped thousands of patients improve their health using homeopathy. “My objective is to build a complete profile that includes all aspects of the patient’s emotional and physical makeup.”

Practitioners use a variety of questions to help patients get to the source of their problems and find the appropriate homeopathic remedy: Is the person hot or cold? Heavy or slender? Perspires a lot? Introverted or an extrovert? Rational or emotional, excited or depressed? What does the patient crave?

According to Dr. Ayoubzadeh, medical doctors are pressured to see too many patients and often have too little time with them to get to the real root of their health condition. A basic principle in homeopathy is that “like cures like”—if a substance causes a disease or a condition, that same substance, in a very minute and diluted dose, can cure a similar disease.

The effects of these diluted remedies are first tested for their effectiveness in treating patients by using healthy individuals in double-blind studies. Close to 500 of these remedies have been very well studied and successfully used and many more are always in the process of being tested. It takes four to five years before a new remedy’s effect is properly understood.

What is unique about homeopathic remedies is that they are extremely diluted by a process called “potentisation.” That is, they are diluted so much that the original substance is not physically present, but rather its essence or energy is. And that is why there can be no adverse physical effects to the remedy.

In order for a homeopathic treatment to be successful, the remedy has to match perfectly the state of the patient. Otherwise, it won’t act at all or it will improve the condition only temporarily.

Once taken, the remedy can initiate a “healing crisis” by intensifying symptoms. Thus, remedies simulate and stimulate the body’s natural defence system to finish the healing job it has started, and often afterwards, the symptoms are gone forever.

In acute and infectious disease, in addition to the appropriate homeopathic remedy, Dr. Ayoubzadeh also prescribes a “potentized” form of the actual bacteria or virus—(like cures like, similar to the vaccination process). If there is no significant improvement within 12–24 hours of the homeopathic treatment, he advises his patients to seek appropriate conventional therapy.

Homeopaths believe that all people have inherent weaknesses and predispositions to specific disorders—it is the predisposition that needs to be cured in a patient. These dormant predispositions are triggered by physical, environmental or emotional traumas and result in symptoms and pathologies.

Healing at the emotional level is particularly significant in homeopathy—often a deep form of healing takes place at this level which in turn heals the physical ailment.

Parvaneh Rowshan, a local employment counsellor, has experienced profound healing with Dr. Ayoubzadeh, and consults with him periodically to address any of her health concerns.

"I have complete trust in his approach."

Initially, she saw him for back pain.

"I soon realized that his homeopathic treatments were healing me at a much deeper level—an emotional level. After taking a remedy, my subconscious would be sparked and I'd often have a dream which would resolve an emotional issue, which resulted in my back pain going away. Homeopathy has made a huge, significant positive change in my life—I also know myself and my life objectives better."

Because remedies are based on the distinctive profile of the patient, it connects the whole person.

"The remedy acts as a catalyst to promote healing in every part of the person's life," says Dr. Ayoubzadeh.

"By ridding the body of inherent weaknesses, the patient's general quality of life improves and the process sparked by the remedy significantly diminishes the possibility of the person developing chronic disease."

Kenney, E. (2002, December 29). Homeopathy offers deep and true healing. Ottawa Citizen, p. A12.

Homeopathy note-taking chart

Name of alternative medicine	Homeopathy
Philosophy (approach, main idea, central theme or theory)	
Method (what practitioners actually do)	
Results (benefits)	

Student B: Acupuncture relieves chronic pain

"Acupuncture, a 5,000-year-old practice, literally means "needle piercing." And you'd be well advised not to be phobic about needles if you're considering it for your aches and pains.

The process, however, is virtually painless. Acupuncturists insert small, sterile, stainless steel needles just under the skin at various acupuncture points throughout the body.

The World Health Organization recognizes the practice for treatment of 200 conditions.

"Acupuncture is particularly good for chronic pain relief in those suffering from arthritis or cancer," says Dr. Lienpo Chou, a local acupuncturist, who emphasizes she never tells cancer patients they are going to be cured, only that she can make them more comfortable.

"Acupuncture stimulates circulation," she says. "So, when there is a blockage, for example in the bowels, acupuncture opens it up."

Acupuncturists say their skills are effective in treating pinched nerves, headaches and neck pain. "It's no doubt that people have neck pain and headaches with so many operating computers these days," Dr. Chou says. And for those suffering from neck or back pain, she offers some easy and practical suggestions.

"A lot of neck problems would be solved if people used pillows that give their neck support, and a hard mattress helps a lot of sore backs. In fact, if you have a sore back, take a piece of foam and put it on the floor and sleep on that—it's much better than sleeping on a mattress that's too soft."

Dr. Chou arrived in Canada from China in 1976. She opened her Chinese Acupuncture and Herbs Centre in 1981, where she works six days a week practising acupuncture and preparing Chinese herbal remedies.

An acupuncture treatment for headache, for example, would usually require needles to be inserted into the head. Other needles may be inserted in the hands and feet, as they may be part of the "channel" related to the kind of headache the patient is experiencing. For treatment to be effective, all acupuncture points along the channel related to a particular condition must be used."

Kenney, E. (2002, December 31). Acupuncture relieves chronic pain. Ottawa Citizen, p. A12.

Acupuncture note-taking chart

Name of alternative medicine	Acupuncture
Philosophy (approach, main idea, central theme or theory)	insert small sterile needles under the skin

Method (what practitioners actually do)	
Results (benefits)	

Student C: The hazards around us (environmental medicine)

"Do you have one or a combination of the following symptoms? Fatigue, poor concentration, decreased short-term memory, distractibility, mood swings, irritability or depression. If the answer is yes, there are those who would claim you may be suffering from allergies or environmental sensitivities, often referred to as "environmental hypersensitivity disorder."

Today, environmental pollutants and food additives are far more abundant than in decades gone by.

"It is the 'total load' that has a huge impact on our health," according to Dr. Jennifer Armstrong of the Ottawa Environmental Health Clinic and one of a handful of doctors practising environmental medicine in Canada.

As a result, she suggests there are more cases of autism, learning disabilities and cancer in children. She also believes children are particularly susceptible to pollutants in the air because they breathe more rapidly than an adult and inhale more toxins in relation to their body weight.

Dr. Armstrong is particularly concerned about moulds and pesticides in the environment, both of which she says can have a detrimental effect on people's DNA. Parents' damaged DNA is passed on to their children.

"I teach patients about their health and empower them so they can look after themselves. Initially, patients see us as being quite different, but then they start to see health in a completely new light. For some, it fits like a glove."

Dr. Armstrong became interested in the practice of environmental health when she became environmentally sensitive and found expert help from Dr. John Mclennan. He became her mentor and encouraged her to study environmental medicine.

Many patients Dr. Armstrong sees have already been seen by a number of doctors who were not able to help them.

In her approach to medicine, Dr. Armstrong assesses the symptoms, but also searches out causes.

"I practise conventional medicine with a biochemistry slant that searches out the root cause of illness, often resulting in patients getting much better and needing fewer drugs or none at all."

Patients are routinely tested for elevated levels of heavy metals through hair analysis, or tested for sensitivities to dust, moulds, chemicals and foods. Many other tests examine individual biochemistry, tests not normally done in mainstream medicine.

Dr. Armstrong explains the type of patient she helps. "We treat a wide range of conditions including chronic fatigue syndrome, depression, arthritis, fibromyalgia, severe asthmatics and anaphylactics. An anaphylactic is someone who is so allergic to peanut oil that simply sniffing it could result in them going into shock."

Other treatments include administering vitamins and minerals intravenously to treat allergies. Therapists also look at diet and lifestyle changes, encourage sauna detoxification and use oxygen to detoxify and halt allergic reactions.

Dr. Armstrong is not against all drugs. She says painkillers are necessary in cancer treatment, and antihistamines and antibiotics have important uses. Her concern is that drug research is often undertaken by drug companies and thus may not be entirely objective. She would prefer research be done by independent companies.

Dr. Armstrong likes the idea of bringing together conventional medicine and functional medicine, which is the biochemistry of how the body works, to really get to the root of the problem.

"I feel good about practising environmental medicine," she says. "It makes sense to me, and it gives me great satisfaction to see people getting better—they're happier, they're contributing to their own care and there's a bounce to their walk."

Kenney, E. (2002, December 30). The hazards around us. Ottawa Citizen, p. A13.

Environmental medicine note-taking chart	
Name of alternative medicine	Environmental medicine
Philosophy (approach, main idea, central theme or theory)	
Method (what practitioners actually do)	

Results (benefits)	

Student D: Chiropractors unleash body's 'inherent healing ability'

"Chiropractors are committed to the body's innate ability to heal itself," says Dr. Ken Dick, explaining the central theme of chiropractic care. "By making spinal adjustments, we remove interference in a spine that is misaligned (has a subluxation) or not moving properly, so the body's inherent healing ability can take over."

By working on the nervous system and the spinal column that encases it, chiropractors influence the body's overall health, as the nervous system controls circulation, respiration and the musculoskeletal system.

Dr. Dick works out of the Britannia Chiropractic Clinic and has been practising for 20 years. He was almost born into the practice of chiropractic care. As a child, growing up in a Mennonite community, he never saw a doctor—his parents would take him to the chiropractor when he was sick. Interestingly, the chiropractic and the Mennonite philosophy are similar—both focus on a balanced lifestyle to maintain health. An aligned spine is as important as an aligned lifestyle.

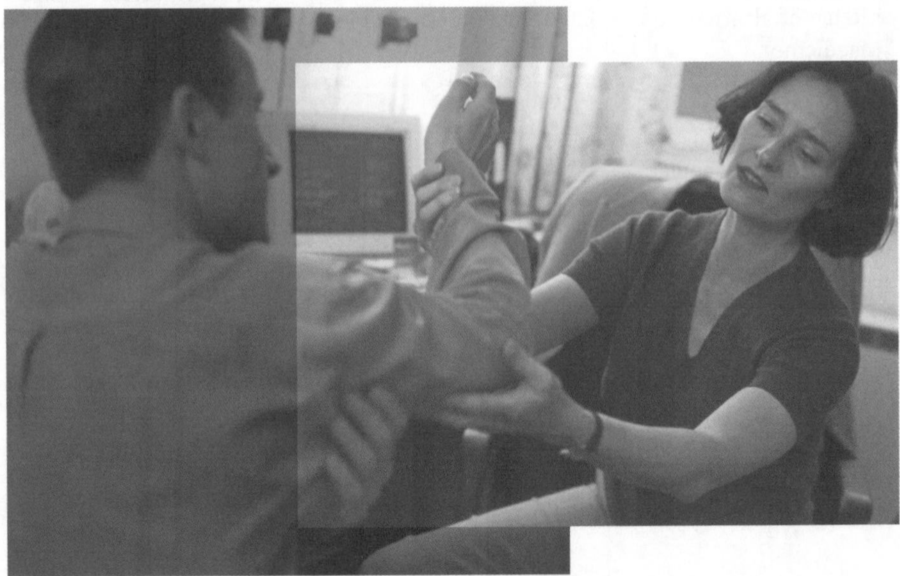

After the necessary paperwork is completed during the initial visit, Dr. Dick does a physical examination. He assesses the spine using a process called motion palpation. Motion palpation is like seeing with your fingers, he said, adding that the feedback he attains from this process "is phenomenal."

He also does a wide range of motion tests and a postural exam. He also tests the reflexes and uses a weigh scale to see if the patient is carrying the same amount of weight on both sides. If need be, he orders X-rays.

He does muscle testing to evaluate the strength and symmetry of the muscles. If the patient is active and in shape with good muscle tone, it is much easier to fix the problem; conversely, if the muscles are weak, the adjustment won't hold as well.

The first month of treatment is the intensive phase in which the chiropractor may see a patient three times a week. This is to enable the tissues to make a discernible change and to alleviate symptoms, particularly pain.

"In the first three or four sessions, I find out how much of a change I can make and which approach to use, as each patient is unique," says Dr. Dick.

After a month he reassesses the spine and may see the patient every two weeks or even once a month.

Why is it important to see a chiropractor regularly?

"It's like seeing your dentist," replies Dr. Dick. "You go back for preventive maintenance."

The second phase of treatment is the rehabilitative phase in which weaknesses and imbalances in the spine are corrected and strengthened.

The third phase is to maintain the adjustments from the first two phases. Adjustments may improve the functioning of many organ systems or even lower high blood pressure.

Chiropractic care can start immediately after birth. Dr. Dick cites an example from his own family. "My second child required a spinal adjustment seconds after his birth because of the position his head was in."

And one of the best-kept secrets of chiropractic care is that pregnant women who follow it have much shorter labours, says Dr. Dick.

Chiropractors often treat osteoarthritis or stiffening of the joints—a common condition of aging. In fact, the number one physical concern that people in retirement have is poor flexibility in the joints. By opening up the joints through adjustments, their range of motion can be much broader.

"Chiropractic care has a definite place in the medical system," Dr. Dick says. "Conventional medicine plays an important role in crisis care—if I'm in a car accident or my appendix bursts I want to go to the hospital, but if my back hurts or I have a headache, I want to go to the chiropractor."

In one year alone, he says he saved dozens of patients from needless surgery.

Kenney, E. (2002, December 30). Chiropractors unleash body's 'inherent healing ability.' Ottawa Citizen, p. A13.

Chiropractic medicine note-taking chart	
Name of alternative medicine	Chiropractic medicine
Philosophy (approach, main idea, central theme or theory)	
Method (what practitioners actually do)	
Results (benefits)	

Student E: Patient, heal thyself (kinesiology)

“Oh, my aching back!

Your back may be sore, but is it the spine that's causing the problem? Or, if you suffer from migraines, you may want to know where such excruciating pain comes from.

Applied kinesiology could provide the answers. The theory behind the practice is that each muscle is related to a specific system, organ or part of the body, and Dr. Jacques Bedard has been using it at his Vanier clinic for more than 25 years.

He has a succinct description for applied kinesiology. “It is to help patients understand why they are not feeling well, help them through the crisis and to teach them how to help themselves be well,” he says. “Ultimately, I want the patient to become the patient-doctor.”

When Dr. Bedard meets a new patient, he begins by listening and observing. This gives him valuable information about where to start looking for the source of the problem. Where the patient actually feels pain may be the end result of the problem.

During muscle testing, the muscles are the messengers. Dr. Bedard "listens" to them in order to find the "keys" that point to the source of the illness or problem, then he makes the necessary adjustment so the body can start to function properly and heal itself.

But how does he do all this?

Take a patient who suffers from severe migraines. "My job," he says, "is to find out the why behind the headache."

He tests the strength or weakness of the patient's muscle while exploring potential sources of the problem throughout the body. "It could be a weakness in the liver system, a condition that manifests itself in migraines."

Dr. Bedard suggests there are three main causes of illness.

Structural problems are related to the spine, sprains and bruising.

A chemical illness is related to how the system deals with stressors in the environment, whether its source is bacterial, viral, pollutants, food additives, or anything related to nutrition.

Then there is the emotional component—stress, trauma, depression can impact significantly on a person's health and well being. "People want to fix the physical, but often emotional aspects are part of the problem."

Dr. Bedard notes that we live in a world with many stressors and, as a result, many physical problems people experience are related to stress.

His solution? "Find your special island of relaxation. Your island is a special place that you visit regularly to find peace and relaxation."

Kenney, E. (2003, January 2). Patient, heal thyself. Ottawa Citizen, p. A14.

Kinesiology note-taking chart	
Name of alternative medicine	Kinesiology
Philosophy (approach, main idea, central theme or theory)	
Method (what practitioners actually do)	

Results (benefits)	

TASK FOUR: Learning word forms

There are many possible word forms relating to alternative medical therapies.

- Fill in the table below to become aware of these word forms. Answers can be found in the readings.

Type of alternative medicine (noun)	Name for practitioner (noun)	Adjective
	Homeopath	Homeopathic (remedy)
Acupuncture		No adjective form
Environmental medicine	Environmental doctor	Environmental (sensitivities)
Chiropractic medicine		
	Kinesiologist	No adjective form

TASK FIVE: Learning collocations relating to doctors

As you may recall, collocations are words that often appear together in recognized mini-expressions (see page 74). The following chart displays collocations with the words *doctor* and *practitioner*.

Collocations for doctor and practitioner

Verb	Noun
see	a doctor a practitioner
go to	
visit	
consult	

- Work with the group that you formed for Reading 2.

- Use the collocations above and your knowledge from the articles to describe the kind of doctor or practitioner you visit when you:

1. have a pain in your shoulder or knee?

   When I have a pain in my shoulder, I ***see*** *an acupuncturist.*

2. have a sore back?

3. have a cold?

4. have stomach trouble?

5. feel tired all the time?

6. have allergies?

7. break a bone?

8. feel overly anxious or stressed?

- Discuss what happens when you are treated for these kinds of health problems. Do you think the treatment is effective (does it make you feel better)?

LANGUAGE AWARENESS FOCUS: MOVING TO AN ACADEMIC PERSPECTIVE – USING THE THIRD PERSON

The academic perspective is always ***objective***. This means that when you want to speak or write in a formal academic manner, you must present the facts. Your experiences and opinions are no longer useful because they are ***subjective***, based on your feelings and emotions—not the facts.

Sometimes, your instructors may ask you to speak or write about a personal experience, or to express a view based on your own opinions; in these cases, it is acceptable to write about yourself and what you think. However, as you progress in your post-secondary education, your instructors will ask you to read, research and summarize other sources of information. You will need to base these assignments on information that is objective. You will no longer be able to use your own experiences or opinions to support these assignments.

Avoiding the personal perspective in academic writing isn't hard if you know how to revise sentences that are subjective. Look at the following examples.

Personal perspective – first person – subjective	Academic perspective – third person – objective
I think that acupuncture is a good technique to relieve pain.	Acupuncture is a proven technique to relieve pain.
In my opinion, alternative and complementary medicine are different approaches to health care.	Alternative and complementary medicine are different approaches to health care.
Once I went to see a chiropractor, and he really helped me understand that my poor posture was causing problems with my digestive system.	Chiropractors can help people understand how a poorly aligned spine influences other systems in the body. For example, poor posture may cause problems with the digestive system.
My father always took me to see a homeopathic doctor for my allergies because he believed children shouldn't have needles or drugs for allergy problems.	Many people visit homeopathic doctors because they hope to avoid using needles or drugs for treatment.
I know many more people are visiting alternative doctors than ever before.	Americans made approximately 425 million visits to alternative therapy providers during 1990.[1]

TASK SIX: Moving from the subjective to the objective

- Now try converting these sentences from a subjective perspective to an objective perspective.
- Use information from the articles in Reading 2.

1. I never believed a homeopathic doctor could help reduce my back pain—until I went to see one.

2. In my opinion, acupuncture can help many people.

3. I was hoping Ginseng would make me smarter for my exams, but it didn't help me at all.

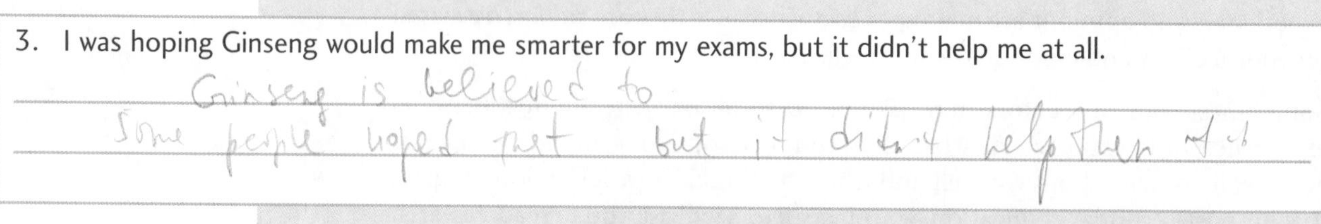

1. Flint, V. (2001, January). How to use alternative and complementary medicine [Electronic version]. Retrieved April 2003, from www.webmd.com

4. Like more and more people these days, I suffer from environmental sensitivities.

5. My chiropractor says that the body has an innate ability to heal itself.

WARM-UP ASSIGNMENT

TASK SEVEN: Writing a short compare or contrast essay

- Write a short compare or contrast essay. In order to keep the essay relatively short, review the chapter content to this point and decide whether you will write about the similarities or differences between Western and alternative medicine.

In a compare or contrast essay, you must organize and explain similarities or differences in ways that make sense. Refer to the Models Chapter (page 210) for more information about compare and contrast essays. Be sure to write using an objective, third person, academic perspective. Use parallel structure when necessary.

When you receive feedback from other students or your teacher on this assignment, you will have information that you can use to improve your performance on the final assignment.

LISTENING: DIFFERENTIATING BETWEEN ALTERNATIVE AND COMPLEMENTARY MEDICINE

You will listen to a recording of Dr. Barrie Cassileth explaining the difference between the terms *alternative* and *complementary*.

TASK EIGHT: Listening and taking notes

Part A: Pre-listening vocabulary building

Here are some key words that you will need to know to understand the audio segment. The key words are in bold in the sentences below. The parts of speech are listed in parentheses.

- Read the sentences and discuss with a partner what you think the words mean.
- You can ask students from other groups if you aren't sure. Consult your dictionary only as a last resort.

1. Mathematicians must be very **rational** (adj.) thinkers. They use logic to solve problems.

2. Combining psychology with biometrics is an **integrative** (adj.) approach to training that may help elite athletes excel.

3. Her diet is very strict. Every day she follows a **regimen** (n.) of very little food, and lots of physical activity.

4. The SARS virus **invaded** (v.) the populations of Beijing, Hong Kong and Toronto in the summer of 2003. It was an **invasive** (adj.) virus.

5. Physical therapy is an important **adjunct** (n.) to drug therapy.

6. **Physiology** (n.) is the study of how the human body functions. There are many **physiological** (adj.) benefits of complementary therapies.

7. This man calls himself a doctor, but he has no formal education in medicine. He is a **quack** (n.). He tells patients about "cures" that do not work. It is all just **quackery** (n.).

Part B: Listening and note-taking

- Before you listen, read the note-taking outline below. Try to predict what you will hear.
- Listen once without writing anything.
- Listen again and take notes as if you were listening to a lecture.
- Compare your notes with two other classmates.
- Listen again to confirm your answers.

Note-taking outline

Introduction:
Barrie Cassileth is
- a medical sociologist;
- an author;
- in charge of a new integrative medicine program at a top cancer hospital.

What therapies does her program offer?
-
-
-

Every rational **complementary** therapy. Complementary, not alternative.
What is the problem with terminology in this area?

CAM stands for

There is a vital distinction between alternative and complementary therapies:
- Characteristics of alternative medicine (for cancer)
- Characteristics of complementary therapies

It is important to separate the two kinds of therapies.
If we put them together, it is too easy to throw them all out.

Categories of complementary medicine

- mind-body therapies, such as:

  Benefits of these therapies:

- body work therapies:

  Benefits of these therapies:

- music therapy

  Benefits of this therapy:

- Discuss with your class the differences between alternative and complementary medicine.
- Take notes on the discussion. This information will help you with your final assignment.

SURVIVAL ACADEMIC SKILL: AVOIDING PLAGIARISM BY REFERENCING

Copying another person's words or ideas is called plagiarism, and it is considered an academic "crime." As there are serious academic penalties for students who plagiarize, plagiarism is a significant concern for students and professors alike. Generally, there are two types of plagiarism:

Type One: copying another person's *words*.

Type Two: copying another person's *ideas*.

Providing references for other people's words and ideas is one way to avoid plagiarizing. When you provide a reference, you let the reader know who originally wrote or said the referenced words, or who first came up with the referenced ideas.

You have probably seen references before; in fact, there are a number of references in this textbook. Briefly discuss with your class the elements that should be included in a reference, (for example, the author's name). What else does a reference require? Your teacher may write the elements on the board.

Referencing words and ideas is easy; however, referencing them accurately can be difficult. You must combine all the reference elements in the proper order while using the proper punctuation. To confuse matters, there are also a number of different referencing styles, such as the American Psychological Association (APA) style and the Modern Languages Association (MLA) style. Each style demands that reference elements be placed in a different order with unique punctuation.

This textbook uses the American Psychological Association (APA) style because it is widely used in the social sciences, and therefore will be useful for many students.

Type One: Referencing another person's words

When you want to include another person's words in your own writing, follow these rules:

1. **For short quotes** (less than a few lines long), place quotation marks around the words and include a footnote or endnote number after the quote. A footnote will place your reference at the bottom of the page; an endnote will place your reference at the end of the document.

   EXAMPLE: Conventional medicine traditionally focused on physical health, and not emotional health. However, "more and more doctors—and patients—recognize that mental states and physical well-being are intimately connected."[2] This has brought about a great change in the way conventional medicine is practised.

2. **For longer quotes** (more than a few lines long), separate the quote from your own writing by indenting. You don't need to use quotation marks.

   EXAMPLE: The connection between mind and body seems logical.

   > The brain, after all, is only another organ, and it operates on the same biochemical principles as the thyroid or the spleen. What we experience as feelings, good or bad, are at the cellular level no more than a complex interaction of chemicals and electrical activity.[3]

   This has brought about a great change in the way conventional medicine is practised.

2. Lemonick, M. (2003, January 20). The power of mood. Time, 161 (3), 38.

3. Lemonick, M. (2003, January 20). The power of mood. Time, 161 (3), 38.

Type Two: Referencing another person's ideas

It is also considered plagiarism if you use another person' ideas without referencing them. Here are some general guidelines to help you avoid using another person's ideas improperly.

1. It isn't considered plagiarism if you write about information that is considered general knowledge in your field.

   EXAMPLE: Scientists have made great progress in their understanding of how physical problems are related to depression.

This isn't considered copying another person's ideas (type two plagiarism) because it is a widely known fact in the field of medicine. Many researchers have agreed that this is a true statement, and many people have written about this idea in a variety of ways.

You must learn what information is "widely known" in your field. You will learn which ideas are common ideas as you continue to study your major.

If you aren't sure whether an idea is widely known or not, you should probably reference the information to be certain to avoid plagiarism.

2. It is considered plagiarism if you write about a specific idea without providing a reference to explain its origins. Specific ideas are usually:
   - an author's unique idea;
   - the results of specific research;
   - a statistic.

   EXAMPLE: Research that has been done by Dr. Oz suggests that patients who listen to calming music and use meditation before surgery recover faster than patients who don't.[4]

This information requires a reference because it discusses the results of specific research.

Formatting references

Students often want to write references for information that they find in a) books, b) newspapers, c) magazines and academic journals, and d) Internet articles. This textbook will provide you with the general format for these sources of information, but you will find many more examples in the American Psychological Association's publications and on its website.

a) Referencing books

EXAMPLE:

author's family name — date of publication — edition number - omit if none — main location of publisher's office

Tuckwell, K.J. (2004). Canadian Marketing in Action (6th ed., p. 208). Toronto: Pearson.

author's initials for his/her first name(s) — book title (underlined) — page number for specific information — publisher's name

4. Oz, M. (2003, January 20). Say "om" before surgery. Time, 161 (3), 43.

b) Referencing newspapers

EXAMPLE:

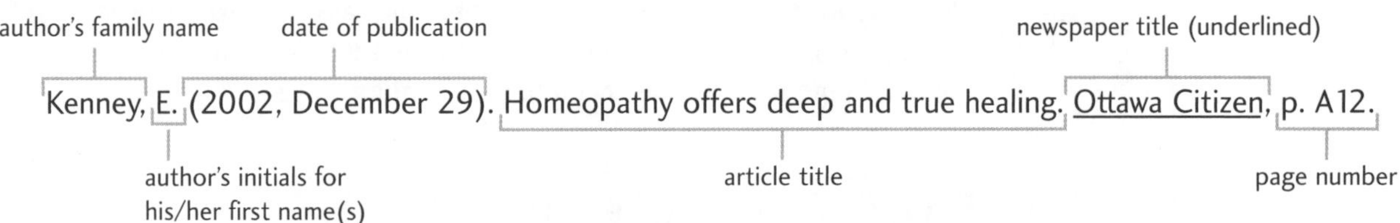

c) Referencing magazines and academic journals

EXAMPLE:

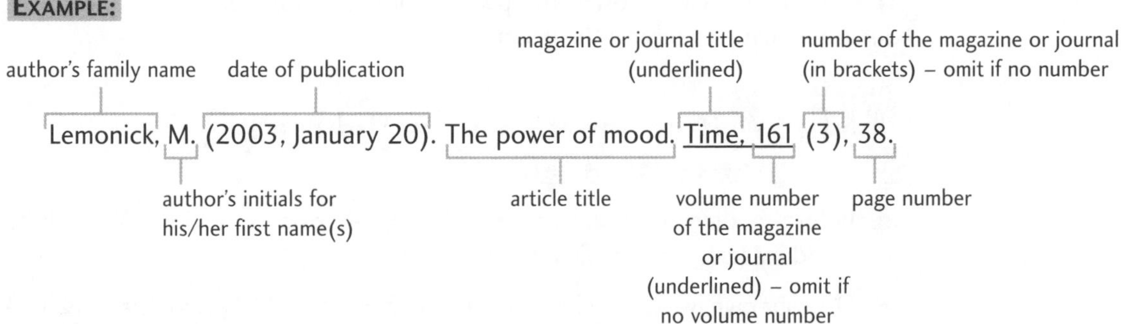

d) Referencing Internet articles

Referencing Internet articles is especially difficult as quite frequently one—or possibly many—of the standard reference elements aren't found within the articles. You should refer to the APA website to stay informed about the evolution of referencing formats for Internet articles.

EXAMPLE:

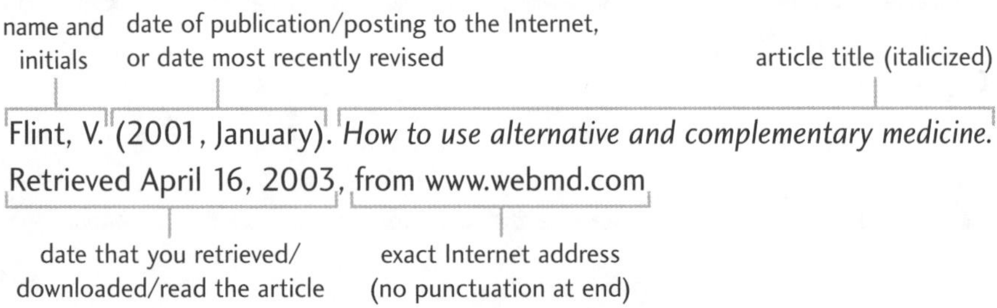

TASK NINE: Writing references

- With a classmate, write a reference for each of the following:
  1. this textbook, or a textbook that you have with you;
  2. a newspaper article that your teacher has brought to class, or one that you have with you;
  3. a magazine or academic journal article that your teacher has brought to class, or one that you have with you;

4. an Internet article that your teacher has brought to class, or one that you have with you.

- When you have finished, your teacher may ask you to write your reference(s) on the board. Compare your references with those of other students. Remember to use accurate punctuation.

READING 3: HOW TO COMBINE COMPLEMENTARY AND TRADITIONAL MEDICINE

This article describes how some people combine complementary and traditional medicine to receive the benefits of both.

TASK TEN: Writing short answers and reading for comprehension

- Before reading the article, read the comprehension questions. You will be asked to scan for specific information.
- On your own, write short answers to the questions. Make sure that you have enough detailed information to support your answers.
- When you have finished, check with a classmate to make sure that you understand the content. Fill in any gaps that you might have.

1. The article introduces three people. Read the article once quickly and gather as much information about the three people as possible. Fill in the chart below with the descriptions of the people.

Person	Details / Description
Dini Petty	
Dr. Elaine Chin	
Penny Kendall-Reed	

- Now read the article again more slowly to find the answers to these questions.

2. What problems did Dini Petty have when she saw her family doctor and her naturopath?

3. What benefits do Dr. Chin and Penny Kendall-Reed provide to their clients?

4. Why was Dr. Chin dissatisfied with practising traditional medicine?

5. The article mentions a "spectrum from prevention to treatment." If patients are interested in preventing illness, which form of medicine is most useful for them? If patients are interested in curing illness, which form of medicine is most useful for them?

6. Are all natural medicines safe?

7. What type of medicine do you think will be practised most in the future?

Physician and naturopath combine healing talents to offer their patients a new blend of health care

"At 57, former broadcaster and consummate dynamo Dini Petty looks and feels 20 years younger.

She credits much of her youthful appearance and energy to a new approach to health care that marries traditional and alternative medicine under one roof.

"I have more vitality. My body is more toned than it was 20 years ago. I look forward to wearing a bathing suit now. My goal is to peak at 60 and hold it," says

Petty, who is enrolled in a longevity program designed to combat the ravages wrought by aging.

She used to run back and forth between her family doctor and her naturopath but found that frustrating.

"I'd go to my family doctor and he'd pooh pooh my natural therapies and my naturopath would just roll his eyes at my medical questions. There was such a gulf between them—and as the patient, I was left to figure it all out on my own," says Petty.

Now she has the best of both worlds under the care of Dr. Elaine Chin, a family doctor and Penny Kendall-Reed, a naturopath, who work "synergistically" as a team at the Beresford Clinic on Avenue Rd. in Toronto.

"We provide an opportunity for patients to have one-stop service for their health care needs. It's a preventive, multi-disciplinary model that we need in the larger context of our health-care system," says Chin, who also has an MBA.

"We offer a safe environment where traditional and natural medicine work together. We don't do anything that's not scientifically proven. We share charts and are in constant communication about how we're treating patients," says Kendall-Reed, who is trained in natural remedies such as acupuncture, herbal supplements and homeopathy.

The set-up allows them to collaborate with each other while concentrating on their individual areas of expertise to treat the patient. "It's allowing each health-care practitioner to do what they know best," says Chin. "How can you argue with that? I know a little about natural medicine, but not a lot so why should I meddle in it?"

She used to work in a traditional family practice, but found it less than satisfying. When patients came in for their annual physical, Chin would typically order blood work and check their weight and blood pressure.

Ninety-nine percent of the time she'd tell patients they were "fine."

"But are they really fine when they're a little bit overweight, or their cholesterol, blood sugar or blood pressure is a little up?" asks Chin. Patients routinely left with nothing more than a caution to watch their salt intake and eat less fat. But in reality, the "alarm bells" should have been going off, says Chin.

"That's the fundamental reason why I stopped practising that way because I knew when the patient walked out my door, many of them walked out with future potential diseases."

In their integrated practice at Beresford, Chin or Kendall view illness and healing on a spectrum from prevention to treatment. One or the other of them will take the lead role with a patient depending on the condition being treated.

"If we're talking about something like obesity, natural medicine would take the lead role in terms of diet, exercise and supplements because it's a condition that's easily reversible. In the case of cancer, the roles are reversed and traditional medicine would take the lead, while natural medicine plays a supportive role," says Kendall-Reed.

The arrangement allows patients, many of whom are afraid to tell their doctors that they're using alternative therapies, to be open and honest about what they're taking.

"People think because something is natural, it's completely safe, but that's not necessarily true," says Kendall-Reed.

For example, cancer patients who combine their prescription medication or chemotherapy with herbal supplements could suffer severe side effects, drug interactions or reduce the effects of their therapy.

"There are a lot of products out there claiming to be the magic bullet or the cure-all for a certain disease. Patients can run into trouble if they try to dabble in it by themselves," says Chin.

It costs $145 for an initial consultation with Chin and Kendall-Reed and $85 an hour thereafter. The clinic also offers customized programs geared to specific conditions, such as weight loss, longevity (anti-aging) and menopause management. They come with hefty price tags, ranging from $490 to $5,500. It also provides plastic surgery, hair transplantation and "organic" beauty services.

None of the costs are covered under OHIP, but may be eligible for reimbursement under some employer-sponsored health plans. About half of Chin's patients ask for naturopathic intervention, typically more women than men.

"To us, this is the medicine of the future. We're not just treating disease, we're actually preventing it and improving people's quality of life," says Chin. Adds Kendall-Reed: "People aren't sitting back and taking their health for granted anymore or just relying on traditional medicine to make them better."

Yelaja, P. (2002, June 21) Bridging the medical divide. Toronto Star.

FINAL ASSIGNMENT

TASK ELEVEN: Writing a compare and contrast essay

- Write a compare and contrast essay to explain the similarities and differences between alternative and complementary medicine. Use an academic perspective to explore what you know about alternative and complementary medicine. Quote and refer to information from the chapter readings and listening task, using appropriate references when required.

Refer to the Models Chapter (page 210) for information about compare and contrast essays.

CHAPTER 6

Vaccine Safety

QUICK OVERVIEW

READING

Read book, magazine and Internet articles in order to acquire key information about vaccine safety. Use scanning and other "read smart" strategies to find the information.

WRITING

Write short answers to questions and take notes while listening. Practise paraphrasing in order to avoid plagiarism. Write a paraphrase. Then write a process essay that incorporates a paraphrase of information from the chapter.

LISTENING

Listen to a lecturer discuss how scientists determine whether a causal or temporal relationship exists between vaccines and adverse reactions to vaccines.

DISCUSSION

Discuss how you feel about vaccine safety, exchange information from the readings and compare your answers with those of your classmates.

LANGUAGE AWARENESS FOCUS

Learn about the problems associated with writing in the third person/present tense, and how to avoid them.

SURVIVAL ACADEMIC SKILL

Learn how to paraphrase in order to avoid plagiarism.

WARM-UP ASSIGNMENT

Write a short paraphrase.

FINAL ASSIGNMENT

Write a process essay that incorporates a paraphrase of chapter content.

Most of us have experienced the prick of a needle at some point in our lives. Although we may not like needles, we usually allow doctors or nurses to vaccinate us because we believe that the injection will allow us to resist a certain disease. However, this isn't the case for everyone; in fact, a growing number of people have begun to question the benefits of vaccines. Some even refuse to have their children vaccinated against deadly diseases that used to kill thousands of children.

GEARING UP

TASK ONE: Developing vocabulary

Work with a partner and look at how the boldfaced words are used in the following sentences.

- Write the part of speech for the boldfaced words in the parentheses: *n* for noun; *v* for verb; *adj.* for adjective; *exp.* for expression. The first one has been done for you.
- Check with other students to be sure that you understand the meaning of the word.

1. The doctor filled the **syringe** ( ) with the **vaccine** ( ).
2. The idea that **vaccination** ( ) might prevent disease began with an English doctor who noticed that once people had recovered from a disease, they did not **contract** ( ) the same disease again.
3. In order **to be vaccinated against** ( ) a disease, you must have a **needle** ( ).
4. The needle **injects** ( ) a milder and inactive form of the disease into your body.
5. Once the **inoculation** ( ) is complete, your body will develop **immunity** ( ) to the disease. In other words, it **will resist** ( ) the disease in the future.
6. The doctor **vaccinated** ( ) all the children; now the children are **immune** ( ) to sickness.
7. The **immunization** ( ) program had a goal of vaccinating 90 percent of people over the age of seventy-five against the **flu** ( ).
8. **Adverse** ( ) reactions to routine vaccinations are **rare** ( ).

TASK TWO: Finding synonyms and discussing attitudes

Synonyms are words that have the same meaning. Using synonyms can add variety to your speaking and writing. It can also help you paraphrase (express in your own words) someone else's ideas.

Part A: Grouping synonyms

- Group the synonyms together.
- Pay attention to the forms of the words.

EXAMPLE: immunize (v), vaccinate (v), inoculate (v)

- immunize (v)
- syringe (n)
- vaccination (n)
- adverse (adj.)
- vaccinate (v)
- inoculation (n)
- negative (adj.)
- get (v)
- injection (n)
- contract (v)
- immunization (n)
- needle (n)
- inoculate (v)
- inject (v)

Part B: Discussing injections

- In a group of three students, use some of the synonyms above to discuss how you feel about injections.

1. What is your attitude towards injections?
2. Have you ever had a bad experience with injections?
3. Do you think that vaccines are important for preventing diseases?
4. Do you think that all vaccines are safe?
5. Are there any reasons why you would refuse to be vaccinated?

READING 1: IMMUNIZATION SCHEDULE

This reading contains the immunization schedule for infants and children. It lists all the vaccinations that a child should have in order to be considered completely vaccinated in Canada.

TASK THREE: Forming an opinion

Each "x" in the schedule represents at least one injection.

- Count the x marks. Do you think there are too many needles for a young child? Do you think children really need this many injections?

Routine immunization schedule for infants and children

"Children need different vaccines at different ages. It is important for children to be immunized on time according to the recommended schedule. For more information, contact your doctor or public health nurse.

Age at vaccination	Diphtheria Tetanus Pertussis Poliomyelitis	Hib[1]	Mumps Measles Rubella	Tetanus Diphtheria or Tetanus, Diphtheria Pertussis[2]	Hepatitis B[3]	Chickenpox[5] (Varicella)	Pneumococcal[5]	Meningococcal[5]
Birth					Infancy			
2 months	X	X					X	X
4 months	X	X					X	X
6 months	X	X			or		X	X
12 months			X			X	X	
18 months	X	X	X[4] or					or
4-6 years	X		X[4]		Preado-lescence			
14-16 years				X	(9-13 years)			X

Notes:

1. *Haemophilus influenzae* type b (Hib) requires a series of immunizations. The exact number and timing of each may vary with the type of vaccine used.
2. Tetanus-Diphtheria vaccine, an "adult type" preparation, contains less diphtheria toxin than the preparation given to younger children and is less likely to cause reactions in older persons. It is recommended at 14–16 years of age and every 10 years thereafter. The shot is also available in combination with the acellular pertussis vaccine, which is recommended as a booster around 15 years.
3. Hepatitis B requires a series of immunizations. In some jurisdictions, they may be administered at a younger age.
4. Two-dose programs for MMR are given in all territories and provinces. Second dose MMR is given either at 18 months or 4–6 years of age. If the child is past the age at which the second MMR is recommended, the second dose can be given 1–2 months after the first.
5. The costs of these vaccines are not covered by all provincial/territorial health plans. You may have to pay for them yourself.

Source: Canadian Paediatric Society
Phone: (613) 526-9397 Fax: (613) 526-3332
www.cps.ca; www.caringforkids.cps.ca

READING 2: FREQUENTLY ASKED QUESTIONS ABOUT VACCINE SAFETY

This reading contains a list of frequently asked questions and answers about vaccine safety from Health Canada's website.

TASK FOUR: Pre-reading vocabulary building

Familiarize yourself with the names of children's diseases. Try to complete this task without a dictionary.

- Match the disease with the symptoms.

Disease		Symptoms
1. Autism		a) Causes diarrhea in babies. Can result in dehydration and death.
2. Asthma		b) Causes muscle degeneration ranging from twisted arms and legs to an interruption of breathing. Can be fatal.
3. Allergies		c) Causes the body to lose its ability to process sugar. Can be fatal.
4. SIDS (Sudden Infant Death Syndrome)		d) Causes brain damage. Prevents people from forming emotional attachments to friends and family.
5. Febrile Seizures		e) Causes a red, spotty and itchy rash on the skin. Lasts for a week or two before disappearing.
6. Pertussis (Whooping Cough)		f) Causes the unexplained death of infants while they sleep.
7. Hyperactivity		g) Causes a swelling of the brain. Can be fatal.
8. Diabetes		h) Causes respiratory damage. Prevents people from breathing easily. Can be fatal.
9. Polio		i) Causes coughing that is difficult to stop. Can be fatal.
10. Chickenpox		j) Can cause a variety of negative reactions ranging from itchy eyes and runny noses to severe shock and death.
11. Smallpox		k) Causes a loss of consciousness and muscle contractions due to a very high fever.
12. Encephalitis		l) Causes an inability to sit still and concentrate.
13. Rotavirus		m) Causes a red, spotty, itchy rash. Can be fatal.

TASK FIVE: Taking notes and discussing main ideas

- Read the questions and answers in the reading below.
- In the margins, take short, point-form notes based on the information in the answers.
- When you have finished, compare your notes with those of another student. Do you both agree on the main points for each answer?

When you have finished comparing your notes, try this activity to help you remember the reading content and to practise chapter vocabulary:

1. Student A closes the textbook.
2. Student B reads the questions to Student A.
3. Student A answers the questions orally, providing the main points without looking at the reading.
4. Switch roles: Student A asks Student B the questions.

- Discuss with the class how you feel about vaccines now. Do you feel that vaccination is safe?

The questions and answers that follow, adapted from a number of sources, are intended to assist in counselling about immunization; the wording and style are targeted at a general audience. The answers expand on the key messages about vaccine safety listed in Box 1 while addressing the common misconceptions listed in Box 2.

Box 1

Key messages on vaccine safety in Canada

- The vaccines used in Canada are extremely effective and extremely safe.
- Serious adverse reactions are rare. The dangers of vaccine-preventable diseases are many times greater than the risks of a serious adverse reaction to the vaccine.
- Health authorities worldwide take vaccine safety very seriously. Expert committees in Canada investigate reports of serious adverse events.
- There is no evidence that vaccines cause chronic diseases, autism or sudden infant death syndrome. Alleged links—for example between hepatitis B vaccine and multiple sclerosis—have been disproved by rigorous scientific study.

Box 2

Common misconceptions about vaccines

- Vaccines are not safe.
- Vaccines cause serious side effects. Vaccines are linked to chronic diseases.
- Vaccines are not necessary. The diseases are gone.
- Vaccines contain poisonous substances.
- Vaccines weaken the immune system.
- Natural medicines provide safer protection.
- There are greater risks from the vaccines than from the illnesses they can prevent.

Q: Do vaccines work?

A: Yes. Vaccines work very well in preventing specific diseases. They are so effective that most of the diseases they prevent are now rare in Canada. Some people do not develop full immunity after being vaccinated. This is why some immunization programs include a second or third dose of a vaccine. For some diseases, we need "booster" doses because the protection of the vaccine wears off over time. However, no vaccine will work for 100% of the people who receive it. How often a vaccine might fail to work varies with each type of vaccine and each vaccine product. For more details, please see the chapters on specific vaccines in the *2002 6th Edition Canadian Immunization Guide*. Some vaccines also work by creating "herd immunity." When most people in a community have received a vaccine for a particular disease, the chance of an outbreak of that disease is greatly reduced. This "herd immunity" protects the small number of people who cannot be immunized for medical reasons or for whom the vaccine did not work. For herd immunity to be effective, however, as many people as possible must be vaccinated.

Q: Are vaccines safe?

A: Yes. Vaccines are among the safest tools of modern medicine. Serious side effects are rare. For example, severe allergic reactions can occur, but they very rarely do. In Canada, this kind of reaction has occurred less than once in every one million doses of vaccine, and there are effective treatments for this condition. The dangers of vaccine-preventable diseases are many times greater than the risks of a serious adverse reaction to the vaccine. For information on who should not receive specific vaccines, please see the Contraindications and Precautions section of each vaccine chapter in the *2002 6th Edition Canadian Immunization Guide*. Minor side effects from vaccines, on the other hand, are common. Many patients get a mild fever after immunization or soreness where they receive the injection. These reactions are a nuisance, but do not usually last long. They can be part of the body's normal response to the vaccine.

No one in the field of public health takes the safety of vaccines for granted. Vaccine safety is an international concern. Information on possible safety concerns is communicated very rapidly among different countries. This careful monitoring ensures that public health authorities can act quickly to address concerns. In addition, research continues to improve vaccines.

Some examples follow:

- In 1999, some babies in the U.S. developed a rare form of bowel obstruction after receiving a new vaccine to prevent rotavirus infection (a cause of diarrhea, sometimes severe, in infants). Pre-licence studies had suggested that there might be an increased risk of this condition, and monitoring effectively picked up the problem. (In the first 1.5 million doses of rotavirus vaccine, 15 cases of bowel obstruction were reported.) Use of this vaccine was stopped in the U.S., and the manufacturer withdrew its request to license the vaccine in Canada.
- The oral polio vaccine (OPV), introduced in the 1950s, prevented hundreds of thousands of polio cases. It was also found to cause a form of paralysis once in every 3 million doses. A vaccine that uses inactivated virus (IPV) is now used almost exclusively throughout the world and cannot cause even this rare adverse event.
- The original whole-cell pertussis (whooping cough) vaccine sometimes caused high fever, seizures or collapse. A vaccine was developed that uses only part of the cell of the pertussis bacterium. This vaccine has fewer side effects and is now used instead.

In considering the safety of vaccines, it is important to look at both risks and benefits. If there were no benefits from a vaccine, even one serious side effect in a million doses could not be justified. If there were no vaccines, however, there would be many more cases of disease, more serious side effects from disease, and more deaths.

The examples from countries that have stopped or decreased their immunization programs have illustrated this fact many times in recent years. The diseases we can prevent with vaccines can lead to pneumonia, deafness, brain damage, heart problems, blindness and paralysis in children who are not protected. We are fortunate in Canada to have vaccines for diseases that still kill and disable children throughout the world every day. The risks of *not* getting immunized are a lot greater than any risk of immunization itself.

Q: How are vaccines made and licensed in Canada?

A: Vaccines for humans are regulated in Canada by the Biologics and Genetic Therapeutics Directorate of Health Canada. Like all medicines, vaccines must undergo several stages of rigorous testing before they are approved for use. The Bureau also supervises all aspects of vaccine production by the manufacturers. Before any vaccine is licensed and approved for use in Canada, the factory where it is manufactured must be inspected to ensure that all stages of production meet the requirements for safety, sterility and quality control. Before release by the manufacturer, each batch of vaccine is tested for safety and quality under guidelines specified by the Biologics and Radiopharmaceuticals Evaluation Centre. Most safety tests are carried out by both the manufacturer and, independently, by the laboratory of the Bureau. Once vaccines are in use, Canada has several systems in place to ensure that they are carefully monitored and that any problems are dealt with quickly. These systems are described in the section "Adverse Events" in the *2002 6th Edition Canadian Immunization Guide.*

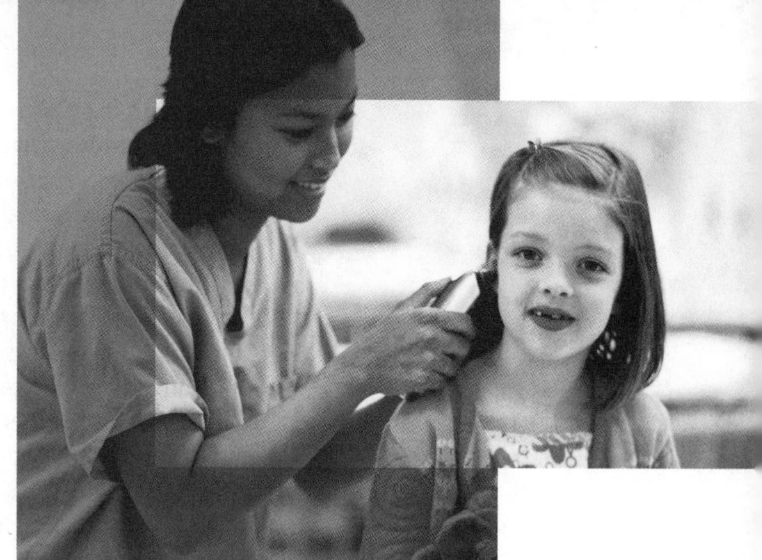

Q: What would happen if we stopped immunizing?

A: Experience from other countries shows that diseases quickly return when fewer people are immunized:

- Ireland saw measles soar to more than 1,200 cases in the year 2000, as compared with just 148 the previous year, because immunization rates fell to around 76%. Several children died in this outbreak.
- A large outbreak of rubella (German measles) occurred in Nebraska in 1999. All 83 cases in this outbreak involved adults who had not been immunized. Most of them came from countries where rubella immunization is not routine. The outbreak spread from a meat-packing plant to the general community, including several pregnant women and two daycare centres. The greatest danger from rubella is to infants, who may be born with congenital rubella syndrome if their mothers are infected during pregnancy.
- In 1994, there were 5,000 deaths due to diphtheria in Russia after the organized immunization system was suspended. Previously, Russia (like Canada) had had only a few cases of diphtheria each year and no deaths. Diphtheria toxoid came into routine use in the 1930s, but even today diphtheria remains a severe disease. About one person in 10 with diphtheria still dies in spite of medical treatment.
- In the U.K., a major drop in rates of immunization against pertussis (whooping cough) in 1974 was followed by an epidemic of more than 100,000 cases and 36 deaths in 1978.
- Japan had 13,000 cases and 41 deaths from whooping cough in 1979, after only 30% of children received pertussis immunization. In earlier years, when most children received the vaccine, Japan had only a few hundred cases of whooping cough and no deaths.
- Sweden had a similar experience with pertussis. When vaccination programs restarted, the number of cases fell once again.

Q: Why do we still need vaccines if the diseases they prevent have disappeared from our part of the world?

A: It is important to continue vaccine programs for four basic reasons:

- First, unless a disease has completely disappeared, there is a real risk that small outbreaks can turn into large epidemics if most of the community is not protected. The only disease that has been entirely eliminated in the world so far is smallpox. Some diseases, such as tetanus, are caused by bacteria that live naturally in the soil. The risk of diseases like tetanus will never disappear, so continued immunization is important.

- Second, no vaccine is 100% effective. There will always be some people who are not immune, even though they have had their shots. This small minority will be protected as long as people around them are immunized.
- Third, there are a small number of people who cannot receive vaccines. These may be people who have previously had a severe allergic reaction to a component of the vaccine, or they have a medical condition that makes receiving vaccines too risky for them. These people are not protected from disease, and for some diseases it is very important that people around them are immune and cannot pass disease along to them. By protecting themselves, immunized people can also protect those around them who are vulnerable to disease.
- And fourth, most vaccine-preventable diseases are still common in other parts of the world. Travellers can carry them from country to country. If we are not protected by immunization, these diseases will quickly spread. For example, most cases of measles in Canada today can be traced to someone who travelled here from a country where measles is more common.

Q: Why can't I take a chance that my child won't get sick, as long as most other people are vaccinated?

A: Unvaccinated children have a much greater chance of getting the disease than children who have received the vaccine.

Two recent studies of disease outbreaks in the U.S. illustrate this concern. Children whose parents chose not to have them immunized against measles were 22 to 35 times more likely to get measles than were immunized children. Children who did not receive the vaccine for pertussis (whooping cough) were almost 6 times more likely to get whooping cough than immunized children; the risks were even higher for the younger children (children < 11 years old), who were 62 times more likely to get measles if they were not immunized and 16 times more likely to get pertussis in these outbreaks.

Unimmunized children also add to the risk for children who cannot receive vaccinations or for whom the vaccine did not provide full protection from disease. People who are not immunized can be carriers of disease and pose a risk to those around them, even if they do not get sick themselves.

Q: Do vaccines weaken the immune system?

A: No. Vaccines strengthen the immune system to protect children and adults from specific diseases. This is true even for newborn infants. Infants and children are exposed to many kinds of germs every day, through normal eating, drinking and playing. Scientists estimate the immune system can recognize and respond to hundreds of thousands, if not millions, of different organisms. The vaccines recommended for children and adults use only a small portion of the immune system's "memory." Infants need to be protected with vaccines because they are more likely to get very sick from the diseases that vaccines can prevent, such as diphtheria, whooping cough and meningitis due to *Haemophilus influenzae* type b (Hib). The recommended immunization schedule for infants in Canada is carefully timed to ensure that newborns and older babies get safe and effective protection from the diseases that are most likely to seriously harm them.

Q: Can natural infection or a healthy lifestyle be effective alternatives to vaccines?

A: Vaccines create immunity to specific diseases without causing the suffering of the disease itself. Children do develop immunity to many different germs through their everyday exposure to these infections. However, the diseases we can prevent with vaccines kill and disable children. For some diseases (e.g., tetanus and meningitis) the vaccine creates stronger immunity than natural infection does. Boosting the immune system in general through herbs or vitamins does not offer specific protection from the viruses and bacteria that cause vaccine-preventable diseases. For infants, breast-feeding offers protection against some infections, such as colds, ear infections and diarrhea, because the infant receives immune-boosting proteins in the mother's milk. Despite its many benefits, however, breast-feeding does not protect infants from the specific diseases we can prevent with vaccines. Vaccines also use a natural mechanism to keep us healthy by taking advantage of our natural immune response. A vaccine stimulates antibodies so that if we are exposed to that specific virus or bacterium in the future, our immune system can mount an effective attack.

Q: Why do we need vaccines if we have better hygiene and sanitation to help prevent disease in Canada?

A: Better living conditions have been important in controlling some kinds of infectious diseases, such as diseases spread by dirty water. For the specific diseases that vaccines can prevent, however, disease rates only began to drop dramatically after the vaccines for those diseases were licensed and came into widespread use:

Measles vaccine was first approved in Canada in 1963. Sanitation and living conditions in Canada have not changed greatly since that time. Before immunization, almost everyone got measles. For many children, the disease was serious: about 5,000 were hospitalized every year, and 50 to 75 children died. Today, because the vaccine is in wide use, there are few cases of measles in all of North and South America, including communities where living conditions are much poorer than in Canada.

Meningitis (infection around the brain) and other severe infections due to Hib were common until just a few years ago. About one in every 300 Canadian children developed Hib disease by age 5. About 100 infants died each year from Hib meningitis, and many more suffered brain damage or deafness. Immunization against Hib became routine in the early 1990s. Since then, Hib disease has almost disappeared in Canada, from about 2,000 cases a year to less than four cases in the year 2000. Sanitation is no better now than it was in 1990, so it is hard to credit anything but the widespread use of Hib vaccine for this dramatic improvement.

Many children in Canada still get very sick from pertussis (whooping cough) each year, and every year one child dies from this disease. Nearly all of the children affected got the disease because they were not immunized against pertussis.

Q: What about reports that vaccines are linked to chronic diseases or problems such as sudden infant death syndrome (SIDS)?

A: Vaccines are sometimes blamed for conditions that are poorly understood. A child's first year of life is a time of tremendous growth and development, and it is a time when serious problems may start to appear. It is also the time when most vaccines are given, but this does not mean that vaccines cause these problems. Many of our vaccines have been in use for decades with no evidence of long-term adverse effects. Still, research to ensure the safety of vaccines continues. Anti-vaccine books and websites claim that vaccines cause autism, seizure disorders, multiple sclerosis (MS) or Crohn's disease, among other health problems. These connections have never held up to scientific scrutiny. Recent research using the best scientific methods and reviews of studies from around the world provide very strong evidence that

- MMR vaccine does not cause autism or inflammatory bowel disease.

- Hepatitis B vaccine does not cause multiple sclerosis or relapses of pre-existing MS.
- Pertussis vaccine does not cause brain damage.
- Childhood vaccines do not increase the risk of asthma.
- Vaccines do not cause SIDS. (Fortunately, we have learned that other factors, such as sleeping position and second-hand smoke, *are* linked with SIDS, and successful public education campaigns about these factors have helped to reduce the rate of SIDS in Canada.)

More extensive discussion of specific vaccine concerns is available in the resources for patients and parents listed in the *2002 6th Edition Canadian Immunization Guide.*

Q: Is immunization compulsory in Canada? Does my child have to be immunized?

A: Immunization is not compulsory or "forced" in Canada, but we do have regulations that help ensure that as many people as possible are protected by vaccines from the diseases they prevent. Some provinces require certain vaccines to be given before a child can enter school, but these are not mandatory in the usual sense of the term. Rather, parents (or children, if they are old enough to give consent) are required to declare a choice of whether to have their child (or themselves) immunized or not. If they choose not to, the child may be told that he or she must stay home from school if there is an outbreak of disease. This rule is designed to keep unimmunized children from getting sick and to keep the outbreak from spreading. School entry regulations also give parents an opportunity to bring their child's immunizations up to date. Health care workers may also be required to have certain vaccinations, such as Hepatitis B vaccine and an annual flu shot. If they refuse, they may be required to stay away from work during an outbreak. This practice protects their patients, who could be in grave danger if they became ill with a communicable disease.

Conclusion

Because the diseases that vaccines can prevent are so rarely seen by the general public today, it is understandable that vaccine safety concerns have such a high profile. Careful and timely counselling can help patients weigh the benefits of vaccines and the risks of disease, as well as the small risk of the vaccine itself. By providing vaccines in a climate of appropriate informed consent, including discussion of the common misconceptions that are circulating, immunization will maintain its status as one of the most effective preventive measures in the history of medicine. ”

Vaccine Safety. *Frequently asked questions.* (n.d.). Retrieved November 7, 2003, from Health Canada Website: http://www.hc-sc.gc.ca/pphb-dgspsp/dird-dimr/vs-sv/index.html

LANGUAGE AWARENESS FOCUS: USING THE THIRD PERSON/PRESENT TENSE – PROBLEMS AND SOLUTIONS

Most academic writing is completed in the third person/present tense because

- academic writing should have an academic perspective (third person) to show objectivity (see Chapter Five, page 107); and
- academic writing discusses facts or repeated actions (present tense).

Writers may choose to use the present tense, third person, *singular* perspective (he, she, it, everybody, anyone, nothing), or the present tense, third person, *plural* perspective (they).

If you use the present tense, third person, singular perspective, you may have problems with a) subject-verb agreement in the present tense and b) pronoun-antecedent agreement.

a) Subject-verb agreement in the present tense

Remember to add "s" or "es" to a present tense verb to agree with a third person, singular subject. Subject-verb agreement must also be continued in adjective clauses.

EXAMPLES:

1. A *vaccine works* by allowing the body to develop immunity to a disease before the *disease strikes.*
2. *Fear* of possible adverse reactions *convinces* some parents not to vaccinate their children.
3. *Extensive media coverage,* which *increases* awareness of adverse reactions to vaccines, often *does* not reflect the real likelihood of an adverse reaction occurring.
4. Parents want all possible *information* that *relates* to vaccine safety.

Problem: **Often students forget to make verbs agree with third person, singular subjects.**

Solution: **Switch to a third person, plural perspective.**

EXAMPLES:

1. *Vaccines work* by allowing the body to develop immunity to diseases before the *diseases strike.*
2. *Fears* of possible adverse reactions *convince* some parents not to vaccinate their children.
3. *Extensive media reports,* which *increase* awareness of adverse reactions to vaccines, often *do* not reflect the real likelihood of an adverse reaction occurring. (There is no plural form of "media coverage.")
4. Parents want all possible *statistics* that *relate* to vaccine safety. (There is no plural form of "information.")

b) Pronoun-antecedent agreement with the third person, singular

Remember to make your pronouns agree in number and gender with the antecedent (the corresponding noun).

EXAMPLES:

1. A *parent* may think *his or her* child's risk of experiencing an adverse reaction is low as *his or her* child is healthy and *he or she* is well informed about vaccine safety. (problem: is awkward)
2. A *child* may find *his* skin becomes red and itchy, or *his* arm may be sore at the injection site. (problem: excludes female children)

Problem: **Using singular pronouns can be awkward, or can exclude either males or females.**

Solution: **Switch to a third person, plural perspective.**

EXAMPLES:
1. *Parents* may think *their* child's risk of experiencing an adverse reaction is low as *their* child is healthy and *they* are well informed about vaccine safety. (isn't awkward)
2. *Children* may find *their* skin becomes red and itchy, or *their* arms may be sore at the injection site. (includes both male and female children)

Of course, it isn't always possible to switch to a third person, plural subject. If it isn't feasible to shift to a third person, plural perspective, you can look specifically for these errors (subject-verb agreement and pronoun-antecedent agreement) once a draft of the writing is complete.

Tip: It may be helpful to proofread sentence by sentence, from the bottom of the writing to the top, so that you can focus on grammatical correctness instead of information presentation.

TASK SIX: Shifting to the present tense, third person, plural perspective

- Revise these sentences to eliminate problems that occur when writing in the present tense, third person, *singular* perspective.
- Shift these sentences into the present tense, third person, *plural* perspective.

1. A newborn infant should be vaccinated to avoid the possibility that she may contract a disease early in her life.

   Newborn infants

2. An unvaccinated child that live long enough to be exposed to a disease can contract that disease.

   Unv- d children

3. A vaccine which reduce the chance of death is beneficial to society.

   Vac

4. Sometimes, a person can't be vaccinated. He or she may have a severe allergic reaction to some part of the vaccine, or his or her immune system may be too weak to receive the vaccine.

5. A tourist who accidentally expose himself to a disease may bring his sickness back to his country.

SURVIVAL ACADEMIC SKILL: AVOIDING PLAGIARISM BY PARAPHRASING

As you now know, copying another person's words or ideas is called plagiarism, and it is considered an academic "crime." In Chapter Five, you learned why plagiarism is a serious concern, and how you can avoid it by providing a reference for the quoted information. You can also avoid plagiarism by paraphrasing. If you choose to paraphrase another person's words or ideas, you will still need to reference your source.

Although you may use quotes to express specific ideas, it is best to use your own words when writing your assignments. Expressing another person's words or ideas in your own words is called paraphrasing.

Characteristics of a good paraphrase:

- The paraphrase has the same meaning as the original writing.
- The paraphrase is roughly the same length as the original writing.
- The original words and structures of the source, except for technical words or very common words ("public domain" words), have been rephrased.

The following techniques will help you paraphrase successfully. Usually, you will use more than one technique to paraphrase well.

a) Use appropriate synonyms

EXAMPLES:

syringe →	needle
disease	sickness
vaccination	immunization
develop immunity	acquire resistance

Some words from the original text, such as the names of people, countries, religions, diseases and scientific terms, cannot be changed because they have no synonyms.

b) Change the sentence type

To use this technique, you must ask yourself, "What is the sentence structure of the original writing?" Once you have answered this question, you can change the sentence structure to help you avoid plagiarism.

EXAMPLE: The original sentence structure → Independent clause
"The successful use of vaccines in preventing disease means most parents of young children in Canada today have never seen a life-threatening case of diphtheria, polio, or even measles."[1]

1. It's your health: Misconceptions about vaccine safety. (n.d.) Retrieved November 7, 2003, from Health Canada's Website: http://www.hc-sc.gc.ca/english/iyh/medical/misconceptions.html

1. Change the sentence structure. → Independent clause + dependent clause

   Most parents of young children in Canada today have never seen a life-threatening case of diphtheria, polio, or even measles because the use of vaccines in preventing disease has been successful.

2. Add appropriate synonyms → Paraphrased sentence

   The majority of Canadians these days don't experience dangerous diseases like diphtheria, polio or measles as immunizations to eliminate sickness have worked.

c) Change the voice from active to passive— or from passive to active

EXAMPLE: Original source → active voice

"Unfortunately, a small minority of people actively oppose immunization."[2]

1. Change to passive voice.

   Unfortunately, immunization is actively opposed by a small minority of people.

2. Add appropriate synonyms → Paraphrased sentence

   It is disappointing that vaccination is rejected by a tiny segment of the population.

d) Change the parts of speech

To use this technique, change nouns into verbs, adjectives into adverbs, verbs into adjectives, adjectives into nouns and so on.

EXAMPLE: Original Source

"Vaccines (n) strengthen (v) the immune system to protect (v) children and adults from specific diseases."[3]

1. Change the parts of speech wherever possible.

   Vaccination (n) makes the immune system stronger (adj.) for the protection (n) of children and adults against specific diseases.

2. Add appropriate synonyms.

   Immunization creates a strong immune system in order to resist certain sicknesses that may cause damage to people.

3. Change the sentence structure and voice (from active to passive).

   A strong immune system that resists deadly diseases is created by immunization.

---

2. It's your health: Misconceptions about vaccine safety. (n.d.) Retrieved November 7, 2003, from Health Canada's Website: http://www.hc-sc.gc.ca/english/iyh/medical/misconceptions.html

3. It's your health: Misconceptions about vaccine safety. (n.d.) Retrieved November 7, 2003, from Health Canada's Website: http://www.hc-sc.gc.ca/english/iyh/medical/misconceptions.html

Quick tips to help you paraphrase successfully:

- You may need to use more than one technique to paraphrase successfully.
- You must understand the original writing before you try to paraphrase it.
- When you have finished your paraphrase, it must make sense.

TASK SEVEN: Practising paraphrasing

- With one or two classmates, paraphrase the following sentences.
- Compare your answers with those of other students. Is one paraphrase better than another? Why or why not?

1. Vaccines are safe for almost everyone although very rarely there are people who experience adverse reactions.

2. Some mild side effects are experienced by most people after they are immunized.

WARM-UP ASSIGNMENT

TASK EIGHT: Paraphrasing

- Now that you have learned how to paraphrase, return to Reading 2: Questions and Answers. Select an answer from one of the frequently asked questions.
- Paraphrase the answer to the question using the techniques that you just learned.

When you have received feedback from your teacher or peers for this assignment, you will have information that you can use to improve your writing in the final assignment.

READING 3: TWO STORIES ABOUT VACCINE RISK

These two readings can be found on the Vaccine Risk Awareness Network (VRAN) website. VRAN is a volunteer organization based in British Columbia that is dedicated to raising awareness of the risks of vaccines.

TASK NINE: Taking notes and drawing conclusions

- Pair up with a classmate. You will each read one of the two stories about the possible negative effects of vaccines.

Story	Student reader
Student A: Stacy's story	
Student B: Katie's story	

- As you read your story, complete the appropriate chart below.
- When you have completed the chart, check with another student who read the same story, and make sure that your information is accurate and complete.
- Then exchange information with your partner. As you listen to your partner, fill in the chart for the other story.
- When you have finished, discuss whether you believe vaccination to be safe or not.

Stacy's story
In point form, and in chronological order, retell the events of the story:
Do you believe that the negative effects the victims experienced (multiple sclerosis and death) resulted from their vaccinations?
Do the victims have scientific proof to demonstrate that their outcomes resulted from their vaccinations?

Katie's story
In point form, and in chronological order, retell the events of the story:
Do you believe that the negative effects the victims experienced (multiple sclerosis and death) resulted from their vaccinations?
Do the victims have scientific proof to demonstrate that their outcomes resulted from their vaccinations?

Student A: Stacy's story

"Everyone is having it. It will protect you for the rest of your life." That's the message 17-year-old Stacy Moon got about the hepatitis B vaccine when a public health nurse wanted her to have it. It sounded good, so Stacy agreed to have the recommended 3 doses. Six hours after receiving her 3rd dose at Penticton Health Unit, the teenager began to feel tingling in the fingertips of her right hand. Within a few days, numbness had spread up her arm; she couldn't hold a pen or glass or even open a door. By the 3rd week following the shot, Stacy was numb from her toes to her ribs, couldn't hold her balance and found it difficult to walk. In the following few months visits to her doctor, neurologists and Vancouver for an MRI scan resulted in the diagnosis ... multiple sclerosis, **MS!**

Right from the start, Stacy and her mother thought the Hep B shot was to blame. The pair spent countless hours doing research to verify the possibility of a connection. Stacy obtained the vaccine package insert which she should have been shown before receiving her first shot, and was shocked to find MS listed, along with lupus, Parkinson's Disease, rheumatoid arthritis, Guillain-Barre Syndrome, SIDS and autism as rare but possible adverse reactions. A UBC

MS specialist agreed with their conclusion that the vaccine brought on the MS and was to be the pivotal witness in a lawsuit they filed against the Medical Services Commission, the Okanagan Similkameen Health Region and SmithKlineBeecham Inc, the vaccine maker. The writ of summons alleged that these defendants knew or ought to have known of the risk of developing MS and should have informed Stacy or her family of this.

The lawyers for the defendants never met with Stacy and her lawyer to discuss the possibility of settling out of court. They did send her letters asking her to drop the case, but she would have none of that. Referring to the vaccine maker, she says, "I was never scared to fight them, even though they are a billion dollar company." She asked her lawyer to reply telling them to "Bring it on!" However, just when she and her lawyer needed the UBC specialist to testify, he left for New Zealand for 13 months. Stacy felt sabotaged, deflated and suspicious: "I think 'SmithKline' paid him to leave. All of the other doctors who were an option at one point, we could not use for my case. I studied the whole Hep B vaccine issue and its astonishing ... for long term side effects, basically it has hardly been tested at all, yet they still proceed to vaccinate with it. I have piles of papers explaining everything you would want to know about the hepatitis B vaccine. I thought we could use this information, but because none of it was proven evidence, we could not use any of it. On Nov 4th, 2002 my case went in front of a judge and was dismissed with costs. Now 'SmithKline' wants me to pay their lawyer fees. Too bad for them, I have no money. Having MS, I am on a disability pension, which gives me $781.00 per month. It pays my rent, bills, some groceries and gas in my car. The money is usually gone the same day I get it. After all that, I am broke until the following month. Try as they may, they will get nothing from me; it's a lost cause for them to even try."

When her disease was diagnosed, Stacy was put on medication to slow its progression. She was angry and suffered from depression, sometimes crying herself to sleep at night. She knew her future had changed the day of her 3rd Hep B shot. It had been her goal to study marketing at BCIT but the limits to how far she can walk and the fatigue she experiences has made attaining that very unlikely. She says "It's the whole process of walking that makes pretty much everything some sort of task." In fact, any job prospects are limited due to the unpredictable nature of her disease. Whether she will ever be able to have children is also questionable. One thing she is certain of is that if she does have children, she will never have them vaccinated.

Today, Stacy's condition remains fairly stable. She has had to find medication to eliminate bladder problems she developed and is still taking the medication, which slows the advancement of MS. In a way, her disease has made her a stronger person. She still is angry but says, "I have to live with it, and in turn I dealt with it and am doing very well. I can't just be depressed about something I cannot change." And she's determined to have her piece of justice. She says, "I want to make as much noise as I can to let everyone know the dangers of vaccination. I want to go on TV talk shows, get articles in the paper, every paper across Canada. Once 'SmithKline' hears what I am doing, they may just pay me to shut up; that was one of their options in the beginning. If there is any way you can help me accomplish this feat, please let me know. I refuse to back down, to let them take advantage of the innocent people and children. I will fight with all I have for as long as it takes. People really need to know this; they need to know what they are doing to themselves and their children before this happens to any more people. So, do your research before going for any vaccine. Please do not put yourself at risk by getting a vaccine you do not need; I am living proof as to what just may happen to you."

Although Stacy focuses her disgust on the vaccine maker, those who should have provided her full information before obtaining her consent are certainly not blameless. They should have told her that the risk of getting the disease is minimal and, for her age group, may be less than a serious risk from the vaccine. Health Canada statistics reveal that during the 4 years, 1997–2000, an average of only 15 teens, 15–19 years old had hepatitis B each year in BC and only 46 in all of Canada. Unfortunately for Stacy, it is a gargantuan task to gain compensation for vaccine injuries in BC and most of Canada. A federal compensation scheme has been proposed and is supposed to be in place by 2005. So far, little has been heard about it. As Stacy discovered, Canada's legal system requires definitive proof of causality. Due to the limited, often biased and inconclusive scientific studies performed to date, this, in all probability, is impossible to attain. For people such as Stacy we can only hope that, very soon some high quality independent research is funded and uncovers the evidence needed. ”

"Stacy" (n.d.). *Stacy's story*. Retrieved March 11, 2004, from Vaccine Risk Awareness Network Website: http://64.41.99.118/vran/news_art/stories/story_stacy.htm

Student B: Katie's story

by Katie's mom Mary, October, 2001

“Nineteen years ago, my husband, Terry, and I were blessed with the birth of our second child, Katie Marie. She was absolutely beautiful. Her complexion was olive, her eyes dark blue and her black hair was unusually thick, with gold frosted tips. We joked that Katie looked like she had just stepped out of a beauty salon! I remember the attending nurses at Katie's birth also remarked how much Katie looked like her daddy. And it was true—she had the same shaped face and coloring as her dad. We were thrilled with our new baby daughter! She was a healthy, contented newborn, who nursed well, and gained weight according to schedule. She was indeed the perfect baby!

Our son, Peter, was 20 months old at the time his sister was born. He adapted well to his new sibling. Life was good. We knew that we were so fortunate to have two wonderful children.

I took Katie to her well baby check up at two months of age. Since her older brother was fully vaccinated and healthy, I was anxious that Katie, too, be vaccinated. I was certainly aware of the benefits of vaccination. I believed that vaccination was a totally safe and effective procedure. I had no idea that childhood vaccines could harm babies. Naively, I believed that vaccines were thoroughly tested and would not be allowed on the market if they were not completely safe.

I had never been given information regarding the risks and side effects of vaccination by my family doctor. Therefore, I did not make an informed decision in choosing whether or not to vaccinate my children. In fact, I was never informed that I had a choice in choosing to vaccinate or not. The doctor did not ask about my family medical history to find out if my children were high risk for an adverse reaction.

Katie received the DPT-Polio vaccination in August 1983. Within 48 hours I noticed that she fell into a very deep sleep. I was not alarmed as it was a very hot, humid summer. Since we did not have air conditioning in our home, I thought that perhaps the heat was affecting her and that was the reason that she slept so much. Katie would wake up to nurse, but her sucking was weaker and she nursed for a shorter period of time before falling into a deep sleep again.

Approximately 2-1/2 weeks following her first vaccination, Katie developed a very high fever. I took her to our family doctor right away. The blood and urine tests that he ordered were normal and her chest was clear. The doctor stated he did not know what was causing the fever, but wrote a prescription for an antibiotic.

Three days after her doctor's appointment I went to get Katie up from her afternoon nap. I was horrified to note that her left side was completely paralyzed. The left side of her face and her left eye drooped. Katie was admitted to Children's Hospital. The emergency doctors queried whether Katie had suffered a stroke or Western Equine Encephalitis. After five days of extensive testing, including brain scan, EEG, spinal tap, numerous x-rays, Katie was discharged from Children's Hospital with an unknown diagnosis.

I did physiotherapy with her four times throughout the day and once a week brought her to Children's Hospital to meet with the physiotherapist. Gradually Katie began to improve. She could move her little fingers and bend her left arm to her elbow. We were so pleased with her progress. The pediatrician who took over Katie's care after she was hospitalized suggested that I bring Katie back to our family physician for her four month DPT-Polio vaccination. No mention was ever made that Katie's paralysis was related to her vaccination. I now know that Katie experienced a classic reaction to the oral polio vaccine. The time frame to contract polio from the vaccine is fourteen to twenty-one days. Katie fit the profile. Our baby contracted polio from the vaccine, which is a live, attenuated vaccine. She NEVER should have received the second vaccination. However, in my ignorance, I handed over my beautiful baby to receive her second dose of the DPT-Polio vaccine. It was like handing over "the lamb to the slaughter." Katie, once again slept an unusual amount of time. In the medical literature this is referred to as, "excessive somnolence." It is listed in the pharmaceutical product insert as an adverse reaction to the vaccine as it is a sign of encephalitis. Also listed is fever, which Katie also experienced.

Following her second vaccination, once again she did not nurse as vigorously. She failed to gain weight.

About 2 weeks following her vaccination, Katie woke in the middle of the night and screamed for hours. I could not console her. Her scream was high pitched and she sounded like she was in extreme pain. The product insert refers to it as "the encephalitic scream," caused by swelling of the brain. Screaming episodes and persistent crying are also listed in the product insert as an adverse reaction and contra-indication for further vaccination. My mother and sister were visiting from Toronto at the time and my mother who has raised five children said that she had never heard a baby scream in that way before.

The next morning Terry, Katie and I were in the doctor's office recounting the nightmare of the night before. The doctor suggested that perhaps Katie was teething! It was at that point that Terry and I informed the doctor that we wanted to have Katie seen by specialists at Sick Children's Hospital in Toronto. An appointment was made for Katie to travel to Toronto in one month's time.

Katie never did make it to Toronto. She died that night.

Following the doctor's appointment, we brought her home. She appeared to have recovered from the night before. She was happy and playing with a toy that we had just bought for her to strengthen her left arm. She was still wearing her pink dress. I remember her lying on the floor with her brother, her daddy, her grandma and her Auntie all watching adoringly as she pulled the little string down and a clown face popped up. We were all laughing at how clever she was, and Katie joined in our laughter. She was so proud of herself!

That night, before we went to bed, we checked on Katie. I will never forget her face. There was a golden glow surrounding her head, it made me think of a harvest moon. The bedroom was dark—we had not turned on the light—but this incredible golden glow surrounded her face. I believe we were witnessing Katie's spirit leaving her body. I began to do CPR on my infant daughter while Terry phoned for an ambulance.

Katie was declared dead on arrival to Children's Hospital. The doctors continued to work on Katie without reviving her. Our beautiful baby was declared dead on November 8, 1983.

I can't begin to describe the pain we experienced over losing our daughter. All of our dreams and hopes for her died that day. We were denied watching her develop into a young woman and develop her gifts. Our son Peter was denied the enjoyment of growing up with his little sister and our future children, Natalie and Michael, missed out on the opportunity to have a big sister to play with and confide in. We will never know what contributions Katie would have made to this world. To say we were devastated does not do justice to our feelings. I have little memory of the two years following Katie's death. I existed, I cared for my two-year-old son, but my grief was so great, and I was so totally enveloped in it. It was all encompassing. I carried a deep physical pain and heaviness around my heart for years.

After Katie died, we agreed to an autopsy, as we desperately wanted answers. We did not receive the results until eight months later. We were informed that Katie had died from a virus, but the pathologist was unable to identify what type of virus. So basically we were left in the dark.

Fourteen months following Katie's death, Terry and I were on our way to bed, when I said to him, "I want to see what is on The Journal," an investigative show that followed the CBC news. I was transfixed to the television as I heard Edda West debating Dr. Ronald Gold from Sick Children's Hospital in Toronto, regarding the serious adverse reactions and deaths that can occur following childhood vaccinations. Edda's daughter had experienced a serious reaction to her MMR vaccination. It was obvious that Edda had done in-depth research on the vaccination issue. Suddenly I knew in a way that I have never known anything before what had caused Katie's death. It was her childhood vaccination.

I got in touch with Edda the next day and we spoke on the phone for a long time. She was wonderful, supportive and patient. She sent me a thick manila envelope full of information regarding the harmful and lethal effects of childhood vaccines. I will always be so grateful to Edda for this life saving information as I was now pregnant with my third baby and would have had Natalie vaccinated, as we still did not know what had caused Katie's death.

I approached all the doctors, the family doctor, the neurologist, the pediatrician and the pathologist, who Katie had seen, with this new information. Their reaction was very curious and surprising. When I mentioned the possibility of Katie's death being due to her vaccination, not one of the doctors would look me in the eye. They told me that there was absolutely no connection between Katie's death and her vaccination. Not one of them said let's review Katie's records to see when her high fever, loss of weight and paralysis began. I was urged not to think about it anymore and to concentrate on my pregnancy.

In the nineteen years since Katie's death, two of the four vaccines that she received have been removed from the market because of safety concerns. The Sabin oral polio vaccine is no longer used in Canada, because it is well recognized in the medical literature that oral polio vaccine caused paralysis and death in recipients. Curiously, there was no fanfare when oral polio vaccine was discontinued. It was very quietly removed from the market. No mention was made of the countless children who died or who developed paralysis from this tainted vaccine.

Katie received the whole cell pertussis vaccine, which also was withdrawn from the market in Canada, in favour of the Japanese acellular pertussis. Since the 1930s when whole cell pertussis was licensed, it was well documented that it could cause permanent seizure disorders, encephalopathy resulting in permanent brain damage and death in some children. Statistics for adverse reactions were never kept, and still aren't, so we will never know how many infants have died as a result of childhood vaccines.

These babies' deaths were swept under the carpet, as if they never existed, as if these wee babies were never loved and provided so much joy to their families. Their lives were expendable for the so-called "greater good" of others.

In nineteen years, the truth about the cause of Katie's death as due to her vaccination has still never been recognized by the medical profession. Despite the fact that Katie exhibited a classic reaction to the oral polio vaccine, with fever, high pitched screaming, paralysis and death, all listed in the product insert and on the Report of a Vaccine-Associated Adverse Event Form from Health Canada, her death has never been recorded or listed as due to the oral polio vaccine.

So even in death, she has not been granted the dignity of the truth of how she died. As Katie's mother and her advocate, I will continue to fight for her truth and the truth of countless other babies who have been sacrificed for an immunization program that refuses to look at the mounting casualties from the war on microbes.

"Katie's Mom" (n.d.). *Katie's story*. Retrieved March 11, 2004, from Vaccine Risk Awareness Network Website: http://64.41.99.118/vran/news_art/stories/story_katie.htm

READING 4: TIPS ON EVALUATING INFORMATION

This reading provides tips on how to evaluate anti-vaccine information, such as the two stories that you have just read. It provides a list of characteristics that are typical of anti-vaccine information.

TASK TEN: Thinking critically

- Read the tips and determine how many of these characteristics are demonstrated in "Stacy's story" and "Katie's story."
- How do you evaluate "Stacy's story" and "Katie's story?"

"In your search for information about vaccines, you will probably come across sources you're not sure about. The questions below will help you judge whether or not the information is reliable. These questions were written specifically for information obtained from the Internet; but they are useful to ask of any media source, including newspapers, magazines, radio, tabloids, pamphlets or books.

What is the source of the information?

- The website should clearly identify the person or organization that produced it.
- The site should provide a way to contact the provider of information.

Has the medical information been reviewed by scientific experts?

- If yes, the experts should be identified, including their credentials (degrees, positions, etc.).

Is there a date indicating when the information was last revised?

- If yes, is it current?

Is there scientific evidence to support the claims?

- If yes, the site should provide sources (e.g., articles from medical journals) for the scientific evidence (e.g., studies, reports, statistics).

Is the site certified by the Health On the Net Foundation?

- Health On the Net (HON) Foundation is a Swiss not-for-profit organization working to help Internet users find useful and reliable on-line medical information. HON has developed a set of guidelines for health sites. Sites that meet the criteria can use the HON seal to show they follow the code of conduct. The HON site (www.hon.ch) also has a checklist to help users judge whether a given site would meet the criteria.

Anti-vaccination websites. A recent study of 22 websites that oppose vaccination found that the sites shared a number of features (*Journal of American Medical Association,* 2002, vol. 287, pp. 3245–8).

- They made the same false claims about vaccines.
- They all had links to other anti-vaccination sites.
- Many promoted alternative systems of health care—such as homeopathy, naturopathy and chiropractic—as being superior to vaccination.
- More than half provided anecdotes about children who had allegedly been damaged by vaccines.

False claims made on anti-vaccination websites include the following:

- Vaccines cause illnesses whose causes are unknown, such as autism (from MMR and/or DTaP), SIDS, immune dysfunction, diabetes, seizures, brain damage, attention deficit disorder, antisocial behaviour, asthma, allergy (100% of sites).
- Vaccines erode immunity or harm the immune system (95% of sites).
- Vaccine producers or government regulators are responsible for an underreporting of adverse reactions because they cover up the truth about such events (95% of sites).
- Vaccine policy is motivated by profit: manufacturers make enormous profits on vaccines, which influences vaccine recommendations and promotes cover up of reactions (91% of sites).
- Vaccines are ineffective or produce only temporary immunity (82% of sites).
- Compulsory vaccination violates civil rights (77% of sites).

- Rates of disease declined prior to the use of vaccines due to improved nutrition (73% of sites).
- Lots of vaccines cause severe reactions (55% of sites).
- There is an increased risk of reactions from multiple simultaneous vaccines (50% of sites).
- Homeopathy, naturopathy, alternative medicine and breastfeeding enhance immunity better than vaccines.

If you are in doubt about any information you read or hear, discuss it with your health-care professional. ”

Gold, R. (2002). Tips on evaluating information. In Your Child's Best Shot: A Parent's Guide to Vaccination (pp. 300–302). Ottawa: Canadian Paediatric Society.

LISTENING: TEMPORAL VERSUS CAUSAL RELATIONSHIPS

TASK ELEVEN: Taking notes from a lecture

- Before listening, discuss with the class what you think the listening segment will be about.
- Listen to the information and take point-form notes in the outline below.
- When you have finished listening, compare your notes with those of another classmate.
- Then listen to the recording again to confirm your answers.

Listening outline

Title: Temporal versus causal relationships

- Today, parents worry about
- Years ago, parents worried about

Adverse (negative) reactions

Mild:

Severe:

How do scientists determine whether a vaccine causes an adverse reaction?

Example:
Event A is

Event B is

- A causal relationship is

- A temporal relationship is

Six criteria used by scientists to determine temporal or causal relationships

1. Unique and specific outcome:

2. Positive association in animal experiments:

3. Alternative reasons for the relationship:

4. Demonstrable biological mechanism:

5. Positive relationship in the frequency of events:

6. Likelihood of coincidence:

   - A vaccine related example:

READING 5: HOT SHOTS

This is an excerpt from a longer article about vaccine safety.

TASK TWELVE: Skimming for information

This excerpt can be divided into four sections.

- Look at the following section titles and match each title with the appropriate section of the article. You will need to skim the article to determine where each section starts and finishes.
- Discuss your results with the class.

Section titles

MMR and autism

DPT and SIDS

Real life story of the fear of polio

DPT and brain damage

- For each section, write the section title and answer the questions after reading the article.
- When you have finished answering the questions, compare your answers with a partner's. Check to make sure that your information is accurate and complete, and fill in any gaps that you might have.

Section one: ____________________

1. Why have we been able to forget the horror of many diseases?

2. Why do we hear more about the negative effects of vaccination?

Section two: ____________________

3. In the 1970s, the DPT vaccine was linked to sudden infant death syndrome (SIDS). Japan responded by raising the age at which children received DPT shots from three months to two years. Fill in the blanks to show what happened.

   SIDS deaths ______ Pertussis deaths ______

4. Why is it reasonable to think that DPT has a causal relationship to SIDS? Is it true?

Section three: ____________________

5. One small study linked MMR vaccine to autism. According to Dr. Gold, why is it unlikely that the MMR vaccine is linked to autism?

Section four: ______

6. Why has DPT been linked to brain damage?

______

7. Has a causal relationship between brain damage and vaccinations been proven? What is more dangerous—the DPT vaccine or pertussis itself?

______

"One summer, my mother wasn't allowed to go the park because of polio. She grew up in Windsor, Ontario, in an ivy-clad Tudor house opposite Memorial Park. Directly across the street was the park's snack bar, where she and her friends liked to go for ice cream. But during the polio outbreak of 1937 the snack bar, the playground a little further down the way and, most of all, the wading pool were strictly off limits. "My mother was terrified that I'd pick up germs from someone who had polio," she recalls today. "People were afraid to go swimming. They were afraid to go anywhere there was a crowd."

This generation of parents has never had to worry that their children will catch deadly diseases in the playground sandbox. We worry about car accidents, kidnappers and terrorism, but not polio. We may remember getting our polio shots, but the ravages of the disease itself—the children who died or were crippled for life—we have no recollection of those. We've forgotten that before the polio vaccine was introduced in the mid-1950s, there were several thousand cases in Canada each year. Happily, we don't remember diphtheria or tetanus either. We're not even sure what they look like. Chances are we've heard more about possible adverse reactions to vaccines than we've ever heard about the diseases they were designed to prevent.

When a child dies from whooping cough (pertussis), as a handful still do every year in Canada, it doesn't make the news. But when there's a speculative report of a link between a vaccine and autism, sudden infant death syndrome (SIDS) or asthma, it may end up on *60 Minutes*. That's because, even though deadly and nasty diseases like polio, diphtheria and measles have been virtually eliminated since the introduction of widespread immunization, there's a small but vocal minority that still believes vaccines do more harm than good. The very fact we're engaged in this debate is arguably a luxury of living in a society where vaccinations have erased the memory of these dreadful illnesses that once killed thousands of Canadian children and devastated families.

One of the theories that fuelled anti-vaccine rhetoric in the 1970s blamed the diphtheria-pertussis-tetanus (DPT) vaccine for some cases of SIDS. It gained credence for a while due to claims—later proven to be false—that SIDS virtually disappeared in Japan after that country raised the starting immunization age from three months to two years in 1975. What actually happened was that people stopped making damage claims for DPT-caused sudden infant death, once the shot clearly could not be implicated. SIDS deaths continued during this period. What increased were infant deaths due to pertussis.

It's understandable that someone made this connection, since SIDS has confounded experts for years, and most SIDS deaths occur during the period when babies get three DPT needles. Therefore, it's likely that some SIDS babies will die not long after their last needle. But the proximity of the needle to the death proves nothing. In fact a study found that, if anything, babies who had died of SIDS were slightly less likely to have been vaccinated with DPT.

More recently, the media have reported a supposed link between autism and the measles-mumps-rubella (MMR) vaccine. Cases of autism seemed to be increasing at the same time immunization was on the rise. However, the only scientific data linking autism to the MMR vaccine is a 1998 study that involved just 12 children with autism who also had inflammatory bowel disease (IBD). The theory was that the MMR vaccine may be responsible for the IBD, which may lead to a decreased absorption of essential nutrients, which in turn may damage the brain and cause autism. This theory has never been substantiated. Subsequent studies in the UK and Sweden have found no evidence that the incidence of autism increased after MMR was introduced.

Ronald Gold, a retired Toronto paediatrician, author of the book *Your Child's Best Shot* and part-time consultant to vaccine manufacturers, dismisses the idea. "If measles itself doesn't cause autism, and that's never been shown to be the case, it seems very unlikely that the measles vaccine [a weakened version of the virus] would do that." However, the study got lots of publicity, partly because it was published in the prestigious medical journal *The Lancet*. What got less attention was the editor's note in the same issue, which pointed out the flaws in the researcher's methods.

Perhaps the scariest stories have been the ones linking immunization to brain damage. The vaccine that was implicated most often was the whole-cell DPT vaccine, used in Canada until 1997. The difficulty here is that, like SIDS and autism, some childhood brain or neurological problems appear out of the blue in the first 18 months of life, when a child is never far from his last needle. The

cause is often undetermined, so immunization becomes the scapegoat. However, studies have not been able to prove a causal relationship between brain damage and vaccinations. In fact, one major British study estimated the risk of brain damage due to the DPT vaccine at one in 100,000, while the risk of brain damage from pertussis itself is one in 11,000. In other words, the chance of your child getting brain damage from the disease is nearly ten times greater than from the vaccine that prevents it.

"We'll never be able to definitively prove that no vaccine anywhere ever caused brain damage or death," says Gold. "Science can never prove a negative. But the most reasonable scientific explanation is that, if there is a risk of brain damage from vaccines, it's so small that we can't measure it."

Hoffman, J. (2002, March). Hot shots. Today's Parent, 19 (2), 48–52.

FINAL ASSIGNMENT

TASK THIRTEEN: Process essay

- Write a process essay that answers the following question:

  How did parents become more worried about adverse reactions to vaccines than about the diseases that the vaccines were developed to prevent?

In your essay, include a paraphrase of the following text:

> When a child dies from whooping cough (pertussis), as a handful still do every year in Canada, it doesn't make the news. But when there's a speculative report of a link between a vaccine and autism, sudden infant death syndrome (SIDS) or asthma, it may end up on *60 Minutes*. That's because, even though deadly and nasty diseases like polio, diphtheria and measles have been virtually eliminated since the introduction of widespread immunization, there's a small but vocal minority that still believes vaccines do more harm than good. The very fact we're engaged in this debate is arguably a luxury of living in a society where vaccinations have erased the memory of these dreadful illnesses that once killed thousands of Canadian children and devastated families.[4]

Be sure to reference the paraphrase as a footnote or endnote.

For information about writing a process essay and examples, refer to the Models Chapter (page 206).

4. Hoffman, J. (2002, March). Hot shots. Today's Parent, 19 (2), 48–49.

CHAPTER 7

Risk Perception

QUICK OVERVIEW

READING

Read excerpts from a book and articles from the Internet in order to learn about risk. Identify main ideas, take notes on specific information and answer comprehension questions. Review the information with classmates.

WRITING

Write information in point form to complete a table, write short answers to questions and take notes while listening and reading. Write two summaries to demonstrate your understanding of the chapter content.

LISTENING

Listen to a radio commentary about the factors that increase our fear of risk. Predict how to organize information related to the commentary.

DISCUSSION

Discuss your own attitudes towards taking risks. Share information with your classmates about the readings in order to practise new vocabulary and to ensure comprehension.

LANGUAGE AWARENESS FOCUS

Learn how to express conditional statements.

SURVIVAL ACADEMIC SKILL

Learn how to summarize in order to avoid plagiarism.

WARM-UP ASSIGNMENT

Write a short summary.

FINAL ASSIGNMENT

Write a longer summary.

Are you willing to travel to a city where there is an outbreak of a serious disease? Are you willing to climb a mountain, fly in an airplane or drive a car? There are risks you can avoid and risks you can't avoid. It is natural to fear risks; fearing risks allows you to avoid life-threatening situations. Your reluctance to take risks is based on universal risk response patterns. However, if you are too cautious—or risk adverse—you may miss out on opportunities to study, travel and live well. Only you can decide which risks are too great and which risks are acceptable to achieve the life you want to live.

GEARING UP

TASK ONE: Avoiding dangerous activities

Are you sure that you are safe? Do you expose yourself to unnecessary risks?

- In a group of four students, make a list of all the activities in your day that could be risky or dangerous.
- Once you have made a list, put a check mark in the appropriate column to show if an activity is *avoidable* or *unavoidable*. (You may want to continue your list on a separate piece of paper.)
- Discuss your answers with your teacher and classmates.
  What are the most risky or dangerous activities that you participate in?
  Why do you participate in these activities?
  Are there activities that you can't avoid?

Daily activities that involve risk	Avoidable activities	Unavoidable activities

TASK TWO: Building vocabulary

The boldfaced expressions in the following sentences are often used when people talk about risk.

- Read the sentences and discuss with other students what these expressions might mean.

1. When people **have control over** an activity such as driving, they often don't see their behaviour as **risky**.

2. People are often more worried about a risk than they need to be. Their **risk perception** is not supported by statistical data.

3. Some people have a higher **risk tolerance** than others. For example, some people love to climb mountains, while others are afraid to travel by plane.

4. He didn't understand the **consequences of** his behaviour.

5. Dangerous chemicals can be a **hazard** if you work in a laboratory.

6. The **exposure to** second-hand smoke can increase your chances of **contracting** cancer.

7. Some **cautious** governments want to use the "precautionary principle" to protect their people from **harm**.

READING 1: FINDING OUT ABOUT RISK

The following reading is from the introduction of a book about risk.

TASK THREE: Reading for comprehension

The reading is divided into three parts, so you can identify key information as you read each part.

- Read and answer the questions for Part A, B and C. Read the questions first and use the "read smart" techniques that you learned in Chapter Three (page 47) to find the information.
- When you have finished, discuss your answers with a small group of students. Make sure that your answers are complete. Talk about any differences that you might have.

Questions for Part A

1. Why are people often afraid of progress?

2. What does research show about the risks that we fear?

Part A

"We live in a dangerous world. Yet it is also a world far safer in many ways than it has ever been. Life expectancy is up. Infant mortality is down. Diseases that only recently were mass killers have been all but eradicated. Advances in public health, medicine, environmental regulation, food safety, and worker protection have dramatically reduced many of the major risks we faced just a few decades ago.

Yet new risks have arisen. Hazardous waste. Nuclear power. Genetically modified foods. Mad cow disease. Ozone depletion. Artificial sweeteners. For all the unquestionable benefits of the modern technological world and its scientific power, the march of progress that has given us longer, healthier lives has subjected us to new perils.

We often react to this conflict, of progress on the one hand and risk on the other, with fear. Most of us are more afraid than we have ever been. And not just from any single risk that happens to be grabbing the headlines at a given point in time, whether it's terrorism or West Nile virus. We are afraid, cumulatively, of all the new bogeymen to which our modern existence has exposed us. Many polls find that people feel the world today is more dangerous for humans than it has ever been.

It is true that the industrial and information ages have spawned a whole new range of risks, and raised awareness of those that were lurking all the time. But research suggests that our fears may not match the facts. We may be too afraid of lesser risks and not concerned enough about bigger ones. Polls show a wide gap between what the public and the "experts" think is actually dangerous and what is considered relatively safe. Who's right? There are no simple answers.

Questions for Part B

1. What is the purpose of this section of the reading?

2. What are the four components included in the idea of risk?

Part B

"An anonymous writer once observed, "To risk living is to risk dying." Risk is, indeed, inescapable. But just what is risk? How do you define it? To a stockbroker it means the prospect of losing, or making, money. Same thing for a person at the racetrack or at a blackjack table. For a skier or a bungee jumper or a skydiver, on the other hand, risk has more to do with physical than fiscal health. To the person taking a pill with known side effects, it's about choice. To the person eating food with potentially harmful ingredients that aren't listed on the label, it's about no choice.

At its simplest, risk is the idea that something might happen, usually something bad. But within that simple notion are some important components that you need to understand in order to have a better basis on which to make your personal risk judgments.

You may be hoping that this book answers the common question we all have about most risks: "What are the chances that …?" If you are like most people, you think that risk means *probability*, the likelihood that something will happen, as in "Your risk of dying from X is one in a million." But there is more to risk than just calculating the statistical chances of a certain outcome.

There is also the issue of *consequences*, as in "The likelihood of a nuclear plant meltdown may be low, but it's a risk because it's disastrous if it does happen." A full definition of risk must take into account not just the probability of an outcome, but its severity. Generally, risk involves an outcome that is negative. You might say, "The odds of winning the lottery are …" but you wouldn't say that winning the lottery is a risk. And the more severe the outcome, the higher we judge the risk to be.

A complete definition of risk must also include the presence of a *hazard*, as in "That compound is a risk. It causes cancer in lab animals." If something to which we're exposed isn't hazardous, it isn't a risk. We're all exposed to a lot of cotton in the clothes we wear. So what.

Which brings up the fourth major component of risk, *exposure*, as in "Flooding isn't a risk. I live on a hilltop." If a substance is harmful to test subjects, but we're never exposed to it, it doesn't pose a risk. The risk of being eaten by a shark doesn't exist in Kansas. A hazard can't do you any harm if you are out of harm's way.

So a more complete way of thinking about risk might read: *Risk is the probability that exposure to a hazard will lead to a negative consequence.*

It's helpful to keep all these elements in mind when thinking about risk. Take out any one of those components, and the definition is incomplete. Each one involves characteristics that help you understand risks more completely and keep them in clearer perspective.

Questions for Part C

1. Why is it important to have accurate information about possible risks?

2. Summarize the main factors that increase our perception of risk (more afraid of) and decrease our perception of risk (less afraid of) in the table below. For some points in the reading, you may be able to write an entry in both sides of your table. Use your own words, and write in point form.

Factors that increase our perception of risk	Factors that decrease our perception of risk
• New risks are more frightening than old risks	• Risks,
• Human-made R.	•
•	•
•	•
•	•
•	•
•	•
•	•
•	•

3. How did risk perception play a role in evolution?

____

____

____

4. What fact supports the belief that risk perception helps people survive?

____

____

____

5. What explains individual differences in risk perception?

____

____

____

Part C

"People are disturbed, not by things, but by the view they take of them."
—Epictetus

As we wrote earlier, the facts about risk are only part of the matter. Ultimately we react to risk with more emotion than reason. We take the information about a risk, combine it with the general information we have about the world, and then filter those facts through the psychological prism of risk perception. What often results are judgments about risk far more informed by fear than by facts.

The terrorist attacks on the World Trade Center in New York and on the Pentagon and the subsequent anthrax attacks in the fall of 2001 are an example. Many of us were afraid, and rightly so. But some people responded by driving to a distant destination rather than flying, even though the facts clearly showed that flying remained the far safer mode of transportation, even after September 11. Some people bought guns, raising their risks from firearms accidents far more than reducing their risk of being attacked by a terrorist. Many people took broad-spectrum antibiotics even though they had no evidence that they had been exposed to anthrax—but they didn't get an annual flu shot.

Do these judgments make sense? Are they rational? They are not based simply on the facts. But this is how humans respond to risk . . . with our hearts as well as our heads. The psychological study of this phenomenon, known as "risk perception," explains why our fears often don't match the facts.

Risk perception

Humans tend to fear similar things, for similar reasons. Scientists studying human behaviour have discovered psychological patterns in the subconscious ways we "decide" what to be afraid of and how afraid we should be. Essentially, any given risk has a set of identifiable characteristics that help predict what emotional responses that risk will trigger. Here are a few examples of what are sometimes called "risk perception factors."

- Most people are more afraid of risks that are new than those they've lived with for a while. In the summer of 1999, New Yorkers were extremely afraid of West Nile virus, a mosquito-borne infection that killed several people and that had never been seen in the United States. By the summer of 2001, though

the virus continued to show up and make a few people sick, the fear had abated. The risk was still there, but New Yorkers had lived with it for a while. Their familiarity with it helped them see it differently.

- Most people are less afraid of risks that are natural than those that are human-made. Many people are more afraid of radiation from nuclear waste, or cell phones, than they are of radiation from the sun, a far greater risk.
- Most people are less afraid of a risk they choose to take than of a risk imposed on them. Smokers are less afraid of smoking than they are of asbestos and other indoor air pollution in their workplace, which is something over which they have little choice.
- Most people are less afraid of risks if the risk also confers some benefits they want. People risk injury or death in an earthquake by living in San Francisco or Los Angeles because they like those areas, or they can find work there.
- Most people are more afraid of risks that can kill them in particularly awful ways, like being eaten by a shark, than they are of the risk of dying in less awful ways, like heart disease—the leading killer in America.
- Most people are less afraid of a risk they feel they have some control over, like driving, and more afraid of a risk they don't control, like flying, or sitting in the passenger seat while somebody else drives.
- Most people are less afraid of risks that come from places, people, corporations, or governments they trust, and more afraid if the risk comes from a source they don't trust. Imagine being offered two glasses of clear liquid. You have to drink one. One comes from Oprah Winfrey. The other comes from a chemical company. Most people would choose Oprah's, even though they have no facts at all about what's in either glass.
- We are more afraid of risks that we are more aware of and less afraid of risks that we are less aware of. In the fall of 2001, awareness of terrorism was so high that fear was rampant, while fear of street crime and global climate change and other risks was low, not because those risks were gone, but because awareness was down.
- We are much more afraid of risks when uncertainty is high, and less afraid when we know more, which explains why we meet many new technologies with high initial concern.
- Adults are much more afraid of risks to their children than risks to themselves. Most people are more afraid of asbestos in their kids' school than asbestos in their own workplace.
- You will generally be more afraid of a risk that could directly affect you than a risk that threatens others. U.S. citizens were less afraid of terrorism before September 11, 2001, because up till then the Americans who had been the targets of terrorist attacks were almost always overseas. But suddenly on September 11, the risk became personal. When that happens, fear goes up, even though the statistical reality of the risk may still be very low.

People who first learn about these risk perception patterns often remark on how much sense they seem to make. It's little wonder. These are deeply ingrained patterns, probably ancient behaviours imprinted in us over millions of years of evolution. Long before we had our modern thinking brain, long before humans or primates even developed, only organisms that could recognize and successfully respond to danger survived and evolved. In Darwinian terms, these affective, "irrational" ways of protecting ourselves are adaptive. They help us preserve the species. Evolution selects for this type of behaviour. That belief is supported by the fact that these patterns of risk perception cross cultures, age groups, genders, and other demographic groupings. There are some variations among individuals. Those variations make sense too because different people have different lives, different jobs, different family circumstances, different sets of experiences, different sets of values, and so on. Fearing a risk more if it involves children, for example, means parents will react differently from, say, teenagers. What is frightening to you might not be to your friend. Neither of you is right or wrong. You just each have a unique perspective on the same statistics and facts. But risk perception research shows that underneath our individual differences, we share certain patterns of risk response. ”

Ropeik, D. and Gray, G. (2002). Risk: A practical guide for deciding what's really safe and what's really dangerous in the world around you (pp.1, 4–5, 15–18). Boston: Houghton Mifflin Company.

TASK FOUR: Thinking rationally about risk

- In a group of three students, use the knowledge that you acquired from the reading to explain how the following situation is possible.

Some people drive cars every day, but refuse to fly in airplanes.

LANGUAGE AWARENESS FOCUS: LEARNING THE BASIC VERB FORMS FOR CONDITIONAL SENTENCES

Conditional sentences are useful when you want to discuss risk. They include an ***if-clause*** and a main clause. The likelihood of the main clause depends on the condition of the if-clause.

If-clause (the condition)	Main clause (the outcome)
If people are familiar with a risk,	they will be less afraid of it.

There are three types of conditional sentences.

1. A possibility in the present or future

These sentences show that the condition is possible.

If + present tense	will + simple form
If you expose yourself to the sun,	you will burn your skin.
	can + simple form
If SARS begins to spread again,	the economy can suffer.

2. Unlikely present or future

These sentences show that the condition is unlikely.

If + past tense	would + simple form
If you thought about the consequences of your actions,	you would not behave in this manner.
	could + simple form
If you drove through a red light,	you could be in an accident.

3. Impossible past

These sentences show that the condition is impossible because the time for action has already passed.

If + past perfect tense	would have + past participle
If doctors had known how dangerous the SARS virus was,	they would have acted faster to contain the virus.
	could have + past participle
If scientists had predicted the tsunami sooner,	many people could have escaped death.

TASK FIVE: Practising conditional sentences

- Complete the sentences by writing a main clause to match the if-clause.

1. If our children are at risk, we should take ~~the~~ necessary measures to eliminate this risk.

2. If the government had banned cigarettes, (the cigarettes) would be sold illegaly now.

3. If a risk is a result of a natural cause, ~~they~~ a lot of ~~efforts~~ increased efforts should be applied to eliminate it.

4. If people had no perception of risk, they would estimate the situation inappropriately / inadequately.

5. If patterns of risk perception are the same for all cultures, it is much easier to prevent or eliminate these risks

6. If the U.S. government had known about the terrorist attacks on the Twin Towers, measures would have been taken to detain these terrorists

7. If we are threatened, we should negotiate or respond to the threat

8. If our lives were safer, less people ~~died~~ were dying then.

9. If we were logical about risk, we could foresee the consequences of the risk.

10. If scientists had eliminated mad cow disease there were less victims who suffered from this disease.

SURVIVAL ACADEMIC SKILL: AVOIDING PLAGIARISM BY SUMMARIZING

Plagiarism is copying another person's words or ideas. In Chapter 5, you found out how to avoid plagiarism by quoting and providing a reference for the quote. In Chapter 6, you learned how to avoid plagiarism by paraphrasing and providing a reference for the paraphrase. Another useful way to avoid plagiarism is by summarizing and providing a reference for your summary.

Learning how to summarize is an essential skill for students because professors may ask for formal, written summaries in order to evaluate students' writing skills. In addition, summarizing information is an efficient way to study.

Like a paraphrase, a summary translates another person's ideas into your own words. However, unlike a paraphrase, a summary is approximately one third of the original writing's length. To write a summary, therefore, you must summarize the main points of the writing and eliminate all the details and examples.

To write a summary, try this approach:

- Before beginning your summary, read the original source carefully. Underline only the main points of the writing.
- Begin your summary by referring to the author, title and source of the article.
- Paraphrase the underlined sections of the original source.
- Eliminate the details, examples and repetitious points from your summary.
- Write a reference to acknowledge the ideas contained in your summary.

TASK SIX: Summarizing a paragraph

- With one or two classmates, practise summarizing the following information.
- Include the reference in the footnote below.
- Follow the steps for summarizing above. You may wish to refer to the example of a summary included in the Models Chapter (page 214).

> We live in a dangerous world. Yet it is also a world far safer in many ways than it has ever been. Life expectancy is up. Infant mortality is down. Diseases that only recently were mass killers have been all but eradicated. Advances in public health, medicine, environmental regulation, food safety, and worker protection have dramatically reduced many of the major risks we faced just a few decades ago.[1]

WARM-UP ASSIGNMENT

TASK SEVEN: Writing a short summary

Summarize the factors that increase and decrease our perception of fear from Part C of Reading 1.

- Use your chart from page 155 to help you identify the main points.
- Write your summary using the academic perspective (present tense, third person). Pay careful attention to subject-verb and pronoun-antecedent agreement. Use correct verb forms in conditional sentences.

1. Ropeik, D. and Gray, G. (2002). Risk: A practical guide for deciding what's really safe and what's really dangerous in the world around you. Boston: Houghton Mifflin Company.

- Don't forget to include a reference for the reading at the end of your summary.

Refer to the example of a summary included in the Models Chapter, page 215.

Once you have received feedback for this assignment, you will have information that you can use to improve your writing in the final assignment.

LISTENING: RISK PERCEPTION AND SARS

You will listen to a commentary that David Ropeik, the author of Reading 1, made on CBC Radio One.

TASK EIGHT: Organizing information before listening

David Ropeik's commentary includes the nine pieces of information that are listed here out of order.

- Look at the pieces of information and try to organize them in the essay outline.
- Compare your answers with those of a classmate. Do you agree about which pieces of information fit into the different sections of the essay outline? Explain why you organized the information the way you did.

Pieces of information

- Recommendations: How to reduce our fear of contracting SARS.
- Sometimes our fear of SARS can be worse than the disease itself.
- Effects of excessive fear on our bodies: (list of two effects).
- There are four factors that increase our fear of contracting SARS: (list of four factors).
- However, sometimes we are too afraid, and sometimes our fear is dangerous.
- Many people die from serious diseases every day in Canada.
- Effect of excessive fear on our society: (one effect explained).
- Only SARS makes us feel terrible fear.
- Sometimes we must fear fear itself.

Essay outline

Introduction (general information to help the reader focus on the essay topic) • •
Thesis (the main point of the essay) •

Body (detailed information to prove the thesis)

•

•

•

•

Conclusion (restatement of the thesis; may include recommendations for the future, or further questions for the reader to think about)

•

•

TASK NINE: Taking notes while listening

- Listen to this short commentary by David Ropeik. He presents his ideas in a structured way, with an introduction, thesis, body and conclusion.
- Use the outline below to help you take notes while you listen.
- Discuss your notes with one or two classmates. Fill in any gaps that you might have. Listen to the commentary again to confirm your answers.
- Finally, return to Task Eight. Check to see if your organization for the essay outline matches Ropeik's organization for his commentary. Is your organization of information different from his? If your method of organization is different, can you explain which is better and why?

Note-taking outline

Introduction

In Canada, in any given five-month stretch, how many people will die of

pneumonia? __________

influenza? __________

tuberculosis? __________

All of these diseases are like SARS, so why does only SARS evoke so much fear?

Thesis

Might the fear be ________________________ than the disease itself?

Body

There are four factors that increase our fear of risk:

1.

2.

3.

4.

It is certainly legitimate to use our __________ as well as __________ to try and protect ourselves and survive. However, it is safe to say that our fear of SARS is excessive, and that excessive fear is dangerous.

Effects of excessive fear on our bodies:

-
-

Effects of excessive fear on our society:

- When we demand government protection from less threatening risks rather than more threatening risks, the resources spent on the less threatening risks are no longer available to protect us from the more threatening ones, and as a result, some of us left exposed to the more threatening risks die.

Conclusion

We also have to fear ________________________ itself.

Recommendations:

-
-
-
-

TASK TEN: Reviewing information after listening

You have organized the information from the commentary and listened to the actual commentary. You have compared your organization of the information with the organization of the speaker. Review your listening notes one more time.

- Turn your notes over and don't look at them again.
- With your classmates, repeat the information that you heard in the same order, reviewing the speaker's points in the introduction, thesis, body and conclusion.
- With your group, present your information to the class.

READING 2: PRECAUTIONARY PRINCIPLE

Governments play a significant role in protecting their citizens from risks. Governments must attempt to prevent external risks, such as wars, and internal risks, such as environmental disasters. In order to do this, some governments have adopted the "precautionary principle" to guide their decision-making. The precautionary principle is the belief that if an activity (for example, scientific research) may cause harm to human or environmental health, precautions must be taken to prevent harm. The usefulness of the precautionary principle is controversial.

TASK ELEVEN: Reading for meaning and taking notes to answer questions

- Read the following document from the website of the Science and Environmental Health Network. This document presents "frequently asked questions" (FAQs) about the precautionary principle.
- Take point-form notes as you read the questions and answers. When you have finished, answer the questions after the reading.

Frequently asked questions

1. What is the precautionary principle?

The 1998 Wingspread Statement on the Precautionary Principle summarizes the principle this way:

"When an activity raises threats of harm to the environment or human health, precautionary measures should be taken even if some cause and effect relationships are not fully established scientifically." All statements of the Precautionary Principle contain a version of this formula: When the health of humans and the environment is at stake, it may not be necessary to wait for scientific certainty to take protective action.

2. Is there some special meaning for "precaution"?

It's the common sense idea behind many adages: "Be careful." "Better safe than sorry." "Look before you leap." "First do no harm." "Precautionary principle" is a translation of the German Vorsorgeprinzip. Vorsorge means, literally, "fore-caring." It carries the sense of foresight and preparation—not merely "caution."

The principle applies to human health and the environment. The ethical assumption behind the precautionary principle is that humans are responsible to protect, preserve, and restore the global ecosystems on which all life, including our own, depends.

3. Why should we take action before science tells us what is harmful or what is causing harm?

Sometimes if we wait for certainty it is too late. Scientific standards for demonstrating cause and effect are very high. For example, smoking was strongly suspected of causing lung cancer long before the link was demonstrated conclusively. By then, many smokers had died of lung cancer. But many other people had already quit smoking because of the growing evidence that smoking was linked to lung cancer. These people were wisely exercising precaution despite some scientific uncertainty.

When evidence gives us good reason to believe that an activity, technology, or substance may be harmful, we should act to prevent harm. If we always wait for scientific certainty, people may suffer and die and the natural world may suffer irreversible damage.

4. How do we implement the precautionary principle?

The precautionary principle is most powerful when it serves as a guide to making wiser decisions in the face of uncertainty. Any action that contributes to preventing harm to humans and the environment, learning more about the consequences of actions, and acting appropriately is precautionary.

Precaution does not work if it is only a last resort and results only in bans or moratoriums. It is best linked to these implementation methods:

- exploring alternatives to possibly harmful actions, especially "clean" technologies that eliminate waste and toxic substances;
- placing the burden of proof on proponents of an activity rather than on victims or potential victims of the activity;
- setting and working toward goals that protect health and the environment; and

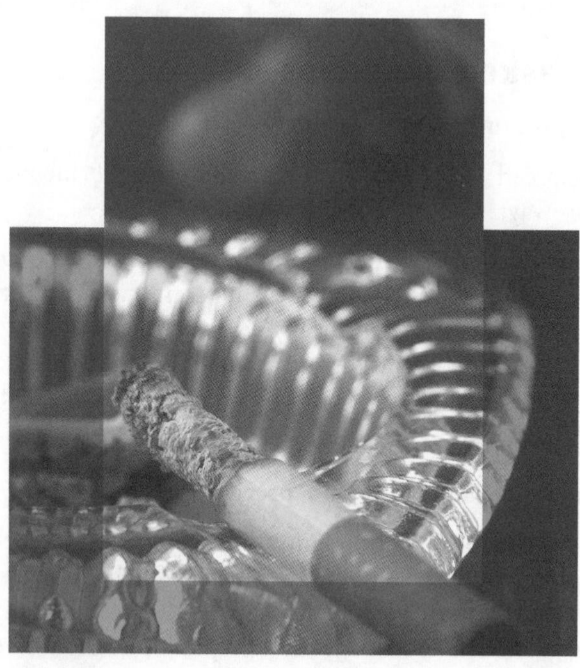

- bringing democracy and transparency to decisions affecting health and the environment.

5. Why do we need the precautionary principle now?

The effects of careless and harmful activities have accumulated over the years. Humans and the rest of the natural world have a limited capacity to absorb and overcome this harm. There are plenty of warning signs:

- Chronic diseases and conditions affect more than 100 million men, women, and children in the United States—more than a third of the population. Cancer, asthma, Alzheimer's disease, autism, birth defects, developmental disabilities, diabetes, endometriosis, infertility, multiple sclerosis, and Parkinson's disease are becoming increasingly common.
- In laboratory animals, wildlife, and humans, considerable evidence documents a link between levels of environmental contamination and malignancies, birth defects, reproductive problems, impaired behaviour, and impaired immune system function. Scientists' growing understanding of how biological systems develop and function leads to similar conclusions.
- Other warning signs are the dying off of plant and animal species, the destruction of ecosystems, the depletion of stratospheric ozone, and the likelihood of global warming.

Serious, evident effects such as endocrine disruption, climate change, cancer, and the disappearance of species can seldom be linked decisively to a single cause. Scientific standards of certainty may be impossible to attain when causes and outcomes are multiple; latent periods are long; timing of exposure is crucial; unexposed, "control" populations do not exist; or confounding factors are unidentified. ”

Science and Environmental Health Network. (n.d.) *Precautionary Principle – FAQs*. Retrieved February 28, 2004, from http://www.shen.org/ppfaqs.html

1. Paraphrase the answer to the first FAQ, "What is the precautionary principle?"

2. What are the English expressions or adages that sum up the meaning of precautionary principle? Do you have similar expressions in your own language that have the same meaning?

3. Do you believe that we should act to prevent harm *before* we have scientific proof that harm is being done, or that we should *wait* for scientific proof to demonstrate that harm is being done before acting?

4. Which of the following examples demonstrates how to implement the precautionary principle?

EXAMPLE 1: A sample of water at the local water treatment plant shows high bacteria levels. The person who operates the plant immediately shuts down the plant, takes more water samples and reviews the water treatment processes. The whole city loses its water supply for two days, but nobody becomes sick.

EXAMPLE 2: A sample of water at the local water treatment plant shows high bacteria levels. The person who operates the plant decides to take a number of other samples and wait for the results from those samples before deciding what to do. The extra samples show that bacteria levels remain within the safe range. The city's water supply hasn't been shut off, and nobody becomes sick.

5. Which of the statements below is the best summary of the answer to FAQ 5? Explain why you think it is the best.

a) In the document "Precautionary Principle – FAQs," the Science and Environmental Health Network argues that we must adopt the precautionary principle now as the world is showing signs of destruction in the human, animal, plant and environmental spheres. If we wait for science to prove human behaviour is damaging our world, it will be too late to save ourselves.[2]

b) In the document "Precautionary Principle – FAQs," the Science and Environmental Health Network suggests it is important to use the precautionary principle as a guide to decision making now because the effects of negligent human behaviour are beginning to be obvious. Many people suffer from sicknesses related to exposure to toxic substances, animals are showing signs of irregular growth and development due to the damaged environment, and many of the world's natural systems have been disrupted. We should not wait for scientific proof of harm, when scientific proof is so difficult to establish.[3]

2. Science and Environmental Health Network. (n.d.). *Precautionary Principle – FAQs*. Retrieved February 28, 2004, from http://www.shen.org/ppfaqs.html

3. Science and Environmental Health Network. (n.d.). *Precautionary Principle – FAQs*. Retrieved February 28, 2004, from http://www.shen.org/ppfaqs.html

TASK TWELVE: Thinking about the precautionary principle

- Discuss the precautionary principle with a small group of students.
- Think about how the precautionary principle would affect:
  1. an elementary school that is planning to build a climbing structure in the schoolyard for its students;
  2. a shipping company that wants to ship oil through an aquatic preserve;
  3. a medical research proposal to find a cure for cancer by testing a new drug on human subjects;
  4. a company that wants to import a cheaper product from a foreign country.
- When you have finished, discuss with the class whether or not you think the precautionary principle is useful as a guide for decision-making.

FINAL ASSIGNMENT

TASK THIRTEEN: Writing a summary

The following excerpt explains both the pros and cons of adopting the precautionary principle.

- Read the excerpt carefully and summarize the text.

Review the approach to a summary on page 161. You may also wish to refer to the Models Chapter (page 214) for help.

"Our modern world presents us with many new technologies (cell phones) or processes (genetic modification of food) or compounds (statin drugs to reduce cholesterol) that have profound benefits, but which also come with risks. Sometimes we are exposed to these technologies or processes or compounds before the risks have been adequately studied.

In the professional and policymaking world of people who deal with risk, how we should handle this uncertainty is a hotly debated issue. Some people argue that we should thoroughly study anything that might pose a risk *before* we start to use it.

The people on this side of the argument heed the advice of the eighteenth-century British politician Edmund Burke, who said, "Early and provident fear is the mother of safety." They suggest that we should adopt as a matter of law the "Precautionary Principle," the academic term for what most people think of as "Better Safe Than Sorry." These advocates argue that the best way to protect human and environmental health is to treat new compounds or technologies as guilty until proven innocent. They say that while we do this with some things, like new drugs, we don't do it with others, like new industrial chemicals. Advocates of the Precautionary Principle say that we must apply this careful approach across the board.

Others might subscribe to the advice of the American essayist Randolph Bourne, who wrote in his 1913 book *Youth and Life,* "We can easily become as much slaves to precaution as we can to fear. Although we can never rivet our fortune so tight as to make it impregnable, we may by our excessive prudence squeeze out of the life that we are guarding so anxiously all the adventurous quality that makes it worth living." These opponents of a sweeping Precautionary Principle argue that it would deny society many of the benefits of new technologies for years, even decades, until thorough scientific study can be completed. Those that argue against the Precautionary Principle also point out that almost anything carries *some* risk. Under the most rigorous application of the Precautionary Principle, these people claim, it would be hard to approve such things as motor vehicles or prescription drugs or vaccines. They argue that while it makes common sense to err on the side of caution, we should assess risks on a case-by-case basis, rationally weighing them against benefits. They say a blanket Precautionary Principle might deny society a public health advance that could save lives before all the scientific answers are in. ”

Ropeik, D. and Gray, G. (2002). Risk: A practical guide for deciding what's really safe and what's really dangerous in the world around you (pp. 13–14). Boston: Houghton Mifflin Company.

CHAPTER 8

Genetically Modified Foods

QUICK OVERVIEW

READING
Read articles about genetically modified foods in order to learn about how they are created, grown and distributed. Think critically about the information and form your own opinions about it.

WRITING
Take notes while listening and write short answers to questions. Write a short persuasive essay and an extended persuasive essay.

LISTENING
Listen to the opinions of science, human health and environment experts regarding the safety of genetically modified foods.

DISCUSSION
Examine the differences between food in your country and food in Canada. Discuss the answers to the readings and predict possible bias in the readings.

LANGUAGE AWARENESS FOCUS
Learn about the advantages of writing in the passive voice, and how to do it.

SURVIVAL ACADEMIC SKILL
Learn how to detect bias and think critically about information and its sources.

WARM-UP ASSIGNMENT
Write a short persuasive essay.

FINAL ASSIGNMENT
Write an extended persuasive essay.

How much do you know about the food you eat? Do you know where it comes from, how it is grown or if it is genetically modified? In this chapter, you will find out what genetically modified (GM) foods are, how they are produced and whether or not they are considered safe to eat. You will try to answer a difficult question: Are genetically modified foods a danger to human and environmental health, or are they the solution to world hunger?

GEARING UP

TASK ONE: Discussing and surveying

- In a group of four students, discuss the issue of genetically modified foods.
- Use the following questions to guide your discussion. Take notes.

1. What are the differences between food in your country and food in Canada?

2. Do you think some of these differences are a result of genetic modification?

3. Why are scientists developing genetically modified foods?

4. How do scientists develop genetically modified foods?

5. Who benefits from genetically modified foods?

- Take a quick survey of your group members by asking the following question:

  Do you think it is a good idea to eat genetically modified foods?

- Combine your results with those of other groups so that you have a survey of the entire class. Record the results below.

  Yes __________ No __________

Note: At various points throughout this chapter, you will be asked this question again to determine if your opinion and your classmates' opinions have changed.

READING 1: BIOTECHNOLOGY'S EXPANDING MENU

The following charts display some facts about genetically modified foods.

Some quick facts

"**Foods** (May contain genetically modified ingredients)

Soft drinks
Mayonnaise
Canned and powdered soup
Prepared gravy
Processed cheese slices
French fries
Salad dressing
Ketchup
Soy sauce
Soybean paste
Cookies
Crackers
Potato chips
Baby food
Soy milk
Powdered milk
Instant coffee
Pancake mix
Jams and marmalades
Tofu
Pasta
Beer
Veggie burgers
Chocolate bars
Protein shakes
Ice cream
Yogurt
Cereal
Bread
Fruit juices
Artificial sweeteners
Frozen meals

Processed foods (Ingredients may be genetically modified)

Cornstarch
Baking fats
Soy lecithin
Canola oil
Corn meal
Corn oil
Corn syrup
Glucose syrup
Vegetable oil
Vegetable protein
Maltodextrin
Margarine
Riboflavin
Soy protein
Vitamin B2
Xanthan gum
Cryptoxanthin
Emulsifying agents
Monosodium glutamate

Source: The Facts About Genes and Our Food (Swiss Committee for Research and Nutrition)

Coming soon

Edible vaccines: U.S. researchers have stitched a cholera gene into a potato to produce a simpler way to deliver a vaccine against cholera. This work builds on the use of modified raw fruit, such as bananas, to deliver vaccines.

Eggs: Biotech company GeneWorks of Michigan has a flock of genetically engineered chickens carrying a gene that allows them to lay eggs containing drugs for humans.

Rice: Scientists are working to increase the amount of lysine, an important amino acid, in rice. This would reduce childhood blindness caused by lysine deficiency, a serious problem in developing countries. Researchers are also trying to develop varieties for people allergic to rice.

Grapes: University of Guelph scientists are trying to design grapes with a cold-tolerance gene to withstand harsh winters.

Milk: Milk products are being changed to remove ingredients such as lactose, a common allergy-causing protein. Researchers are trying to add other ingredients that milk lacks, such as lactoferrin. This essential form of iron is found in human milk but not cow's milk.

Source: *The Food Biotechnology Communications Network and The New Scientist*

Spears, T. (2000, January 3). GM foods are a boon to farmers, but consumers ask: So what? Ottawa Citizen, p. A8.

TASK TWO: Expanding vocabulary

- Working alone, consider the meanings of the following boldfaced words.
- Without using a dictionary, try to define as many words as you can. If you are unsure about a meaning, ask your classmates for help. Finally, consult a dictionary if there are still unfamiliar words.

1. It was a wet year, so the **crop** of corn had a low **yield**.

2. The scientists discovered how a **gene** from one plant could be moved into another plant.

3. To reduce the number of bugs in the fields, the farmer sprayed with **pesticides**.

4. The weeds in the field were reduced after the farmer applied the **herbicide**.

5. Some potatoes are **resistant** to **pests**.

6. Last year, the average yield from an **acre** of corn was 128 **bushels**.

7. When crop yields increase, it is a **boon** to farmers and the economy.

READING 2: GM FOODS ARE A BOON TO FARMERS

This short article examines the advantages and disadvantages of GM foods.

TASK THREE: Collecting information

- As you read, take point-form notes under the following headings.
- Compare your notes with a partner's. Fill in any gaps that you may have. Discuss your notes with the teacher and the class.

1. Benefits to farmers
2. Potential benefits of GM foods
3. Reasons for consumer caution
4. Benefits to consumers

GM foods are a boon to farmers, but consumers ask: So what?

"If genetically modified foods are to gain widespread public acceptance, they will have to offer consumer benefits rather than agricultural benefits, experts say.

But today's altered crops, with their insect-fighting genes or pesticide resistance, don't attract consumers, says Mark Sears, a professor at the University of Guelph and a leading corn expert.

"Farmers looked at it as a gain, but the general public said, 'Yeah, so what? It doesn't help us any."

Most biotech crops today create foods that have no nutritional difference from "conventional" crops. They focus instead on several areas of benefit to farmers:

- Insect resistance. Corn with a gene from a common soil bacterium, *Bacillus thuringiensis* (Bt) produces a protein that's toxic to certain caterpillars. That gives the plant resistance against the corn borer, which destroys or weakens corn plants.
- Yields. Biotech companies claim a grower can get several bushels more of some crops per acre, often through lower losses to insect pests or competition from weeds.
- Pesticide resistance. Many brands of corn, soybean, canola and other crops are designed to resist a particular herbicide (weed killer spray). For instance, a farmer who plants Monsanto's Roundup Ready corn can spray Roundup herbicide and kill every plant in the field except the corn.

Mr. Sears thinks it's time for biotech companies to focus on qualities like nutrition—something of direct value to the consumer.

"They're working on some rice varieties that are going to have iron and vitamin E, and other nutritional qualities to them. I think they're going to look at oil crops around the world and find those that provide more nutritious oils. Protein's going to be the next one.

"Eventually we're going to have nitrogen fixation in crops that don't have it now—grasses, for instance. These are things that are dreams, really, from the '50s."

Indeed, plant breeders tried in those days to breed for things like nutrition, but couldn't do as much with conventional technologies as they can today with biotech, he said.

In Britain, the British Medical Association's head of research and public policy says the public is right to reject—for now—biotech products that offer them no benefit.

"We have to start with the fact the population is very wary of accepting scientific advice," says Dr. Vivienne Nathanson, a professor of medicine at Stirling University in Scotland.

It's not just Britain's recent scare with mad cow disease: They've learned there are salmonella bacteria in eggs, E. coli bacteria in ground meats, and now genes they don't understand in grain. While some risk is acceptable to the public, Dr. Nathanson says, "If people are going to take a risk, they want to know there's a benefit.

"As there's no benefit, they say, 'Why should I eat it?' In that sense, it's quite a sophisticated argument."

Spears, T. (2000, January 3). GM foods are a boon to farmers, but consumers ask: So what? Ottawa Citizen, p. A8.

TASK FOUR: Categorizing information in a chart

Use the following chart to categorize important information about GM foods. This chart will help you summarize the information from the readings and listening segment of this chapter. It will also help you prepare for the final assignment.

- In the first column, list the *advantages* of GM foods. In the second column, list the *disadvantages* of GM foods. In the third column, list the *outstanding issues* related to GM foods. (Outstanding issues are problems that will require solutions in the future.)
- Add new information to the chart as you complete the different tasks throughout the chapter.

GM Foods

Advantages	Disadvantages	Outstanding issues

TASK FIVE: Learning more collocations

There are a number of collocations in the article in Reading 2.

EXAMPLES: genetically modified foods
high-tech
widespread acceptance
leading expert

As you now know, learning these words as a unit can increase your reading, speaking and writing fluency, as well as your listening comprehension.

Notice that, in some cases, the words in collocations may be separated by other words (often adjectives), but they still work as a unit to express a clear idea.

Collocation – words occur together	Collocation – words are separated
widespread acceptance	widespread public acceptance
leading expert	leading corn expert

- Match the words in the column on the left with the words in the column on the right to create some of the collocations from Reading 2.

1. to have resistance		a) disease
2. all around		b) benefits
3. mad cow		c) resistance
4. consumer/agricultural		d) against
5. insect/pesticide		e) the world

LANGUAGE AWARENESS FOCUS: USING THE PASSIVE VOICE

Although the active voice is much more common than the passive voice, the passive voice can also be useful in writing. Using the passive voice eliminates the active subject of a sentence. You have seen examples of the passive voice in the discussion about academic perspective (Chapter 5, page 107).

Active voice: The subject of the sentence performs the action of the sentence.

EXAMPLE: The scientists modify the tomatoes so that they stay fresh longer.

Passive voice: The object of the sentence becomes the subject, and the verb takes a passive form.

EXAMPLE: The tomatoes are modified (by the scientists) so that they stay fresh longer.

You may or may not decide to include the *active subject* (the scientists) in the sentence by using a *by* phrase, usually after the verb or at the end of the sentence.

The passive voice is useful in the following situations:

- You want to emphasize the action, and not the *doer* of the action. As a result, most lab and experimental reports are written in the passive voice. Science students often use the passive voice in their reports.

  EXAMPLE: Water was added to the sample, and the results were measured. (sentence from a lab report)

- You want to avoid placing blame on a specific person. Businesses may use the passive voice when responding to letters of complaint.

  EXAMPLE: A mistake was made in the calculation of your bill. (sentence from a company letter)

Passive voice formation

Only *transitive* verbs (verbs that take objects) can be shifted into the passive voice. To move a sentence from an active voice to a passive voice:

a) the object of the active sentence becomes the subject of the passive sentence, and
b) the verb changes form. Use a form of the verb *to be* and the past participle of the main verb.

EXAMPLE: **Active:** Most Canadians eat genetically modified food without complaint.
Passive: Genetically modified food is eaten without complaint (by most Canadians).

EXAMPLE: **Active:** The techniques of modern biotechnology make the transfer of genes from one species to another possible.
Passive: The transfer of genes from one species to another is made possible (by the techniques of modern biotechnology).

It is possible to use the verb *to be* in different tenses, depending on the verb tense of the main verb in the active sentence. Whatever tense of the verb *to be* is used, the main verb always follows in its past participle form.

EXAMPLE: **Active:** (main verb in the past tense)
Scientists modified cheese first.
Passive: (*to be* in the past tense)
Cheese was modified first (by scientists).

EXAMPLE: **Active:** (main verb in the present progressive)
Genetic modification is making canola, corn, soybeans and potatoes healthier.
Passive: (*to be* in the present progressive)
Canola, corn, soybeans and potatoes are being made healthier (by genetic modification).

TASK SIX: Moving from active to passive voice

- Working with another student, convert these sentences from the active to the passive voice.

1. Farmers enjoy the benefits of GM foods.

2. The corn beetle, a major pest, damages corn every year.

3. Canadians, unlike Europeans, have eaten GM foods without protest.

4. The government is regulating GM foods to ensure the safety of all Canadians.

5. The scientists moved a gene from one species of potato into the DNA of another species of potato.

WARM-UP ASSIGNMENT

TASK SEVEN: Writing a short persuasive essay

- In order to prepare for your final assignment, write a short persuasive essay to agree or disagree with the following statement:

  Genetically modified foods only benefit farmers.

Remember: A persuasive essay should try to convince your readers to accept your viewpoint. Try to include some of the above collocations in your writing, and use the passive voice at least once. Refer to the Models Chapter (page 207) for an example of a persuasive essay.

When you receive feedback from your teacher and classmates on this assignment, you will have information that you can use to improve your performance on the final assignment.

SURVIVAL ACADEMIC SKILL: DETECTING BIAS

Bias is a person's opinion based simply on whom the person is, where the person lives or which benefits the person may receive by expressing the opinion. For example, a person who is a financial planner will always tell you that you should consult an expert when planning your financial future; sales people will always tell you that you need whatever they are selling; governments will always tell you that taxes are being well spent. These statements are often expressed so that the speakers will receive the benefits that result from your agreeing with them.

When you are reading articles in newspapers, magazines and on the Internet, it is important to be aware that writers may benefit from persuading you that their opinion is correct. They are expressing their bias when they express their opinions. This is especially important to consider when you are reading about or listening to opinions about controversial topics. If you are aware that writers may be biased, you will be better able to evaluate their opinions. (See Chapter 6, page 143, for tips on evaluating medical information.)

TASK EIGHT: Predicting bias

- With a small group of students, try to predict the bias that you would expect these people to have if they were asked about the safety of GM foods.
- Discuss your predictions with the class and explain the reasons behind them.

People with bias	Are GM foods safe to produce and eat? Predicted bias:
The scientists at Monsanto, a huge company that produces genetically modified seeds	
The Canadian Food Inspection Agency (CFIA), the government department responsible for ensuring that foods are safe for Canadians to eat	
The scientists at the National Wildlife Federation, an environmental organization that promotes protection of the environment	
Concerned parents who don't realize that they are feeding their children genetically modified foods	

READING 3: WHAT AM I EATING?

This reading was written by the CFIA. This is the government agency that is responsible for approving the safety of new foods (including GM foods). It was written to provide information to the public about genetically modified foods.

TASK NINE: Collecting and evaluating information

Group Work

- Before you begin, form groups of four. Consider the source of the information that you are about to read. Discuss whether you believe that the CFIA is *in favour or not in favour* of GM foods. Do you think there will be any bias in the reading? Write your prediction here.

  I predict ______________________________

- Assign each group member a section of the reading.

Section	Headings	Student reader
1	What are genetically modified foods? Where do GM foods come from? How many GM food products are permitted in Canada?	
2	Are GM foods evaluated for safety? How long does it take to assess the safety of GM foods? What does the government look at in its safety assessment of agricultural products?	
3	What about foods? What about the long-term safety of GM foods? What is the concern about allergies? How are concerns about allergens being addressed?	
4	Have concerns been raised about herbicide-tolerant plants?	

- Answer each question in your section with point-form notes.
- Before sharing your information with your group, meet with the other students who read your section of the reading. Compare your answers and notes.
- Return to your original group and discuss your answers and notes. Group members should take notes during the discussion so that all students have information from all sections of the reading.
- Check whether or not your prediction at the beginning of the task was correct. Was there a bias in the reading?
- Once you have finished discussing your notes, return to your chart from Task Four (page 177). Fill in any additional information that you have.

Section 1

1. What are genetically modified foods?

___

___

2. Where do GM foods come from?

___

___

___

3. How many GM food products are permitted in Canada?

Section 2

1. Are GM foods evaluated for safety?

2. How long does it take to assess the safety of GM foods?

3. What does the government look at in its safety assessment of agricultural products?

Section 3

1. What about foods?

2. What about the long-term safety of genetically modified foods?

3. What is the concern about allergies?

4. How are concerns about allergens being addressed?

Section 4

1. Have concerns been raised about herbicide-tolerant plants?

Section 1

What are genetically modified foods?

Genetically modified (GM) foods, also called "biotechnology-derived foods" or "novel foods," have had one or more inheritable characteristics intentionally changed by altering the genetic makeup of the food. This is done to add, remove, or modify a characteristic of the food. For example, a plant might have its genetic makeup modified to make it resistant to a particular plant virus. A food may also contain GM food ingredients that have had their genetic makeup altered. Canola oil, for example, is a GM food that is contained in many processed foods.

Where do GM foods come from?

Genetic modification is not something that is new to our food system. Selective breeding and cross-breeding are methods of genetic modification that have been used by farmers for generations. For example, historically, farmers have genetically modified corn through cross breeding to produce products like "Peaches and Cream" corn. What is relatively new is the ability to make specific changes to the genetic make-up of a plant or animal using modern methods of genetic modification. This technology makes it possible for farmers to grow plants that are resistant to pests by triggering genes to produce certain types of enzymes that pests do not like.

How many GM food products are permitted in Canada?

The Canadian Food Inspection Agency (CFIA) shares responsibility for the regulation of products derived from biotechnology including plants, animal feeds and animal feed ingredients, fertilizers and veterinary biologics. For genetically modified crop plants, the CFIA assesses the potential risk of adverse environmental effects; authorizes and oversees import permits, confined trials, unconfined release and variety registration.

Health Canada is responsible for assessing the human health safety of products derived through biotechnology including foods, drugs, cosmetics, medical devices and pest control products. In the case of novel foods, each safety assessment considers the process used to develop the novel food, its characteristics compared to those of its traditional counterpart, its nutritional quality, the potential presence of any toxicants or anti-nutrients, and the potential allergenicity of any proteins introduced into the food.

Fifty-one types of genetic modification in crops have been approved by Health Canada for food use in Canada. Crops so far approved include:

- corn, including strains resistant to corn borers and herbicides;
- canola, including strains resistant to herbicides;
- potato including strains resistant to Colorado potato beetles;
- tomato including strains that ripen slowly;
- squash;
- soybean;
- flax;
- cottonseed oil; and
- sugar beet.

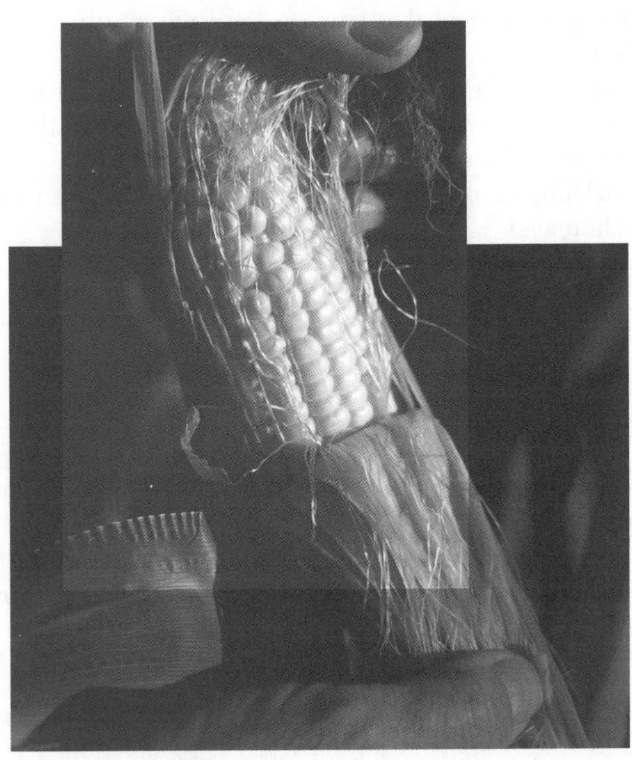

Section 2

Are GM foods evaluated for safety?

Yes. Before a GM agricultural or food product can be produced and marketed in Canada, it must undergo a number of scientific safety assessments. These assessments are designed to determine that the product is not dangerous for humans, animals, or the environment. Government of Canada evaluators conduct these safety assessments, taking into consideration expert advice from the global scientific community and the latest scientific literature.

Together, the CFIA and Health Canada are responsible for assessing the safety of GM agricultural and food products. They have a strict process in place, which is consistent with international standards.

How long does it take to assess the safety of GM foods?

It takes seven to ten years to develop, test, and thoroughly assess the safety of genetically modified food products.

What does the government look at in its safety assessment of agricultural products?

The CFIA assesses new agricultural products for safety and effectiveness. The Agency sets safety standards for seeds, plants, animal feeds and feed ingredients, veterinary biologics, and fertilizers, including those that are produced through modern biotechnology.

Before becoming a food, GM plants are subjected to several years of confined research field trials. During this time their interaction with the broader environment is restricted. The information from the research field trials is then used in another safety assessment that looks at the environmental impacts of the plant, including:

- the potential of the plant to become a weed or to invade natural habitats
- the potential to affect wild plants that are related to the modified plant
- the potential for the plant to become a new plant pest
- the potential impact of the plant or its gene products on other species (including humans)
- the potential impact on biodiversity

Section 3

What about foods?

Health Canada assesses the safety of all foods developed through biotechnology. Scientific evaluators with expertise in chemistry, microbiology, molecular biology, nutritional sciences, and toxicology look at the following:

- how the food crop was developed and what changes were made in the plant's molecular structure
- how the GM food compares in composition and nutrition with its counterpart food that has not been modified

- whether the GM food contains new toxins (substances that may cause harm to animals, humans, or the environment)
- whether the GM food may cause allergic reactions

At any point in the assessment of GM foods, the government may ask for additional research or testing from the food producer or manufacturer. Only if all of Health Canada's stringent criteria are met, is a GM food approved for sale in Canada.

The government maintains up-to-date information on new scientific research and new types of food and agricultural products. This helps keep government regulations current and effective.

What about the long-term safety of GM foods?

Another of Health Canada's key responsibilities is to monitor potential long-term health trends associated with health products and food, including biotechnology-derived products. If Health Canada has any concerns about the safety of a product while doing the scientific assessment, it is not approved for sale in Canada. After nine years of reviewing the safety of GM foods, Health Canada has not found any scientific evidence showing that GM foods are any less safe than their traditionally produced counterparts.

On the environmental side, the government is developing a plan to study potential long-term and cumulative effects of genetically modified organisms (GMOs) on biodiversity, wildlife, and other parts of our ecosystem. The knowledge gained from this research will be used in both policy and regulatory decision-making. Also, Agriculture and Agri-Food Canada, in consultation with the CFIA, is doing a research project—which will last for at least 12 years—to examine the potential long-term environmental impacts of approved and commercially available modified crops such as corn, potatoes, and canola.

What is the concern about allergies?

With an increasing awareness of the potential for allergic reactions to foods, consumers (and particularly those with known allergies) are concerned that through genetic engineering, genes from a food to which they are allergic may be transferred to an unrelated food. In addition there is some concern that transferring genes to another organism could create new allergens.

How are concerns about allergens being addressed?

It is important to recognize that consumers are not alone in their concern about potential food allergens. The food industry is extremely concerned about the potential for allergic reactions to their products. Health Canada is responsible for the safety of the Canadian food supply.

Before any genetically modified micro-organism or plant is approved by Health Canada as a safe food, it must undergo a thorough assessment. Part of that assessment, as described in Health Canada's Guidelines for the Safety Assessment of Novel Foods Vol. II: Genetically modified micro-organisms and plants, includes explicit consideration of potential allergenicity of the novel food.

Based on detailed information provided by the developer of the product, the potential for allergenic response to the product would be considered by looking at the history of both the host and donor organisms and the modification that has been undertaken. Health Canada would require clear labelling if there was any health or safety concern related to allergens.

Section 4

Have concerns been raised about herbicide-tolerant plants?

Yes. Some people have raised concerns that herbicide-tolerant plants will breed with other plants and weeds, creating weeds that are hard to control. Some have dubbed these "**superweeds**." If a herbicide-tolerant plant successfully breeds with another plant that is considered a weed, it could create a version of the weed that is resistant to regular doses of that particular herbicide. Agricultural experts, including those at the CFIA, concur that this is possible. However, the term "superweed" suggests that the weed cannot be controlled in any way. Scientific research and historical practices in agriculture indicate that this is not the case.

First, traits can be transferred only to **closely related plants**. Several of Canada's major crops (such as corn, tomatoes, potatoes, and soybeans) don't have weedy relatives in Canada that they could transfer their traits to, so there is no potential for hard to control weeds to develop from these crops.

Second, regarding those crops that do have "weedy" relatives, there are many other ways of controlling weeds that become tolerant to herbicides. Farmers have traditionally used **a number of methods to manage weeds** that have become herbicide-tolerant, whether naturally or through genetic modification. For example, they may:

- use a different herbicide to control the weeds
- till the land immediately before they plant their seed
- use herbicide mixtures to treat fields
- rotate the herbicides they use
- use non-chemical weed control methods such as silage and green manure
- rotate the crops planted in a field
- swath at the optimum crop stage

As a further precaution, the CFIA requires developers who are granted approval for new herbicide tolerant plants to have a **herbicide tolerant crop stewardship plan** that details steps farmers can take to minimize the chances of weeds becoming herbicide resistant. They are also working with industry to develop similar stewardship plans for plants that have already been approved.

Others have raised concerns about what happens if a plant becomes tolerant to **more than one herbicide.*** This can happen when herbicide-tolerant plants breed together. The offspring (new plants) may be tolerant to more than one herbicide. The new plants have combined characteristics from each of the parent plants.

* There have been some reports of canola that is tolerant to three different types of herbicides. This is very rare.

This process is called "**gene stacking.**" Gene stacking is not unique to plants developed through biotechnology. Field plants may become tolerant to more than one herbicide if the herbicides are not used properly to manage weeds. Farmers use the methods listed above to manage these sorts of weeds, as well.

Concerns have also been raised that herbicide-tolerant plants will take over other cultivated areas or natural habitats. Studies have shown that herbicide-tolerant plants cause no more problems than do other plants—unless that specific herbicide is the *only one* used to get rid of weeds and other competing plants.

Studies have also shown that domesticated plants, such as crop plants, do not survive well without human care. This means that a herbicide-tolerant plant that grows outside a farmer's field has little chance of surviving or breeding with other plants. In 2001, a 10-year study was published that looked at four types of genetically modified crop plants. It found that the plants **did not survive well in the wild** and are no more likely to invade non-farm habitats than their unmodified counterparts. The study, by M. J. Crawley et al, called "Biotechnology: Transgenic crops in natural habitats" can be found in the journal *Nature*, volume 409, pages 682-683 (2001).

CFIA (2003, 2004). *Fact sheets/Frequently asked questions*. Retrieved February 3, 2005, from http://www.inspection.gc.ca/english/sci/biotech/gen/queste.shtml

TASK TEN: Surveying the class for second opinions

- Ask your teacher to survey the class again for a response to this question:

  Do you think it is a good idea to eat GM foods?

- Have the results changed since your first survey (page 173)? Why or why not? Record the results for comparison purposes.

  Yes __________ No __________

LISTENING: HIGH-TECH HARVEST

This recording is a lecture that discusses some of the potential disadvantages of GM foods.

TASK ELEVEN: Taking notes to collect more information

- Before listening to the recording, look at the following note-taking outline (page 190) and try to predict what you will hear.
- Listen to the recording once. After listening, take a few minutes to review your notes.
- Discuss your answers with a small group of students. Fill in any gaps that you may have in your notes. Transfer your new knowledge to your Task Four chart (page 177).

Note-taking outline

Dangers of GM foods

- 3 categories of dangers
  1.
  2.
  3. Dangers to human ethics

1. Dangers to human health
   -

   For example:

   Another example:

2. Dangers to environmental health
   -

   For example:

   Another example:

3. Dangers to:
   a)

   b) Money made by GM companies

More details about a) Scientists controlling evolution

Examples:

More details about b)

First

Second

Lecture summary First: Then:
Finally: a) b)
New task:

TASK TWELVE: Surveying the class for third opinions

- Survey the class again by asking the following question:

  Do you think it is a good idea to eat GM foods?

- Record the results.

  Yes __________ No __________

- The class has now been surveyed several times. Have the survey results changed? Why? Why not? Discuss this as a class.

READING 4: GENETICALLY MODIFIED FOODS: THE BATTLE COMES TO CANADA

This newspaper article presents issues that Canadians face concerning GM foods.

TASK THIRTEEN: Building vocabulary and reading for meaning

There are five sections in the reading. You will read all the sections.

- Do you expect to find any bias in the newspaper article? Why or why not? Discuss this as a class.

Part A: Pre-reading vocabulary building

- Before you begin to read, work with one or two partners to define the bold-faced vocabulary words from the reading. Consult a dictionary only as a last resort.

1. Separating GM crops from conventional crops is impossible to avoid. It is **inevitable** (adj.) in the future.

2. The **segregation** (n) of GM crops from conventional crops is likely to be a nightmare.

3. No one knows exactly what should be done. The farmers are in a **quandary** (n).

4. There are many new GM foods that are still at the research and development stage. They are **in the pipeline** (exp.) and will be sold in the markets when the testing stage is complete.

5. There have been a number of studies that suggest GM foods aren't safe to eat. Other scientists have **denounced** (v) these studies, and have **discredited** (v) the research. No one believes that the results are correct.

6. The CFIA is very careful about testing foods to be sold in the Canadian marketplace. It has a **sound** (adj.) inspection process.

7. The public does not want an unsafe food product to be **foisted on them** (exp.). People want the CFIA to listen to their concerns.

Part B: Reading for meaning and collecting information

- Answer the questions for each section of the reading.
- Discuss your answers with a group of four students. Compare your notes and fill in any gaps that you may have.
- Work together to review your answers and transfer any new information that you may have about the benefits, risks and outstanding issues of GM foods to your Task Four chart (page 177).

Section 1

- Take notes under these headings.

Separation of GM crops from non-GM crops
seems inevitable complicated process

Uncertainties surrounding GM foods

segregation of crops
supply chains → retailers → distributors →
processor → farmers

The quandaries regarding GM foods

spread from farm kitchens to the halls of power

Section 2

List the pros and cons of GM foods in the chart below.

Pros	Cons
• can repel all sorts of blights & insects greater control over the range of crops	may have unknown environm effects

Section 3

1. Which denounced and discredited studies have been presented to show that GM foods are unsafe for human consumption?

Arpad Pustai
Cornel Univ
Iowa State Univ
Switzerland

2. What are biotech companies doing to combat studies like these?

formed a number of industry alliances
& set aside a lot of funds

3. What is the future of GM companies like Monsanto, DuPont and Novartis?

Section 4

4. Which problems may prevent further development of GM foods?

Section 5

5. What are the main questions that food regulators, critics and environmentalists are asking about GM foods?

How can the GM foods can be known to be safe when no long-term testing has been done?

How can governments can claim that GM foods are safe when they rely on studies provided by m-n companies who want their product approved quickly

Section 1

"It's supposed to be quick and easy: a simple litmus test that tells Stan Vanden Bosch whether he has any genetically modified soybeans in his silos.

He crushes a single bean in a thumb-sized tube, adds a spot of clear solution, and stirs in a strip of white paper. Within minutes two red stripes appear on the paper—proof positive that the Chesterville farmer's soybean has been genetically engineered to resist a brand-name herbicide.

Mr. Vanden Bosch, whose Eastern Ontario granaries take in more than 30,000 tonnes of corn and soybeans from the region's growers, is demonstrating a new crop-detection kit made by a Delaware-based company called Strategic Diagnostics Inc.

The market for such tests is growing because consumers around the world are demanding that food makers know whether genetically modified staples are in their products. That means farmers like Mr. Vanden Bosch are staring at a future in which separating genetically modified crops from conventional varieties, along with routine crop testing, seems inevitable.

"I think it's going to be a nightmare," he says. "It's such a complicated process that nobody knows how this is going to happen."

There are any number of uncertainties surrounding genetically modified foods, and segregating crops is just one of them. Consumer fears are being passed along the supply chain to retailers, distributors, processors and farmers. As a result, growers who are fans of genetically modified seeds are wondering what they should plant next spring. Farmers across Canada are key suppliers of genetically altered foodstuffs to foreign markets.

While Mr. Vanden Bosch doesn't grow genetically modified soybean, he accepts shipments from farmers who do. He also grows genetically modified corn.

But because of the uncertainties over what the market will bear, he is planning for half of this spring's crop to be conventionally bred corn. For the other half, he's planting a variety that has been genetically tailored to contain a built-in pesticide.

"We have to do what the market tells us," he says. "At the same time, if North America decided to grow just non-GM (genetically modified) corn this year, there wouldn't be enough seed to go around."

The quandary over genetically modified foods has spread from farm kitchens to the halls of power. Countries, including Canada and the U.S., that export these staples wonder whether there will be foreign markets for their genetically altered goods.

The biotech companies behind these products are worried about the long-term business prospects for their technology. The investors backing these companies wonder about the short- and long-term wisdom of putting tens of millions of dollars behind products that consumers overwhelmingly dislike.

And despite efforts to phase out genetically modified ingredients from processed foods, the world's processing giants and grocery chains can't be sure what they're selling their customers these days.

Section 2

"But at the core of the debate over genetically modified foods is the biggest uncertainty of all: the effects of transferring useful genes from microbes and other organisms into the plants we eat.

For now, these proprietary gene-splicing techniques create crops that can repel all sorts of blights and insects. Some can also withstand the herbicides that zap the weeds around them. Hundreds more are in the pipeline, among them plants that will make industrial chemicals and drugs for medicine.

In the future, the technology promises to boost a crop's nutritional value, speed up its growing time or simply produce foods that taste better and last longer. Biotech companies say genetic modification is progress because it gives farmers greater control over the range of crops that can be grown cost-effectively. It could also reduce the amount of weed-killing chemicals used and increase yields.

That, the industry argues, could benefit not only consumers in industrialized countries who want cheap, high-quality food, but also people in impoverished nations who are desperate for a cure to malnutrition.

But critics believe GM crops may have unknown health and environmental dangers that should be investigated before the food is sold to the public. "There's been no long-term testing on what this does to human health and animal health," says Maude Barlow, chairwoman of the Council of Canadians, a nationalist lobby group.

The Ottawa-based organization is part of a coalition of health and environmental activists that is calling for the Canadian government to stop approving new kinds of genetically modified foods, at least until they are properly tested.

Critics say that in the case of human health, the risks include potential allergic reactions to genetic changes that are not completely understood. On the issue of environmental impacts, a number of scientists believe that, in some cases, foreign genes in plants can pass into their wild, garden-variety relatives and spontaneously breed unkillable "superweeds." They could also harm some beneficial insects while stimulating pesticide resistance in others.

As for the claim that biotechnology can help alleviate world hunger, activists point out that distribution—not production—is the cause of food shortages. Indeed, the genes and methods behind genetic modification are tangled in a web of patent protection that affects the ability of researchers in developing countries to deliver the technology to poor farmers.

Caught between these two extremes are the scientists attempting to understand the implications of the new technology. But even academic researchers are finding their work attacked amid a knot of social, religious, environmental and food safety concerns.

Section 3

"Last February, when British researcher Arpad Pusztai presented the first evidence that genetically engineered food had potential health hazards by damaging the immune systems of rats, fellow researchers at Britain's Royal Society denounced his findings as flawed and inconclusive.

Other studies from Cornell University, Iowa State University and Switzerland, pointing to unexpected effects of genetically modified crops on insects that benefit the ecosystem, were similarly discredited as being dubious science.

But despite flaws in these early experiments, the questions behind them are still valid, says Lucy Sharratt of the Sierra Club of Canada. "Studies like this are just the beginning. They should point us towards asking more questions and furthering these studies."

Meanwhile, biotech companies have formed a number of industry alliances and set aside tens of millions of dollars to fight what they view as a nasty and hysterical campaign that has misrepresented their products. The companies are funding scientific research, organizing educational forums and lobbying legislators, regulators and farm groups.

Delaware-based DuPont Co. has announced it will form an advisory panel of environmental and biotech leaders to guide the company's business decisions. Officials at Monsanto Co. of St. Louis and Switzerland's Novartis AG have also pledged to do a better job of communicating with the public.

Behind such efforts is industry's acknowledgement that it hasn't done enough to win consumer confidence for its products. Monsanto chairman Robert Shapiro—the industry's chief booster—admitted as much when he addressed Greenpeace activists in London.

"Our confidence in this technology and our enthusiasm for it has, I think, widely been seen—and understandably so—as condescension or indeed arrogance. Because we thought it was our job to persuade, too often we forgot to listen," Mr. Shapiro said.

The companies are walking a fine line. While downplaying the concerns of consumer advocates, they must also generate enough hype to entice investors. That's particularly true of Monsanto, the industry leader, which has spent $8 billion U.S. in the past three years gobbling up seed companies and transforming itself from a farm chemicals giant into a "life sciences" concern. Its rival, DuPont, spent an estimated $7.7 billion U.S. to acquire Pioneer Hi-Bred International Inc., making it the world's No. 1 seed supplier.

Having put so much money behind farm biotechnology, and become so closely identified with it, the future of these companies is now tied to the future of genetically modified foods. That means the way companies go about influencing public opinion is critical.

Investment analysts predict the sector will see a downturn in sales of genetically modified seeds this year—the first time since 1997 that the market has stagnated.

"I think we're in for a two- to three-year period where additional market share for these seeds is going to be flat to down," says Sano Shimoda of Bioscience Securities Inc., a U.S.-based investment bank and brokerage firm. "Perceptions create reality in the marketplace, even if those perceptions are based on ill-informed judgments."

For the short-term, he adds, companies like Monsanto, DuPont and Novartis will see revenues dip and stock prices fluctuate. At the same time, Wall Street will stay away from investments in early-stage plant biotech companies developing the next generation of genetically engineered products.

But those jitters will pass because "this technology is going to create lots of value-added products that go beyond food and feed," says Mr. Shimoda.

Section 4

"So far, however, momentum is working against industry.

Last year, environmentalists trashed fields of genetically altered crops in Germany and France while in Britain, top grocery chains vowed to phase out such ingredients from their own lines of processed foods. Europe's largest food-makers, including Nestlé, Unilever and Cadbury, have made similar pledges, as have U.S. and Canadian manufacturers such as Gerber, HJ Heinz and McCain Foods.

Officially, the European Union has rejected some types of genetically modified corn and canola, including several varieties from Canada. It has also said no new biotech foods will be approved during the next three years. While some small-scale field trials are under way in all 15 E.U. states, no genetically altered crops are farmed commercially at the moment.

Other countries, such as Japan, Australia and New Zealand, want special labels to identify anything that may have genetically modified ingredients in it.

But the story is different in Canada and the U.S., where objections have so far not reached the fevered pitch seen in Europe, and where governments continue to fund and champion biotech research. Consumers, at least until now, have eaten genetically modified foods without much fuss, though nothing is labelled, nor is it required to be.

The issue could eventually reach the highest levels of international trade, namely the World Trade Organization. The U.S. and Canada want Europe and other key export markets to ease what they say are technical trade barriers on certain types of genetically altered crops.

They also resist demands for mandatory labelling for fear that, if given a choice, consumers will discriminate against foods made from genetically modified ingredients. It would also add prohibitive costs to the food industry if everything must be tested and labelled at every stage of production, the countries argue.

"Genetically modified food is not a trade issue per se, but it has huge implications for trade," says Karl Mielke, an agricultural economist at the University of Guelph.

Section 5

"The issue also tests the credibility of Canada's food-safety system, which has traditionally enjoyed a reputation for sound and rigorous inspection. But when it comes to genetically engineered foods, Canadian food regulators are facing the same questions that have confronted their European counterparts.

How can these new crops be known to be safe when no long-term testing has been done? How can governments claim that genetically modified foods are safe when they rely on studies provided by multinational companies who want their products approved quickly for market?

Sceptics also ask why the federal government simply assumes that a seed whose genetic makeup has been directly reprogrammed is considered to be substantially the same as its unmodified cousin.

Indeed, if genetically engineered products are so similar to conventionally bred varieties, critics argue, why do biotech companies fight so aggressively to protect their products with patents? "I think that's a very important and glaring contradiction," says Ms. Sharratt of the Sierra Club.

Consumer advocates want the regulatory system to be more open so the public doesn't believe such products are being foisted on them by authorities who are seen to be cosier with industry than with shoppers.

In Canada, those who speak for the biotech companies also argue that giving the public a better idea of how their food is vetted and approved would be a good start towards boosting consumer confidence in genetically modified products.

"I don't believe it's the government's responsibility to sell products or to stand behind products. That's our job," says Joyce Groote, executive director for the industry association, BIOTECanada. "But I do think it's their job to at least talk about what they do. And what they do is regulate those products to ensure they're safe before they can be sold."

The issue is expected to heat up in the coming months as Canadian activists pressure the government to introduce long-term testing and mandatory labelling of genetically modified foods. ”

Tam, P. (2000, January 3). Genetically modified foods: the battle comes to Canada. Ottawa Citizen, pp. A1, A8.

FINAL ASSIGNMENT

TASK FOURTEEN: Writing an extended persuasive essay

- Write an extended persuasive essay of approximately five pages. Refer to the example of a persuasive essay in the Models Chapter (page 215). Review your summary of the chapter content by looking at your Task Four chart (page 177).
- Respond to one of the following statements.

  The advantages of GM foods are greater than the disadvantages. Agree or disagree and explain why.

  OR

  GM foods are only a short-lived trend and will not last beyond the next decade. Agree or disagree and explain why.

  OR

  GM foods have the potential to solve the problem of world hunger. Agree or disagree and explain why.

Models Chapter

This chapter provides models of the writing assignments that you may be required to write as you progress through this textbook. All of the assignments are about water, allowing you to see how the same information can be arranged to meet the demands of different writing assignments. Before most of the model assignments, you will find

a) instructions to highlight the key characteristics of the writing assignment and

b) the outline that the writer used to prepare for the writing assignment.

MODEL ONE: SHORT ANSWER TEST

How to write short answers

In the first sentence,

- repeat the important words from the question;
- respond to the first word in the question (for example, *what, when, why, how, explain, define*).

In the rest of the short answer,

- provide correct and detailed information to answer the question;
- organize the information (for example, first to last, simple to complex).

Question 1: What is the water cycle?

Writer's plan

- Sky to earth to sky (vapour to liquid to vapour)
- Rain and snow falls
- Falls on ground, rivers and oceans
- Evaporates from land and returns to atmosphere

Answer

The **water cycle is** the process of water movement from the sky to the earth, and back to the sky again. Water is a vapour in the atmosphere, but changes to liquid rain or solid snow as it falls to earth. Once on land, the water flows into the earth, rivers and oceans. The water will then evaporate and become a vapour again, as it returns to the atmosphere.

Question 2: What are the differences between a watershed and an aquifer?

Writer's plan

Watershed	Aquifer
• All land from which water drains into a common body of water • Is natural—not based on political borders • Example	• Water in the ground • Water travels downwards until it hits rock • Aquifer is the layer of water above the layer of rock • Can be large or small • Example

Answer

A **watershed is** all the land from which water drains into a common body of water **while an aquifer is** an underground layer of water found just above a layer of rock.

A watershed is a natural dividing line that does not reflect political borders. As a result, countries may share watersheds. Canada and the United States share a number of watersheds, such as the Pacific Watershed west of the Rocky Mountains that drains into the Pacific Ocean, and the Great Lakes-St. Lawrence watershed that drains into the Atlantic Ocean.

An aquifer, or layer of water stored underground, **is** created as water from rain or melting snow sinks into the ground. Aquifers are important because people drill wells down to the aquifer to find water. Canada and the United States also share a number of large aquifers.

Question 3: How can we conserve water around our homes?

Writer's plan

Two ways to conserve water:
a) use less water—repair, collect rain, be water efficient
b) avoid contamination—use non-toxic cleaners, reduce pesticide and salt use

Answer

People can conserve water around their homes in two ways. First, they can use less water. By repairing leaky taps and toilets, collecting and using rainwater, reducing water use for the lawn and using water-efficient showerheads and taps, people can save a significant amount of water. Second, people must avoid contaminating their water supply with toxic cleaners, fertilizers, pesticides and salt.

MODEL TWO: SURVEY

How to organize a survey

A survey is designed to collect information from people (respondents/participants). To create a survey, you should:

- decide what information you want to gather (limit yourself to finding out one or two pieces of information);
- select two different groups of respondents you want to find out information about (for example, men and women, older and younger, Chinese and Canadian);
- write a hypothesis—a sentence that explains what you expect to discover;
- ask five or six questions that will give you the information that you want, including yes/no questions, multiple choice questions or Likert scale questions (to which participants can answer a) always, b) often, c) sometimes, d) rarely, e) never);
- write the questions so that you can easily record the respondents' answers;
- conduct the survey (ask the survey questions);
- ask the same number of respondents from each of the groups;
- summarize the information in a table;
- consider whether or not your hypothesis was correct and try to explain why or why not based on the information that you have obtained.

Example survey

Hypothesis: Older people use more water than younger people.

1. How old are you?
   ◉ 13–30 ○ 31 and over
2. How many showers or baths do you take per day?
   ◉ Less than one, or one ○ Two ○ More than two
3. On average, how many times do you flush the toilet per day?
   ○ One–three times ◉ Four or five times ○ Six times or over
4. How many times per week do you use the clothes washer?
   ○ Less than once, or once ○ Twice ○ More than twice
5. How many times per week do you use the dishwasher?
   ○ Less than once, or once ○ Twice ○ More than twice
6. Do you water your lawn?
   ○ Yes ○ No

Table: Summary of survey results

Questions	Total number of 13–30 (10)			Total number of 31 and over (10)		
1. How old are you?	**% total** 50%			**% total** 50%		
2. How many showers or baths do you take per day?	**<1 or 1** 7	**2** 3	**>2** 0	**<1 or 1** 10	**2** 0	**>2** 0
3. On average, how many times do you flush the toilet per day?	**1–3** 0	**4–5** 8	**>6** 2	**1–3** 0	**4–5** 4	**>6** 6
4. How many times per week do you use the clothes washer?	**<1 or 1** 5	**2** 5	**>2** 0	**<1 or 1** 0	**2** 0	**>2** 10
5. How many times per week do you use the dishwasher?	**<1 or 1** 2	**2** 7	**>2** 1	**<1 or 1** 0	**2** 0	**>2** 10
6. Do you water your lawn?	**Yes** 0	**No** 10		**Yes** 4	**No** 6	

MODEL THREE: REPORT

How to write a report

A report is designed to explain data or information. The following guidelines will help you write an effective report.

- Divide the report into sections. Many reports are divided into *introduction, methods, results* and *discussion* sections. However, your sections will depend on the information that you need to explain.
- Select logical section headings.
- In your introduction section, explain why the information was collected.
- In your methods section, explain how the information was collected.
- In your results section, explain what you discovered. You may include tables or charts in this section.
- In your discussion section, highlight the value of the report's results, mention any limitations of the report and provide your ideas for further research.

Example report on the model survey

Writer's plan

Introduction	• general information about fresh water • importance of conservation • importance of public education campaigns to encourage water conservation • what segment of the population would be best to target with these campaigns? • hypothesis

Methods	• explain survey design • explain participant selection (by age)
Results	• hypothesis correct • summarize major results: – younger people have showers more frequently – older people use toilets, dishwashers, clothes washers and lawn sprinklers more frequently – overall, older people use more water than younger people
Discussion	• limitations – is water use related to age or size of household? • more research needs to be done to target water reduction campaigns effectively

Introduction

Water conservation is becoming an important issue as world population increases. Although the world is covered with water, 97 percent of that water is salt water, and much of the remaining 3 percent is held in glaciers in the north and south poles. Only a small percentage of the earth's water is available to support human life. Water conservation is essential if people want to preserve their quality of life. The expression, "Think globally, act locally," encourages individuals to reduce their water consumption.

Scientists and governments are trying to educate people to reduce their water consumption, and protect the quality of existing water. In order to do this, individuals should use less water by repairing leaky taps, collecting and using rainwater, buying water-efficient bathroom fixtures, eliminating grass-watering, and reducing the use of toxic cleaners, fertilizers, pesticides and salts. Although most people are aware they should be conserving water, many people do not actually make an effort to reduce their water consumption where it counts most: in the home. The public needs to be educated about how to reduce and protect water.

To develop effective public education campaigns, it is important to know who uses the most water. Do older people use more water than younger people? If this is true, then the government can target older people with its water use reduction campaigns. If younger people use more water, then the government can target younger people in these campaigns. This survey was based on the hypothesis that older people (31 and over) used more water than younger people (13–30).

Method

The survey was designed to cover all the areas where water is often wasted in the home: showers (baths), toilets, clothes washers, dishwashers, and lawns. There was one question for each of these areas. Here is a list of the questions.

1. How old are you?
   (This question divided the respondents into "younger" or "older" age groups.)
2. How many showers or baths do you take per day?
3. On average, how many times do you flush the toilet per day?
4. How many times per week do you use the clothes washer?
5. How many times per week do you use the dishwasher?
6. Do you water your lawn?

Showers (which use up to 85 litres per day),[1] toilets (which use up to 12 litres per flush), clothes washers (which use up to 45 litres per wash), dishwashers (which use up to 9 litres per wash), and lawn sprinklers (which use up to 36 litres per minute) consume a large amount of water per day. These questions were designed to find out if the individuals were using less or more water.

Twenty people completed the survey. These people were selected, based on their age, so that half the survey population was between 13 and 30, and half was older than 30. Children younger than 13 were not surveyed because these individuals probably do not have the responsibility for cleaning their homes and clothes, and therefore, probably use less water than adults, who have greater responsibility in these areas.

Results

The results prove the hypothesis correct. Older people (31 and over) use more water than younger people (13–31). For only one question (Question 2), the results show that older people use less water than younger people; more senior people have fewer showers per day, consuming less water in this area only. The answers to the third question demonstrate that older individuals consume slightly more water than younger individuals by flushing the toilet more times per day. One hundred percent of both older and younger people said they flushed the toilet more than four times per day, yet 60 percent of older people flushed more than six times per day compared to only 20 percent of younger people. This suggests that more senior individuals are flushing slightly more often than younger individuals.

Responses to Questions 4 and 5 clearly show that older people use significantly more water per day than younger people. In response to the questions, "How many times per week do you use the clothes washer, and the dishwasher, 100 percent of more senior people said they use these appliances more than twice a week. For these same questions, 100 percent of younger people said they used the clothes washer two times or less per week, and 90 percent said they used the dishwasher two times or less per week. These differences result in significantly reduced water consumption for younger people.

Similarly, when asked if they water their lawns, 100 percent of younger individuals responded "No" while only 60 percent of older individuals answered "No." As a result, younger people were again using less water than older people.

Discussion

The results support the hypothesis that older people use more water than younger people. Older participants used the toilet, clothes washer, dishwasher, and sprinkler more frequently than younger respondents. Older individuals only used less water in the shower, as they had fewer showers than younger people.

It is possible that age is not the reason why more senior people use more water than more junior people. All the older respondents had children, and therefore larger households than the younger respondents. It is likely that having children

1 All estimates taken from Agriculture Canada (1999). Water Management (Best Management Practices Series). Ottawa, Ministry of Agriculture and Food.

results in more clothes and dishes to wash, and possibly more toilets to flush during the day. Of the younger people in the survey, only one of them had children. It is suggested that any follow-up survey should divide the respondents according to whether they have children or not.

More research should also be done to determine whether water reduction campaigns should be aimed at younger or older people, or if some other segment of the population should be the focus of encouragement to reduce water use.

MODEL FOUR: SHORT PROCESS ESSAY

How to write a process essay

Process essays are written to explain *how* something is done. Therefore, often a process essay explains the steps in a process. The following guidelines will help you write an effective process essay.

- Like all essays, a process essay must have three general sections: an introduction, a body and a conclusion. Unlike a report, you may not use these section titles as headings in the essay.
- The introduction announces the topic of the essay. Although there are many good ways to start an essay, the introduction usually begins with a general statement about why the topic is important.
- The introduction finishes with a *thesis statement*. A thesis statement is a sentence that includes the topic of the essay and the opinion that the essay will present. It may or may not include the main steps of the process that you are writing about.
- The body of the essay will contain a number of paragraphs. For a short process essay, usually each paragraph describes one step in the process.
- Each body paragraph should start with a topic sentence that clearly indicates the topic of the paragraph. If your thesis listed the main steps of the process, you can repeat the key words (or a form of the key words) from the thesis.
- Each body paragraph should finish with a sentence that makes the point of the paragraph clear.
- The conclusion summarizes the main steps in the process. It often finishes with a sentence that restates (but not repeats) the thesis.

Example process essay: How is dirty water cleaned for drinking?

Writer's plan

Introduction: not much water available for use
- Dirty water must be cleaned and reused.
- This is the water treatment process.
- Three steps—sedimentation, filtration and disinfection

Body
- Sedimentation removes tiny particles from the water—alum is added; water thickens; particles stick together and sink to the bottom.
- Filtration—water is passed through a sand filter to remove any remaining waste.
- Disinfection—chlorine is added to remove bacteria; fluoride is added.

Conclusion
- Three steps in the water treatment process provide clean drinking water.

Although the world is covered with water, 97 percent of that water is salt water, and much of the remaining 3 percent is held in glaciers in the north and south poles. Only a small percentage of the earth's water is available to support human life. This means it is important to use less water and avoid polluting water. It also means that people must clean dirty water if they want to have enough water. The process of cleaning dirty water so that it is safe to drink is called the water treatment process. Dirty water is often treated by sedimentation, filtration and disinfection before it is clean.

Sedimentation of dirty water is the first step in the water treatment process. To start, a chemical called alum is mixed into the water to make small particles stick to each other. With gentle mixing, more and more small particles stick together. As a result, the heavy particles that are produced sink to the bottom of the tank, leaving the water cleaner, but not clean enough to drink.

After sedimentation, the water is filtered to remove the remaining particles. The water is passed through layers of stones, called gravel, and sand. These layers form a filter that further cleans the water. Once the water is through the filter, it is free of particles, but it is still not clean enough to drink.

To complete the water treatment process, disinfection destroys any bacteria or viruses that are present in the water. Chlorine, a chemical used to kill bacteria, is added to the water. Chlorine not only kills bacteria during the treatment process, but also maintains the quality of the water as it is carried through the water distribution system. Another chemical, fluoride, may be added to the water to help reduce tooth decay. The overall treatment results in water that is clean and ready to drink.

If dirty water is not treated properly, people and animals may become sick from the dirt and bacteria in the water. The water treatment process is constantly monitored to make sure this does not happen. An effective water treatment process that includes sedimentation, filtration and disinfection is essential if people want enough safe water to drink.

MODEL FIVE: SHORT PERSUASIVE ESSAY

How to write a short persuasive essay

Persuasive essays are written to persuade, or convince, people that a particular opinion about a topic is correct. The following guidelines will help you write an effective short persuasive essay.

- Like all essays, a persuasive essay must have three general sections: an introduction, a body and a conclusion. Unlike a report, you may not use these section titles as headings in the essay.
- The introduction announces the topic of the essay. Although there are many good ways to start an essay, the introduction usually begins with a general statement about why the topic is important.
- The introduction finishes with a *thesis statement*. A thesis statement is a sentence that includes the topic of the essay and the opinion that the essay will present. It may or may not include the main reasons why the opinion of the essay is correct.
- The body of the essay will contain a number of paragraphs. For a short persuasive essay, usually each paragraph explains one reason why the essay opinion is correct.
- Each body paragraph should start with a topic sentence that clearly indicates the topic of the paragraph. You can do this by repeating key words (or a form of the key words) from the thesis.
- Each body paragraph should finish with a sentence that makes the point of the paragraph clear.
- The conclusion summarizes the main reasons why the essay opinion is correct. It often finishes with a sentence that restates (but not repeats) the thesis.

Example persuasive essay

Water is becoming contaminated with a new form of pollution. Medicines, or drugs, used by humans and animals are entering the water system. Governments should make every effort to eliminate water pollution from medicines. Agree or disagree and explain why.

Writer's plan

Introduction: general information

- Where – ground water, surface water and drinking water
- What – types of medicines
- Source – humans and animals

Governments should not eliminate this form of pollution because

1. pollution levels are so low, and
2. money could be spent better elsewhere.

Body

1. pollution levels very low
   - parts per billion, and parts per trillion
   - so much less than prescribed doses
   - only sensitive equipment allows us to find this kind of pollution
2. very expensive to remove medicine pollution from the water
   - levels so low—hard to find, test and monitor
   - money could be spent better in researching the long-term effects of this pollution

Conclusion
- Water pollution from medicines is worrying.
- It deserves further study BUT remember
  1. pollution levels are very low, and
  2. money could be spent on research rather than treatment.

It is well-recognized that water is essential for life, and consequently, water should be protected from pollution. In order to protect the water supply, water treatment processes are designed to eliminate many forms of harmful pollution. Recently, scientists have begun to find a new type of pollution in ground, surface and drinking water. They have discovered that human and animal medicines, such as antibiotics, are polluting the water. People expect governments to eliminate pollution from medicines in their water. However, at the moment, governments should not attempt to remove medicines from the water supply because the levels of this kind of pollution are very low, and the removal of the pollution would cost money that could be spent on research.

The levels of medicine, or pharmaceutical, pollution in the water supply are extremely low. It is true that research in Europe and the United States has found some form of pharmaceutical pollution in almost all ground, surface and drinking water. However, measurements at levels this low have only become possible because of sensitive measurement equipment that was not available to scientists in the past. Scientists measure the amounts of pharmaceutical pollutants in parts per billion, and in some cases parts per trillion. These amounts of pollution from medicine are so low that they are unlikely to cause a crisis in health care in the short term.

In order to remove these low levels of pharmaceutical pollution from water, governments would have to spend a lot of money. The current water treatment processes remove many harmful particles and bacteria from the water, but they are not as effective at removing low levels of pharmaceutical pollution. Only advanced water treatment technologies would remove medicines from the water supply, and even then, some pharmaceuticals might not be eliminated. At this point, the money needed to remove all medicines from water would be better spent on research related to the long-term effects of pharmaceutical pollution on humans and animals.

Although the thought of medicines in the water supply is worrying, it would not be useful for governments to spend large amounts of money to change current water treatment processes to try to eliminate all pharmaceutical pollution. This kind of pollution is so minimal that it is difficult to measure. Furthermore, low levels of medicines are not likely to cause health problems in the short-term. Instead of spending large amounts of money to modify water treatment processes, governments should spend money on research to identify the long-term effects of exposure to low levels of pharmaceuticals.

MODEL SIX: COMPARE AND CONTRAST ESSAYS

How to write compare and contrast essays

Compare and contrast essays are written to show the similarities and differences between two items. When you compare items, you show the similarities; when you contrast items, you show the differences. The following guidelines will help you write effective compare and contrast essays.

- Decide what points of comparison or contrast you wish to explain to your reader.
- Decide which pattern of organization fits your information best. There are two standard ways to organize a compare and contrast essay: block style organization and point-by-point style organization. Generally, block style organization is best for less technical information while point-by-point style organization is best for more technical information. Both styles of organization are demonstrated here.
- Like other kinds of essays, a compare and contrast essay has three general sections: an introduction, a body and a conclusion. Unlike a report, you may not use these section titles as headings in the essay.
- The introduction announces the topic of the essay. Although there are many good ways to start an essay, the introduction usually begins with a general statement about why the topic is important.
- The introduction finishes with a *thesis statement*. A thesis statement is a sentence that includes the topic of the essay and the opinion that the essay will present. It may or may not include the main points of comparison or contrast.
- The body of the essay will contain a number of paragraphs. For a short compare and contrast essay, usually each paragraph explains one point of comparison or contrast.
- Each body paragraph should start with a topic sentence that clearly indicates the topic of the paragraph. You can do this by repeating key words (or a form of the key words) from the thesis.
- Each body paragraph should finish with a sentence that makes the point of the paragraph clear.
- The conclusion summarizes the points of comparison and/or contrast. It often finishes with a sentence that restates (but not repeats) the thesis.

Example compare and contrast essay

Compare and contrast two different technologies that could be used to solve water shortages.

Writer's plan for a block style compare and contrast essay

Compare and contrast desalination with atmospheric water vapour processing
- both are ways of producing pure drinking water
- some differences in source, waste products and final product

Desalination
- explain the process; give an example
  - source – ocean water
  - waste products – salty brine
  - final product – salty (transport inland)

Atmospheric water vapour processing
- explain the process; give an example
  - source – water vapour in the air
  - waste products – none
  - final product – very pure

Desalination and water vapour processing are useful because
- sources are accessible
- few waste products
- final product = drinking water

Block style essay

Desalination, or the process of removing salt from ocean water, and atmospheric water vapour processing, or the process of turning water vapour into water, are both ways of producing drinking water for human consumption. Although desalination and atmospheric water vapour processing are distinct because they extract water from unique sources, and produce different waste and final products, both are useful to increase the amount of water available for use.

Producing drinking water from salty ocean water is the process of desalination. This process is used in the Middle East, where Saudi Arabia operates the largest desalination plant in the world. The source of water for desalination plants is ocean water. As ocean water is 97 percent of the world's water, there is a large supply of water that could be processed with desalination technology. The process does result in some unwanted waste products. Desalination plants produce a salty brine, as well as some chemical wastes that must be properly disposed of. If the waste products are simply returned to the environment, they will pollute rivers and groundwater, but they can be properly managed so the environment is not damaged. Finally, the desalination process works by removing the salt from ocean water; however, it is impossible to remove all the salt. Therefore, the final product of desalination is drinking water with a salty taste.

Atmospheric water vapour processing pulls water vapour from the air, cools it, and condenses it into drinking water. After an earthquake hit Taiwan in 1999, water vapour processors produced enough water to supply the military soldiers who were helping the relief efforts. The main source of water for this kind of treatment is humid air, which is free in large quantities. As for waste products, it is true that in order to cool the water vapour, a refrigerant is used. However refrigerants, also found in refrigerators and dehumidifiers, can be used for long periods of time before they become waste. The final product of atmospheric water vapour processing is appealing too. It is one of the cleanest forms of water. Pollutants in the air that adhere to rain drops do not stick to water vapour; consequently, the final product of this process is very pure.

Both desalination and water vapour processing technology are useful methods for producing clean drinking water in countries where there is a lack of natural water supply. The sources of water for these processes are easily available, their waste products can be properly managed so they don't harm the environment, and the end products are clean drinking water for human consumption.

Reference: Jacobs, D. (2002, December 28). Water, water everywhere. Ottawa Citizen, p. A3.

Writer's plan for a point-by-point style compare and contrast essay

Compare and contrast desalination with atmospheric water vapour processing
- both ways of producing pure drinking water
- some differences in source, waste products and final product

Source of water:
- desalination – ocean water
- water vapour processing – air

Waste products
- desalination – salty brine
- water vapour processing – none

Final product:
- desalination – tastes salty
- water vapour processing – pure

Water vapour processing and desalination are useful because
- sources are accessible
- few waste products
- final products = drinking water

Point-by-point style essay

Desalination, or the process of removing salt from ocean water, and atmospheric water vapour processing, or the process of turning water vapour into water, are both ways of producing drinking water for human consumption. Although desalination and atmospheric water vapour processing are distinct because they extract water from unique sources, and produce different waste and final products, both are useful to increase the amount of water available for use.

Each of these water creation technologies has a unique source of water. Producing drinking water from salty ocean water is the process of desalination. This process is used in the Middle East, where Saudi Arabia operates the largest desalination plant in the world. The main source of water for desalination plants is ocean water. As ocean water is 97 percent of the world's water, there is a large supply of water that could be processed with desalination technology. Alternatively, atmospheric water vapour processing pulls water vapour from the air, cools it, and condenses it into drinking water. After an earthquake hit Taiwan in 1999, water vapour processors produced enough water to supply the military soldiers who were helping the relief efforts. The main source of water for this kind of treatment is humid air, which is free in large quantities. Each process is based on an abundant natural resource.

Every technology must be evaluated to determine if it produces waste products that will be dangerous to the environment. Desalination technology does result in some unwanted waste products: a salty brine, as well as some chemicals. If the waste products are simply returned to the environment, they will pollute rivers and groundwater, but they can be properly managed so the environment is not damaged. Similarly, water vapour processing uses a refrigerant to cool the water vapour. However refrigerants, also found in refrigerators and dehumidifiers, can be used for long periods of time before they become waste. Both processes produce waste products that need to be disposed of properly.

The taste of the final products is also a significant consideration when evaluating water technologies. The desalination process works by removing the salt from ocean water; nevertheless, it is almost impossible to remove all the salt. Therefore, the final product of desalination is drinking water that tastes salty. In contrast, the final product of water vapour processing is one of the cleanest forms of water. Pollutants in the air that adhere to rain drops do not stick to water vapour; consequently, the final product of this process is very pure. However, both processes produce drinking water for human consumption.

Desalination and water vapour processing technology are useful methods for producing clean drinking water in countries where there is a lack of natural water supply. The sources of water for these processes are easily available, their waste products can be properly managed so they don't harm the environment, and the end products are clean drinking water for human consumption.

Reference: Jacobs, D. (2002, December 28). Water, water everywhere. Ottawa Citizen, p. A3.

MODEL SEVEN: PARAPHRASE

How to write a paraphrase

The goal of a paraphrase is to restate the ideas of another author without copying the author's words. Paraphrasing is an effective way to avoid plagiarism. Use the following guidelines to write a paraphrase.

- All paraphrases start with a reference to the original author. Common ways to start paraphrases are the following:
  In her 2000 article, (author's name) states that ...
  In his book of 2000, (author's name) suggests that ...
  According to (author's name) in her article of 2000,...
  (Author's name) website maintains that ...
- A paraphrase is approximately the same length as the original writing.
- To restate the main ideas of an author without repeating the same words, you may use writing techniques such as finding synonyms for key words, changing the structure of the sentence, changing word forms and changing the voice from active to passive (or passive to active). See pages 133–135 for examples of these writing techniques.
- You may need to use more than one of these writing techniques to complete a successful paraphrase.

Example paraphrase

Paraphrase the following text:

"Because water belongs to the earth and all species, decision-makers must represent the rights and needs of other species in their policy choices and actions. Future generations also constitute "stakeholder" status requiring representation in decision-making about water. Nature, not man, is at the centre of the universe. For all our brilliance and accomplishment, we are a species of animal that needs water for the same reasons as other species. Unlike other species, however, only humans have the power to destroy ecosystems upon which all depend and so humans have an urgent need to redefine their relationship to the natural world."

Reference: Barlow, M. (1999, June). *Protecting water: Ten principles.* In Blue Gold Special Report. International Forum on Globalization [Electronic Version]. Retrieved March 31, 2001, from http://www.thewaterpage.com/blue_gold_principles.htm

Example paraphrase:

In her 1999 paper "Protecting Water: Ten Principles," Maude Barlow states that as all species must have water, politicians should consider the requirements of all species as they make decisions. The next generation should also have some say in water policy. The universe does not revolve around humans, but the earth itself. Humans have achieved great successes, but they still require water for life, just like all other species. Yet it is man alone that has the capability to damage ecosystems that all other species need to survive. Consequently, people must re-establish their connection with nature as soon as possible.

MODEL EIGHT: SUMMARY

How to write a summary

The goal of a summary is to restate the ideas of another author without copying the author's words. Summarizing, *like paraphrasing*, is an effective way to avoid plagiarism. Follow these guidelines to write a summary.

- All summaries, like paraphrases, start with a reference to the original author. Common ways to start summaries are the following:
  In her 2000 article, (author's name) states that ...
  In his book of 2000, (author's name) suggests that ...
  According to (author's name) in her article of 2000,...
  (Author's name) website maintains that ...
- A summary, *unlike* a paraphrase, is approximately 1/4 to 1/3 the length of the original writing.
- To summarize an original text, you should:
  1. read the original text carefully;
  2. underline the main points of the original text, leaving out supporting details, repetitions and examples;
  3. paraphrase the underlined sentences.
- To paraphrase the underlined sentences, you may use writing techniques such as finding synonyms for key words, changing the structure of the sentence, changing word forms and changing the voice from active to passive (or passive to active). See pages 133–135 for examples of these writing techniques.

- You may need to use more than one of these writing techniques to complete a successful summary.

Example summary

Summarize the following text:

"Water, like air, is necessary for all life. Without water, humans and other beings would die and the earth's systems would shut down. Modern society has lost its reverence for water's sacred place in the cycle of life as well as its centrality to the realm of the spirit. This loss of reverence for water has allowed humans to abuse it. Only by redefining our relationship to water and recognizing its essential and sacred place in nature can we begin to right the wrongs we have done.

Because water belongs to the earth and all species, decision-makers must represent the rights and needs of other species in their policy choices and actions. Future generations also constitute "stakeholder" status requiring representation in decision-making about water. Nature, not man, is at the centre of the universe. For all our brilliance and accomplishment, we are a species of animal that needs water for the same reasons as other species. Unlike other species, however, only humans have the power to destroy ecosystems upon which all depend and so humans have an urgent need to redefine their relationship to the natural world."

Reference: Barlow, M. (1999, June). *Protecting water: Ten principles*. In Blue Gold Special Report. International Forum on Globalization [Electronic Version]. Retrieved March 31, 2001, from http://www.thewaterpage.com/blue_gold_principles.htm

Example summary:

In her article "Protecting Water: Ten Principles," published in 1999, Maude Barlow states that without water, there is no life. People have forgotten their historical respect for water, and this has permitted them to pollute water. Humans must remember that all species rely on water for life; consequently, politicians must make decisions with the interests of all species in mind, not just human interests. In order to avoid destroying ecosystems that are essential to all life, society must re-establish its connection with nature as soon as possible.

MODEL NINE: EXTENDED PERSUASIVE ESSAY

How to write an extended persuasive essay

Persuasive essays are written to persuade, or convince, people that a particular opinion about a topic is correct. The following guidelines will help you write an effective persuasive essay.

- Like all essays, a persuasive essay must have three general sections: an introduction, a body and a conclusion. In a short persuasive essay, the introduction and conclusion are usually one paragraph long, and the body of the essay has as many paragraphs as you have main points to make. However, in an extended persuasive essay, the introduction and conclusion may be more than one paragraph long, and the body of an extended essay has as many sections as you have main points to make. Each section may or may not be more than one paragraph long.

- The introduction announces the topic of the essay. Although there are many good ways to start an essay, the introduction usually begins with a general statement about why the topic is important.
- The introduction finishes with a *thesis statement*. A thesis statement is a sentence that includes the topic of the essay and the opinion that the essay will present. It may or may not include the main reasons why the opinion of the essay is correct.
- The body of the essay will contain a number of sections. For an extended persuasive essay, usually each section explains one reason why the essay opinion is correct. Each section may or may not be more than one paragraph long. The number of paragraphs per section depends on the content.
- Each section should start with a topic sentence that clearly indicates the topic of the section. You can do this by repeating key words (or a form of the key words) from the thesis.
- Within each section, each paragraph should start with a topic sentence that clearly indicates the topic of the paragraph and how it relates to the main point of the section.
- Each body paragraph should finish with a sentence that makes the point of the paragraph clear.
- The conclusion summarizes the main reasons why the essay opinion is correct. It often finishes with a sentence that restates (but not repeats) the thesis.

Example of an extended persuasive essay

Water redistribution is the key to solving global water shortages. Agree or disagree and explain why.

Writer's plan

Introduction:
Water redistribution is no longer the key to solving global water shortages. There are other methods that will do a better job of eliminating water shortages.

Redistribution:
- historically – redistribution by dams and pipes
- now – too many dams (give numbers)
- no new rivers to dam
- now what?

- Glaciers
- Water bags
- Old oil tanker

These methods of redistribution are not useful.

Are there really water shortages? Some people don't agree with this statement—they say
- aquifers may be only temporarily low – in the process of establishing a steady state we can adapt to sinking ground levels
- scientists will develop new technologies to eliminate the threat of water shortages

However – this is a minority viewpoint

What can be done about water shortages
Other methods:
- desalination
- atmospheric water vapour processing
- elimination of poverty
- education and conservation

Desalination	Water Vapour	Poverty	Education
• ocean water • energy consumption • waste product	• humid air • energy consumption • pure water	• complex • essential to address	• long term • essential

Conclusion:
Water redistribution is no longer the best method to solve water shortages.
Other methods, although they have drawbacks, are much more effective.
Desalination, water vapour processing, as well as the elimination of poverty and education and conservation will be more efficient in solving the world's water shortages.

Water shortages are fast becoming a fact of life, not only in undeveloped countries, but also in developed countries. Even those countries with the money to spend on wells, pumps, pipes, and distribution systems are running out of water. The solution to this problem seems simple. If there is a shortage of water in one place, and an abundance of water in another place, all that is required is the transportation of the water to the area without water. In fact, water shortages are complex problems; simple redistribution of water is no longer the most effective method of solving global water shortages.

Historically, redistribution of water has been very successful at eliminating water shortages. This redistribution was achieved by building dams on rivers, blocking the natural flow of water, and creating a reservoir, or extra water storage, above the dam. And while the dams have created environmental disruptions, they have been successful in sharing water amongst regions. However, today, the world's major rivers have all been dammed.[1] Any river left to be dammed is too small, or too distant. The cost of building dams on the remaining rivers is too high. As a result, the traditional method of redistributing water through a dam is no longer economically possible.

Other methods of redistribution have been proposed. Scientists have tried towing glaciers from the poles to warmer countries where water shortages exist; however, the glaciers melted too quickly.[2] A number of people have tried to float fresh water, contained in huge bags, through the ocean to thirsty countries. But the water bags remain theoretical.[3] Others have suggested water be carried in tanker ships that are too old to carry oil. But the costs of cleaning the tanker ships are too high.[4] There have always been theories about how water could be redistributed, but for reasons of cost and politics, these theories have not been

1. Cameron, S.D. (1999, October/November). Equinox, 107, 33.
2. de Villiers, M. (1999). Solutions and manifestoes. In Water (p. 332). Toronto: Stoddart.
3. de Villiers, M. (1999). Solutions and manifestoes. In Water (p. 328). Toronto: Stoddart.
4. de Villiers, M. (1999). Solutions and manifestoes. In Water (p. 332). Toronto: Stoddart.

achieved. With the limited number of rivers left to dam, and the high cost of other redistribution methods, this is no longer the most efficient way of preventing water shortages.

It is important to consider if there really are water shortages. There are some scientists that believe that although there may be water shortages, there is no crisis. These people point out that shrinking aquifers may simply be moving to a new steady state, and that we do not know enough about replenishment cycles of aquifers to know if they are really disappearing. These scientists suggest humans need only to adapt to sinking ground levels due to ground water withdrawal; and they recommend people put their faith in emerging technologies to solve any water crisis in the future. However, this is a minority view. Most scientists point to prolonged water shortages in undeveloped countries, California, the shrinking of the Aral Sea in former Soviet Asia, and the depleting of the aquifer under Mexico City as examples that a water crisis is not looming in the future, but here now, in the present. The vice-president of the World Bank, Ismail Serageldin states, "The wars of the next century will be about water."[5]

As the majority of scientists believe there really is a water crisis, other ways of addressing the problem of global water shortages must be considered. Desalination, or the process of removing salt from ocean water, is a reality in the Middle East. This solution has the advantage of a water source that is easily available, provided a piece of coastline is accessible. Desalinated water from the ocean can then be pumped inland. This process consumes a lot of energy, and produces some waste products, but these wastes can be properly managed so as not to damage the environment. Desalination is more than just a theory. It works in reality to fight water shortages.

Furthermore, atmospheric water vapour processing is providing hope for many areas experiencing water shortages. Water vapour processing pulls water vapour from warm, humid air, and cools and condenses it into pure water. Processors have been used in countries where there have been natural disasters in order to provide clean drinking water. For example, after an earthquake hit Taiwan in 1999, water vapour processors produced enough water to supply the military soldiers who were helping the relief efforts. The main source of water for this kind of treatment is humid air, which is free in large quantities. This technology is already fighting water shortages.

Len Abrams, in his paper entitled "Poverty and water supply and sanitation services,"[6] argues that poverty is at the root of all chronic water shortages. He states that governments that can't raise taxes to finance water supply systems can't build or maintain a water supply for their populations. Similarly, individuals who are poor do not have enough money to pay for basic services like water and education. Although this is not an easy solution, Abrams concludes that the best way to eliminate water shortages is to fight poverty.

Education about water conservation is also essential in the struggle against water shortages. In order to preserve water quantity and quality, people must

---

5. Cameron, S.D. (1999, October/November). Equinox, 107, 32.

6. Abrams, L. (1999, Nov. 29). *Poverty and water supply and sanitation services*. Retrieved March 13, 2001 from http://www.thewaterpage.com

learn how to conserve water around their homes and industries. Information about waste disposal and pollutants must become common knowledge, so water quality is protected. Again, this is a long-term solution, but still essential in order to eliminate water shortages.

It is clear now that water shortages are becoming a fact of life in all countries of the world. Traditional methods of water redistribution, building dams, are no longer possible, and other redistribution theories are too costly. Other methods, although they have drawbacks, are much more effective at addressing water shortages today. Desalination, water vapour processing, as well as the elimination of poverty and education and conservation will be methods scientists use to solve the global water shortages of tomorrow.

References: Abrams, L. (1999, Nov. 29). *Poverty and water supply and sanitation services.* Retrieved March 13, 2001 from http://www.thewaterpage.com

Cameron, S.D. (1999, October/November). Equinox, 1*07*, 30–39.

de Villiers, M. (1999). Solutions and manifestoes. In Water (pp. 321–365). Toronto: Stoddart.

Notes

58 → R3

R.4.

62

H-RK

1. List 30min

Notes

Who

What

Where

When

6526

600N

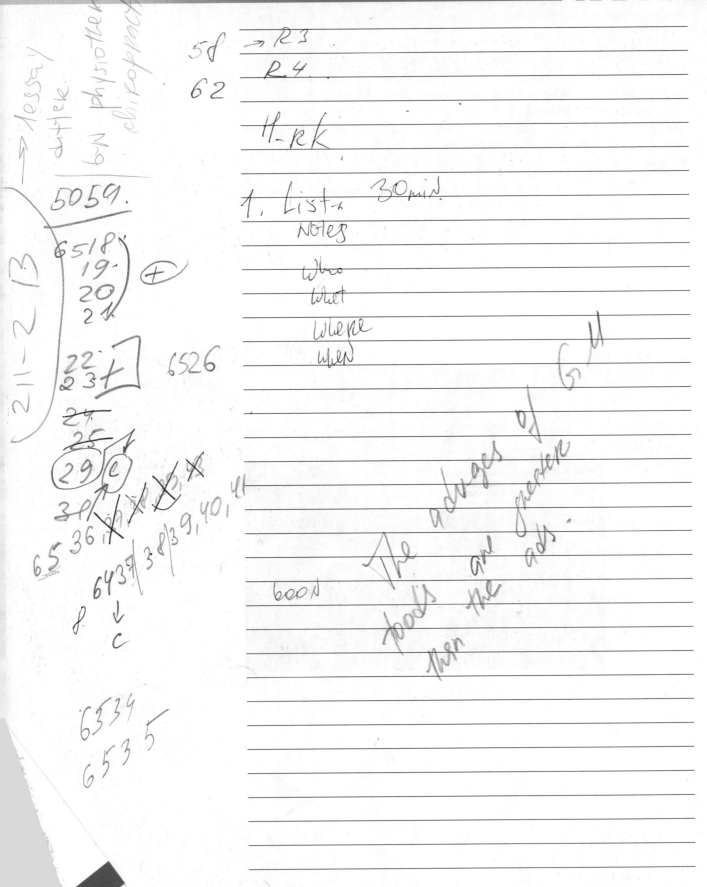

The advanges of foods are greater than the ads.

6534

6535